WILLIAM COX

Blue Mountains Road Builder and Pastoralist

William Cox, JP, in mid-life as a senior magistrate

WILLIAM COX

Blue Mountains Road Builder and Pastoralist

Richard Cox

ROSENBERG

First published in Australia in 2012
by Rosenberg Publishing Pty Ltd
PO Box 6125, Dural Delivery Centre NSW 2158
Phone: 61 2 9654 1502 Fax: 61 2 9654 1338
Email: rosenbergpub@smartchat.net.au
Web: www.rosenbergpub.com.au

National Library of Australia Cataloguing-in-Publication entry

Author: Cox, Richard Hubert, 1931-
Title: William Cox : Blue Mountains road builder and pastoralist /
Richard Cox.

ISBN: 9781921719530 (pbk.)
Notes: Includes bibliographical references and index.
Subjects: Cox, William, 1764-1837.
Mountain roads--New South Wales--Blue Mountains.
Livestock workers--New South Wales--Biography.
Soldiers--New South Wales--Biography.

Dewey Number: 625.7092

Front cover illustration: Convicts repairing the Blue Mountains road, circa 1826, by
Augustus Earle (Nan Kivell Collection, National Library of Australia) with a small
portrait of William Cox as a young officer (Courtesy of Christopher Cox)

Contents

Acknowledgments

This book derives largely from an MPhil thesis submitted at the Menzies Centre for Australian Studies, King's College London. I owe profuse thanks to Professor Carl Bridge and Dr Frank Bongiorno at the Centre.

I have also received valuable contributions from various members of the Cox family, notably Christopher Cox at Burrundulla; James Cox of Anglesea, Victoria; Barrie Cox; Thelma Birrell; Jamie Cox of Longford, Tasmania; and Yvonne and Bryan Cox in New Zealand.

Others to whom I owe a real debt for help and encouragement include Professor Alan Atkinson, Professor John Gascoigne, Dr Grace Karskens and most particularly Babette Smith. Nor should I fail to thank the ever-helpful staff at the Mitchell Library, where the Cox family papers were deposited in 1965.

Richard Cox
Coombe Bissett
England

Metric Conversions

Many measurements, and all historical ones, are given in Imperial form. The equivalents are set out below:

1 mile = 1.60 kilometres

1 acre = 0.40 hectares

1 foot = 30 centimetres

1 pound (lb) = 450 grams

1 yard (3 feet) = 90 centimetres

1 pound (£) = $2

12 pence (d) = 1 shilling

20 shillings (s) = £1

1 guinea (£1 1s) = $2.10

1 gill = 140 millilitres

Foreword:
A Contradictory Character

The stock, when valued, was considered worth twenty five percent more than the purchase money, consequently the farm did not stand Mr Cox in sixpence. What made things even better was that Mr Cox paid him with bills on the regimental agents.

Joseph Holt, Irish rebel and farm manager for William Cox, paymaster of the New South Wales Corps, October 1800[1]

MEMORANDUM

Paymaster William Cox, of the New South Wales Corps, is dismissed the Service.

London Gazette, 16 April 1808[2]

Mr Cox is a Sensible, intelligent Man, of great arrangement, and the best agriculturalist in the colony.

Governor Macquarie, recommending William Cox to be the commandant at Bathurst, 24 June 1815[3]

Let a foreigner, a stranger, be told that it is the Convict, the refuse of our Country, that [*sic*] have performed nearly all the labour that has been done here in the short space of thirty years, and I think he would be astonished.

William Cox to Commissioner Bigge, 7 May 1820[4]

I have received also a grant of land of 100 acres for my Services on the Western road. I have sold it to Mr Cox. He gave me £25 for it, he paid me in money and a cow, and several orders, that I have paid.

James Watson, emancipated for working on the Bathurst road,
in complaint to Bigge, 29 November 1820[5]

There is not a magistrate in the Colony who has given as much of his time to the business of the Crown & the public these ten years past as myself ... If any man ever laboured amidst a den of thieves and a nest of hornets it is myself.

William Cox to Commissioner Bigge, 4 December 1820[6]

What is to be made of these contradictory statements by and about the man who made his name building the first road across the Blue Mountains for Governor Macquarie? William Cox had been dismissed from the army in 1808 for the 'malversation' of the New South Wales Corps' funds, in order to buy himself land. Yet he managed to recover from bankruptcy and become a leading pastoralist in the colony in the 1820s, helping to carry through the pastoralist development which gave Australia its first significant exports, as well as championing the rights of ex-convicts. By the time of his death in 1837 he had become a 'national' figure. The contemporary quotations heading this foreword show that, as well as being a pioneer he was a man whose contradictory character, but constructive actions, not to mention his temperament, make him what one historian calls 'a fascinating if roguish character in early Australian history' and, when building the Blue Mountains road, 'a humane yet seemingly inspiring taskmaster'.[7] Having arrived in the colony in January 1800, in charge of a shipload of convicts on the *Minerva*, when he became noted for his humanity, he went on, after recovering from bankruptcy, to die one of the wealthiest men in the colony. He has many memorials. New South Wales is littered with Cox roads, while a Coxs River runs out of the mountains west of Lithgow. An obelisk stands on Mount York, commemorating his road building achievement, and he has a memorial window in Sydney's St Andrew's Cathedral. Although a Federal Department of Transport building in Canberra was named after him as recently as 1986, few people today know who he was.

The Blue Mountains road was an outstanding achievement by any standard. With a gang of 30 convicts Cox constructed more than 100 miles of roads across appalling terrain, rising to over 4000 feet, in a few days over six months. The road gave access to the extensive grazing around Bathurst, at the time when the colony was expanding and was soon to need more land. At the age of 50 he shared his convict labourers' privations, often sleeping in a bark hut in bitter weather. In this respect he was a forerunner of the distinctively Australian ethos that a leader must prove himself to his men to be accepted by them.

If you were to lay the literary pages devoted to convicts end to end they might almost make a pathway from Sydney to the mountains. Those devoted to the early colonial gentry would barely carpet the drawing room at Government House. Because some made their fortunes – and the colony's – from merino sheep they became known as Pure Merinos. Very little of substance has been written about them since Samuel Bennett's often acerbic *History of Australian Discovery and Colonisation*, published in Sydney in 1865. Many Pure Merino families were bankrupted by the Bank of Australia's crash in 1843 and a catastrophic fall in the value of sheep and cattle. In Bennett's words, 'Castles in the air faded'. William had died in 1837, so never saw this. But the family survived. He had realized early on that the English landed gentry's system of primogeniture and entail was irrelevant in Australia, due to the abundance of land, and he ran his estates as a family enterprise, which was how they survived.

In many ways William's career reflects both the ambitions and the flaws of early Australian development, in what it must be remembered was a harsh and unfamiliar environment. He was a man of determination, an outstanding manager, often more fair minded than his contemporary landowners. He was considerate of the ex-convicts who he recognized had created the colony by their labour. He appreciated that when the British government had sent out female convicts as well as men at the very beginning it was inevitably creating a future generation of free-born British citizens, with citizens' rights. He supported the campaigns for trial by jury and an elected assembly. He had a lifelong concern with improvement, being a founder vice president of the Agricultural Society (still flourishing today) in 1822. Yet he maintained an eighteenth-century view of entitlement to the spoils of office, both as a magistrate and an administrator.

Commissioner Bigge described William in 1822 as one of the six best farmers in the colony.[8] At his home estate of Clarendon on the Hawkesbury he set the pattern of an ambitious landholder, employing large numbers of convicts and also helping deserving men towards emancipation, for which he was heavily criticized by Bigge. He and his contemporary free settlers were driven by the lesson of eighteenth-century England that the ownership of land spelt wealth, power and social position (which was still entirely true when Jane Austen was writing in the early nineteenth century). The pastoralist gentry's eventual failure to retain pre-eminence in the colony has been described by one historian as being 'nearly as significant and as interesting as any success in Australian history'.[9]

All land ownership in the colony depended ultimately not upon the Crown, as the government liked to think, but on the dispossession of the Aborigines. William was aware of their plight, but he did little about it. As a magistrate on the Hawkesbury he proposed tough measures against Aborigines after the murder of settlers in 1816. However, he employed them (as guides) both on making the road in 1814 and as farm workers at Mulgoa later, finding they worked just as well as whites if properly fed and paid. He was also accused of advocating the massacre of Aborigines at Bathurst during the 'Black War' of 1824, although this is far from proven.

As a person William was outwardly strong-minded and straightforward, although described by a daughter-in-law in later life as irascible and not liking to be contradicted, but by then he was 68. He was actually a man of contradictions. His innocent expression in a portrait of him as a young officer hardly prepares one for the stern face of the magistrate. One reason for his not being as well known as his contemporaries, the outstanding example being John Macarthur, is that William seldom courted publicity. He probably never got over the disgrace of his bankruptcy and therefore avoided controversy. Governor Brisbane put him forward for the first Legislative Council in 1824, although only officials were chosen.

A century and three quarters after William's death, Clarendon on the Hawkesbury is long gone, the farm now an RAAF airfield, the name preserved only on a railway station. But his descendants still run the family estate at Mudgee, where land was first acquired in 1821. It continues as an operational family estate. The Coxes still breed racehorses and support the Jockey Club, which they helped to found in 1825. By contrast the Macarthurs' Camden, which encom-passed 60,000 acres in the 1820s, is now almost swallowed up by Sydney and is effectively an entertainment complex and theme park, with paint ball games and one historic colonial house.

MEMOIRS

...OF...

WILLIAM COX, J.P.,

LIEUTENANT AND PAYMASTER OF N.S.W. CORPS,

...OR...

102nd REGIMENT.

LATE OF CLARENDON, WINDSOR.

Sydney and Brisbane :
WILLIAM BROOKS & Co., PRINTERS,

1901.

William's highly eulogistic *Memoirs* were ghosted and published 64 years after his death.

1 An English Gentleman With no Money

The bulk of William Cox's career, with the spectacular ups and downs of a man who was capable of being idiosyncratic, to say the least, was spent in New South Wales. His reason for going there lay in the deprivation and lack of opportunity in rural Dorset, where he grew up, and in Wiltshire, where he lived when first married. His problem was that he was *from* the minor gentry, entitled to a coat of arms, but could not afford to be *of* it. His solution was emigration, although there is an inbuilt mystery about this, since he had a fairly high class clockmaking business in Wiltshire before he joined the regular army in 1795, later transferring to the New South Wales Corps. It must be assumed that the clockmaking was not doing well enough in a time of economic depression, while his father–in–law, who probably supported his business from London, died that year. Even so, it was a curious change of career, most likely prompted by lack of income. As Edna Hickson, a descendant of William's and the editor of a reprint of his *Memoirs,* puts it: 'At the end of the eighteenth century Englishmen with ambition and limited means could look to the Colonies for opportunities to enhance their chances of success in life'.[1]

The War of Independence had closed off North America as a destination for emigrants, except for the wastes of Upper Canada, frozen in winter and plagued by flies and mosquitoes in summer. William might have tried for the East India Company, hoping to make his pile and retire to England a rich man, although cadet entry to the Company was oversubscribed. That he opted instead for a completely new life in a recently established penal colony tells one a good deal not merely about William himself, but also about those other free-settler compatriots who came to form the pastoralist colonial gentry of the colony and who had such a great influence on Australia's early development. Most of them, like John Macarthur, D'Arcy Wentworth, John Piper, William Lawson and in a different way, the colony's chaplain Samuel Marsden, had the same motivation. All escaped unsatisfactory opportunities at home, exploiting military or official appointments to start a new life. They had learnt from the late eighteenth-century society

The timbered frontage of William's birthplace at Wimborne. Inside it is decidedly cramped (Author's photo)

they lived in that the ownership of land spelt wealth and power, even if the possibility of becoming members of a local landed gentry in Australia only became apparent after they arrived.[2]

William was born on 19 December 1764 in the ancient, but isolated, town of Wimborne Minster in Dorset, which lies some six miles from the port of Poole. He had an elder brother, Robert, born in 1754, and two elder sisters, Jane born in 1758 and Anne born in 1762, neither of whom married. His father, Robert, was a ship owner and master mariner at the vast natural harbour of Poole. Shipping was the family business. His grandfather, also William, had traded with Newfoundland. The trade was extremely profitable, Newfoundland having the most prolific fishing grounds in the world. Ships from Poole took salt and general supplies to Newfoundland, shipped salted cod, furs and seal skins from there to the Mediterranean, and returned to Dorset with wine, raisins and olive oil.

In the 1770s some 70 sailing ships made the transatlantic passage every year. From 1600 to 1815 Poole had 'enjoyed an era of great prosperity', which would only end after the Napoleonic Wars.[3] The wealth of the Poole merchants 'equalled, and often exceeded, that of most of the landed gentry of Dorset'.[4] Robert Cox, however, was not a prominent ship owner. In fact the records do not mention him at all. Nor was this was the kind of enterprise a true Dorset gentleman of the period would have run himself, though he might have bought shares in it.

Crossing the Atlantic in small ships was much more dangerous than coastal trading, as one chronicler of Dorset life, Jo Draper, points out.[5] Robert Cox was lost at sea before William was born, leaving his mother not only bereaved, but largely bereft. Robert is known to have made a will – no longer extant – before a previous voyage, which would have provided for his wife. But when he was gone she does not seem to have been left at all well-off financially, despite having help from her father.

On 8 March 1765 Jane Cox had to present herself, supported by her father, Robert Harvey, to provide a bond for £1400 – a considerable sum – to the Official of the Peculiar and Exempt Jurisdiction of Wimborne, and arrange the administration of her affairs. The Jurisdiction had authority over a great deal more than just church matters.[6] Evidently, agreement was achieved. The family remained in their house in King Street, facing the Minster and, in due course, she sent William to the Queen Elizabeth I Grammar School, little more than one hundred yards away round the corner. The Cox home was known then as the Poet's House, because the poet Matthew

Portrait of William's mother at Clarendon (Author's photo)

Prior had lived there in 1664, and probably dates from the late sixteenth century, but was added to in the eighteenth century. Even so, with its low ceilings, half-timbered construction and lathe and plaster walls, this was not a gentleman's residence. It was at best a somewhat poky middle-class dwelling in a dawning age of elegant town houses, such as a few in Wimborne still are (they suffered an onslaught of demolition in the 1950s). It is now known as St Joseph's.[7]

After William and his family moved to New South Wales the matter of what defined a gentleman and what constituted a gentleman's residence would become of disproportionate importance, with William and his sons naming houses to reflect a Dorset ancestry the significance of which had, in reality, been lost. William's origins were of great significance to him. According to an unpublished family genealogy armorial bearings were first allowed to his ancestor Thomas Cox and to Thomas' first cousin, Francis, Prebendary of Wisborough in Chichester Cathedral in 1554. Francis was also King's Almoner. They were descended from John Cox of Monmouth, c.1400. His coat of arms is reproduced in William's *Memoirs*, although the motto of *Fortitudo in Adversis* is commonplace.[8] Francis' son, Sir Richard Cox, was the Clerk Comptroller to the household of King James I. His coat of arms is in the frontispiece of a family bible now in the Mitchell Library. In the 1660s family members settled at Wimborne. According to a family memoir in 1661 'the Revd Henry Cox occupied the church and rectory at Exton. Other family members went to Wimborne, where their landed property "Fern Hill" was at the edge of the Fir Forest, which runs down to Poole, where they became ship owners'.[9] *Burke's Colonial Landed Gentry* merely says that 'the family was at one time seated in Dorsetshire'.[10]

The Cox family coat of arms (Author's photo)

Fern Hill, on the road to Poole, was where William's grandfather had lived. It stood on the edge of the heathland later portrayed in Thomas Hardy's novels as Egdon Heath. A map of July 1795 shows neither Fern Hill nor a forest.[11] However, it is shown in plan view on the Ordnance Survey map of 1811 as a house, though certainly not a mansion, across the road from, and further south than, the country house estate of Merley. There is no indication of a forest (although there is on the 1909 map).[12] This later map does show a square half mile of land behind the house. Today, the whole area east of the road is a housing estate, although there are stretches of conifers further down the road. By the 1780s the land presumably could not provide a living, because Robert Harvey Cox, William's elder brother by ten years, started a factory making fusee chains for watches at the nearby town of Christchurch.

In the compacted form of Fernhill, this house later provided the name for Edward Cox's mansion at Mulgoa in New South Wales, and for one of James' properties in Tasmania, underlining this strong sense of inheritance, which must have been instilled in them by their father and seems to have been a motivating force for both generations. What is harder to understand is why William himself gave the name Clarendon to his estate on the Hawkesbury. Clarendon Park, three miles from the medieval Salisbury Cathedral in Wiltshire, was a royal palace and hunting estate owned by the Plantagenet Kings, but their dynasty came to an end in 1399. By the 1550s, when Francis Cox was the King's Almoner, it was no longer used by the Sovereigns and was given by Charles II to the Royalist Earl of Clarendon in 1651, after the restoration. Yet William must have felt he had a connection there and in 1834 his son James also gave the name to his magnificent mansion in Tasmania, now owned by the National Trust, although that could have been out of filial loyalty. Behind all these names in the colony there lay a clear sense of deprived ancestry in England.

That immediate ancestry is graphically illustrated by two splendid portraits, of William's mother and of her father-in-law, which now hang at the Tasmanian Clarendon.[13] The portraits are compelling, both in ornate gilt frames. William's mother's likeness is of a dark-haired, slightly angular-faced, young lady in an elegant silver/grey gown, with a very full skirt below a tight bodice and having flounced sleeves trimmed with lace. Her slim fingered right hand rests demurely in her lap, her left elbow on a marble and gilt side table, as artists of the time often depicted ladies. Since Jane Harvey was born in 1732 and bore her first child in 1754, but here wears no wedding ring, the picture can be confidently dated at around 1750–52, when she was 20. She was dressed as, and looked like, a lady. That had great importance. Social snobbery is alive and well today in the Shires. It mattered even more then, when it was said that a gentleman could not live properly without a manorial estate.

Equally, the portrait hanging alongside Jane's at Clarendon, of William Cox's grandfather, William the ship owner, depicts him as a fashionable and rich gentleman, with a landscape behind him including the distant sea. Born in 1695, he is here in another typical early eighteenth-century pose, wearing a generous, unpowdered wig right down to his shoulders. His full-length blue coat, perhaps of velvet, has deep pockets and extravagant cuffs, reaching back almost to his elbows. His right hand rests on his hip, his left on the handle of a sword. His wig dates the portrait at before the 1750s, after which time wigs were much shorter, were curled above the nape of the neck and were powdered white.[14] One wonders where Jane would have found wall space for these portraits in the low-ceilinged Poet's House. They were taken to Australia by Commander Nigel Cox, RN, in the 1960s and lent by his son, Tim, to the National Trust in Tasmania.[15]

Happily, Wimborne did have its compensations for the young William. Attending the Queen Elizabeth I Grammar School was to place him among the best educated men in New South Wales when he arrived there, not to mention facilitating his obtaining a commission in the Militia. It would have contributed to his being appointed a magistrate at Parramatta only two years after arriving in the colony.[16] The school was of ancient lineage. In 705 Saint Cuthberga had founded a nunnery at Wimborne, but it was to be seized during Henry VIII's dissolution of the monasteries in 1529. By then the school was already part of the nunnery, having been founded in 1496 with an endowment from the mother of Henry VII. Subsequently some of the land was restored to it by Queen Elizabeth I, who gave the school a new charter in 1562. This was 'for the instruction of all her subjects' sons in learning good manners and virtue, according to the customs of Winchester and Eton' and to be 'general, free and common [open] to all subjects of the Crown.'[17]

Grammar schools were an essential part of English social history from the sixteenth century to the middle of the twentieth. They provided a steady flow of scholars, scientists and professionals to the nation, from the new learning of the Renaissance onwards. Both Isaac Newton and William Shakespeare were the product of grammar schools, which gave as good an education as the more famous public schools. Indeed the most famous, Eton, originated as a grammar school.[18] By William's time the Queen Elizabeth I school was charging fees and educating the sons of the middle and upper classes from a wide area. Two centuries after the Queen made her endowment, to compare her school with the great boarding institutions of Eton and Winchester might have been stretching the imagination. Nonetheless the grammar school boys' education was good enough that they could have gone on Oxford or Cambridge, if their parents could afford it, or they won scholarships.[19]

Aristocratic sons took a different route, often starting with private tutors. William's contemporary, Henry Bankes (1757–1834) of nearby Kingston Hall, attended a private boarding school in Marylebone, London, followed by Westminster School and Trinity Hall Cambridge. He then embarked on a four-year Grand Tour of Italy.[20] William Cox did not go to university. A realization of what he missed is likely to have been behind his leaving funds for his son Thomas, by his second marriage, to go to Cambridge.[21] For the older sons by Rebecca this would not have been possible financially.

Descriptions of the Queen Elizabeth I school were given in the *Memoirs* of David Parry Okeden, a boy who was there in 1779, around the time when William would have been about to leave. He recorded: 'The boys of this school used occasionally to form the school room into a theatre and represented the most celebrated plays to an audience of their friends and the neighbouring Gentry'. According to tradition, one of the duties of the Master was to give instruction in cockfighting on Shrove Tuesday.[22] A previous Usher (second master) had been Fill Cox, BA, of St John's College, Oxford, who died in 1763 and had been a relation.[23] Cock fighting was one of the popular entertainments exported to New South Wales, along with bare knuckle fighting.

William would have left the school when he reached the age of 15. What he did for most of the next ten years is unclear. Neither he nor his older brother, Robert, seems to have considered following in their grandfather's and father's shipping footsteps, possibly because of the drowning, possibly because the Cox shipping operation had collapsed with its owner's death. When dealing with many aspects of William's early life there are so few records that one depends on reasoned speculation as to causes. At the end of the 1780s he worked as an apprentice for Robert in the latter's Watch Chain Manufactory at Christchurch, founded around 1790, ten miles from Wimborne down the River Stour. Here some 500 nimble-fingered women made the delicate fusee chains for the watches of the time. The mechanism is described in the OED as follows: 'there is a conical pulley or wheel of a clock or watch on which the [fusee] chain is wound and which equalises the power of the mainspring'. These tiny chains had 20 links to the inch and were indeed delicate. Robert's building is now the Redhouse Museum.[24]

William could well have met his future wife indirectly through the factory, since her father, James Upjohn, made watches using those chains and had a house in the north Dorset town of Shaftesbury. The *Memoirs* merely say, 'Then he moved to Devizes in Wilts, where he married Rebecca Upjohn in 1789 at the age of 25'.[25] Twentieth-century family researches suggest that William, having been apprenticed to his brother, was then set up 'in that field' in London. This could only have been for a few years in the early 1790s, before he married and they settled in Devizes.[26] Their reason for choosing Wiltshire is not known.

A pivotal aspect of William's motivation for eventually emigrating must have not only been lack of opportunity for young men without a fortune, but the conditions in the countryside, which he saw around him. These were not only intensely miserable for the poor, but offered no career opportunity for an educated young man without a fortune. Broadly speaking, one can identify three influences to which William can convincingly be thought to have responded. The first and most significant was that the ownership of land spelt wealth and power, a theme running through William's entire life. Numerous contemporary writers and later historians confirm this. In the words of one who wrote about emigration to Australia, 'Property was after all the economic prop of gentility'.[27]

Susan Watkins, a biographer of that supreme English social commentator, Jane Austen, explains the imperative of land ownership:

> It was land that counted for everything in English society during the eighteenth century and the early part of the nineteenth century. Wealth, status, political power and even marriage prospects were directly affected by the size of one's property. The squire of a manor was like a little monarch in his village.[28]

Landlords formed the largest unit of economic and social power in Dorset. Even maintaining a modest estate necessitated a capital outlay of about £30,000 for its owner to live the leisured life of a gentleman.[29] This was far beyond anything the Coxes possessed.

The second influence was the value of making improvements. The third was a vivid understanding of the backwardness of Dorset and of the miseries which the enclosures of common land were inflicting on the rural population in the name of progress – and of landowners' profits.

His actions in the colony reveal that one of the qualities William brought with him when he emigrated, as well as humane attitudes, was a strong belief in making improvements. There was certainly stimulus for this in Dorset, if not in Wimborne itself. The nearby town of Blandford Forum, rebuilt after a disastrous fire in 1731 (and today a World Heritage site), was a cultural centre, relatively speaking brimming with ideas. Not so much further away was the city of Bath, where the Bath and West Society, which still runs the annual Bath and West Show, was founded in 1777 'to encourage higher standards of farming'. The society helped to bring into use new crops and new techniques.[30] The Wiltshire County records state that he was a farmer, though not where (but not that he was a clockmaker). If so, as he was an educated man and from Dorset, he was almost certain to have known of the enlightened agricultural initiatives at Blandford and at the Bath and West, if not necessarily being aware of the Enlightenment thinking inspiring them.[31] The aims of the Agricultural Society of New South Wales, of which he became a founder vice president in 1822, were almost identical to those of the Bath and West.

Despite the high clerical status of the Minster, its grammar school, and its being a market town first settled around 300 BC, Wimborne was backward compared with the other Dorset towns of Blandford and Dorchester. So were its transport links. An Act of Parliament of 1755 had denounced the Dorset roads as being 'in a ruinous condition'. In consequence turnpike tolls were instituted, as they later would be on the road from Parramatta across the Hawkesbury. Gradually pack horses and wagons were superseded by coaches and carriers. The *London Directory* of 1772 announced a coach three times a week from London, but to travel on it was an expensive luxury. Most country transport was as depicted in Gainsborough's 1786 painting of *The Market Cart*, laden high with stores and trundling bumpily along a rutted lane on a single pair of huge spoked wheels.[32] Alongside the track is a woodcutter gathering fuel, a favourite addition to Gainsborough's paintings. The enclosures would later have prevented him from doing this.

Although Wimborne had been founded at the confluence of two rivers, which was an important factor for pre-medieval settlement, that value had long waned and by the eighteenth century the town's isolation was mirrored by its lack of economic development. It was away from the uplands where farming revolved largely around the famous Dorset Horn breed of sheep, with its splendidly curled horns. In the 1720s Daniel Defoe was informed that 600,000 sheep grazed the downs within six miles of Dorchester, to the north.[33] The chalk uplands of Dorset and Wiltshire were devoted to sheep, involving water meadows to grow early Spring grass and the folding of sheep into pens at night, to keep them mutually warm and to provide manure for the arable fields in the valleys. The system was 'an integrated whole, with the sheep and grasslands together supplying the manure which maintained corn production.'[34] The production of wool, though vital to peasant families, was subsidiary. In New South Wales, folding turned out to be unnecessary in the quite different physical conditions, but was useful to keep off night attacks by dingoes.

In 1793, four years after William had moved to Devizes in Wiltshire, a thousand women and children were still employed making stockings from fleeces. Set against that, production of cheap cotton goods had increased tenfold in England between 1760 and 1787 and this home industry, where every cottage had its spinning jenny, was soon to be all but destroyed by the products of the new cotton gins. By the time William was grown up many of the Dorset women lived in the poorhouses. That so many women were desperate to find work reflected the virtual extinction of the yeoman class of smallholder and the general rural poverty, which had been created by the enclosures.

There was an enormous disparity between rich and poor, between gentry and labourers. Sir Frederick Morton Eden was an insurance company chairman, who applied the principles of Adam Smith to his investigations into the condition of the poor. He toured much of England in 1795.[35] Writing on *The State of the Poor*, he found that at Blandford 'the rapid rise of the Poor's rates, in this parish, is generally attributed to the high price of provisions; the smallness of wages and the prevailing spirit, among the gentlemen of landed property in this neighbourhood, of consolidating small farms; and the consequent depopulation of villages; the effects of which, it is said, oblige small industrious farmers to turn labourers or servants'.[36] His contemporary, William Marshall, an agriculturalist and originator of the Board of Agriculture in 1793, noted that 'bread is now

[1801] nearly four times its price of late years; beef not more than twice'. But he drew no conclusions from this.[37] Families like William's were forced to: they economized.

Far from poverty being alleviated over the years, it grew worse as the 'improving' enclosures progressed. In the 1820s William Cobbett wrote (on 11 November 1825), 'the honest labourer is fed worse than the convicted felon'.[38] Labouring wages in Sussex were then 7d a day, less than the seven shillings a week which Eden had reckoned a Dorset labourer could not feed his family on thirty years before. Although by then William and his family were in the colony, poverty in England had an effect out there. Eden had deplored 'driving, as we annually do, many thousands of useful hands from us, into distant realms, for want of employment and food'.[39] It drove some of them to New South Wales in two starkly different ways. Gradually mounting rural unrest culminated in the Swing Riots, while the famous Dorset case of the Tolpuddle Martyrs in 1832 led to the men's transportation for trying to form a farm workers' trade union. At a less dramatic level several of Rebecca Upjohn's farm worker relatives were transported for minor crimes of the kind that usually resulted from poverty. The other route was voluntary. Much later, in the 1830s, Dorset yeomen also went to the colony under the assisted emigration schemes, introduced by Viscount Goderich in 1831, described in Chapter 10. Ironically, some of the assisted immigrants came from one of the most troublesome villages in Dorset, Sixpenny Handley, but settled successfully on the Macarthur estates.

William married in 1789 and as food prices climbed during the 1790s he must have found it increasingly difficult to feed a steadily growing family. It was also explicit in Marshall's writings that the owners of landed properties could become richer by improving them and that a tenanted estate gave 'power and authority over persons as well as things'.[40] To cap this, the gentry controlled the local administration in the countryside. The Commissions of the Peace, whose magistrates were known as Justices of the Peace, were chosen from among the local squires and possessed great powers, with control over all manner of appointments. The system had originated with the Tudor monarchs, who employed gentlemen to work for the Crown unpaid, in return for privileges.[41] This power, which also carried political opportunities, was to be mirrored in the colony, where William was a JP from 1810 until his death in 1837, though without exploiting his position politically.

Another dispiriting aspect of English society, happily not replicated in New South Wales, was the political system of the Rotten Boroughs. This remained corrupt until the Reform Bill of 1832. An example local to Wimborne makes the point. The Bankes family had owned the ancient royal castle of Corfe on the Isle of Purbeck, 15 miles to the south of their Wimborne seat, since 1635. During the Civil War it had been reduced to ruins, though with a small village round it. But Corfe retained two seats in parliament. Ralph Bankes sat in parliament for one of those seats in 1659 and thereafter it was effectively a family possession. In William Cox's time Henry Bankes, having returned from his Grand Tour, was elected in 1784, 1789 and 1793. A list of the 1784 election expenses included 'To 45 voters at 13s each'.[42]

William had neither the land nor the capital to maintain himself as a gentleman, which explains what he tried to achieve in the colony, not least for his sons. But that was in the future. In 1789 he came to a turning point, when he married Rebecca Upjohn at Devizes on 1 February. She was two years older than him and would prove herself practical and efficient. Sadly, little is on record about her life in Australia, apart from her later taking a leading role in the Hawkesbury community. Although there is an extant drawing of William's second wife, there is no known picture of Rebecca. As female historians have observed, the activities of women in running their households and bearing children were not deemed worthy of recording, especially the work of pastoralists' wives in New South Wales.

The Upjohn family came from Dorset and many were labourers.[43] But Rebecca's direct ancestors were citizens of repute in Shaftesbury in north Dorset. This small market town stands on the edge of an escarpment, looking south over the Vale of Blackmore, with a famously steep street of medieval houses called Gold Hill. Rebecca's grandfather, Edward Upjohn (1686–1764), was a mason and clockmaker, who had been a trustee of the Holy Trinity church there, while her great-grandfather owned land by the church in 1721.[44] Her father, James Upjohn, was a successful goldsmith and clockmaker in London, which must be why William himself entered the same line of business.

A short account of James' life and travels was printed in 1784, five years before Rebecca's marriage.[45] In it he relates that his own father was ingenious in making the movements of watches. When he was 21 he left home after a quarrel and went to work for a watchmaking friend of the family, making balance wheels and 'Fusee Engines'. In 1743 he arrived in London, again getting work through family friends in the trade, which was a small and close-knit one.

In 1745, at the age of 23, James married Mary Garle, whose brother and father he was employing to make watch springs. Of her he wrote: 'I married for Honey and not for Money, and had a fortune in a Wife, and not a Fortune with one, which to me was far preferable', remarking that 'she took the Man with the comical name of Upjohn'.[46] They settled in St Martin Le Grand in London, near Red Lion Street, Clerkenwell, where Rebecca was born in 1762.[47] She was his ninth child. A recently published study of the Upjohn ancestry shows that he became rich enough to have retired at 60.

Indeed James Upjohn's work was highly valued. He made a pair of musical clocks in 1770 that were valued at £4000 and gold enamelled repeater watches set with diamonds at £300. These were very large sums for the time. He did regular business in the West Country, which would have been continued by his second son, also James, who became his partner and was 36 at the time of Rebecca's marriage. As suggested earlier, William's work at Robert's fusee chain factory all but certainly explains how he met James Upjohn Jnr and so Rebecca. Her father, who was now very well off, presumably welcomed her marrying a gentleman, albeit not a wealthy one, or he would not have permitted it. He is very likely to have helped the couple financially. Perhaps he forgot his own marrying for 'Honey not Money'. Certainly Rebecca, judging from her actions in the colony, inherited her father's energy and capabilities. Whether she also shared his picaresque sense of humour is not known. William Cox was never noted for his humour.

After the marriage, the couple rented a property in Devizes from 1790 until 1795, overlapping with their purchase of one in 1793. The one William bought was an old timbered house in St John's Alley, in the town centre, not far from the old stone market cross and a variety of larger stone-built houses.[48] His own 'tiered' house, with the upper story

The Devizes house where William and Rebecca lived before emigrating, 4 St John's Alley (Author's photo)

projecting above the ground floor, was far from grand, in fact might have reminded him of his birthplace, the beamed Poet's House in Wimborne. The timbered houses of the alley still stand, in their narrow passageway, very close to the town centre and St John Street, where he had his business.

As mentioned earlier, he is described in the County Records

William and Rebecca's first four children were baptized at St John's church in Devizes (Author's photo)

as having been a farmer; being a landowner would helped him to qualify for a commission in the Militia. What only became clear in July 2011, when a clock dealer advertised for sale (for £8250) a handsome longcase clock made by William Cox in 1791–93, was that he 'made' clocks, a craft

learnt both from his brother and his father-in-law. 'Made' is in quotes because it would be truer to say that the maker assembled them, as the dealer explained to this author. The delicately painted dial face of the one advertised came from Wilson in Birmingham, the centre sweep calendar was bought in, the clock's working parts were cast by a specialist firm, the longcase and the finials were made by a craftsman. Finally William put his name to it. The clock, which stands 92 inches high, was the third Cox clock the dealer had acquired. A study of Wiltshire clockmakers confirms him as having been listed in

Longcase clock made by William at Devizes around 1791 (Author's photo)

a 1791 trades directory as a 'Watch and clockmaker' at 1 St John's Street (a short walk from his house). A watch made 'William Cox of Devizes' was reported lost in the *Kentish Post* of 15 December 1795, so he evidently had buyers from outside Wiltshire. He was also a bondsman for marriage licences. [49]

Devizes was described in the Directory of 1791 as a 'populous town … distant twenty two [miles] from Salisbury … the buildings are old and of the most part of timber … The post passes through from London to Bristol at nine 'clock and takes letters from Devizes to the westward; returns every night from Bristol … to London. Three stage coaches stop at the Bear Inn in this town every morning and evening on their way to and from Bath'.[50]

Thus communications, vital to a businessman, were good and William would have no problem keeping in touch with his father-in-law, who in all probability helped him to find buyers outside Wiltshire.

This raises the question of how, being in trade, William became an officer in what was effectively the gentleman's club of the Militia. The *Memoirs* describe him as 'of good estate and served in the Wiltshire Militia'.[51] But he does not appear in the Militia records, of which Major Peters, the archivist, writes 'for the period in question are scant and for the officers virtually non-existent'. Peters also comments: 'the fact that William was a watch maker I feel does not mean he was just "in trade", but in a highly skilled and respected profession. As such it would not have been too difficult for him to have been commissioned in the Wiltshire Militia.'[52] And, of course, William had been born into the minor Dorset gentry and been well educated. What is indisputable is the entry of his commissioning into the regular army in the *London Gazette* of 7 July 1795, which states 'William Cox, Gent, to be Ensign, without Purchase, vice Stopford, promoted'.

Peters writes: 'It was fairly commonplace for Militia officers to transfer their commission to a Regular Army Regiment, especially during the period from 1795 when there was a danger of invasion from France and of a Rebellion in Ireland, which the French threatened to support'. William was to learn all about the Irish rebellion when he sailed to New South Wales in charge of men convicted for their part in it. The *Memoirs* say that: 'During the French wars he got a taste of the anxieties of hostility, but he longed for action' and so joined the 117th Foot.[53] France had declared war on England and Holland on 1 February 1793. The Militia's use outside the country was not permitted, but there is nothing to prove that he transferred to the regular army because he longed for action. *Burke's Colonial Gentry* even states that he served in the French Wars, of which his Army List regimental postings provide no evidence.[54] It is much more probable that what he longed for was regularly paid employment.

William's rank of ensign was the lowest for a commissioned officer, which he must have held in the Militia. The Militias in southern England were ostensibly formed as a defence against potential invasion by the French, but the underlying reason was for the control of rural domestic unrest. Officers from the gentry were allocated sections of a county for their men to guard. William would have certainly needed money to be accepted. The way it worked was that the Clerks of the Peace assessed the right of landowners or their sons to obtain commissions, which they did by proving income from their land under the provisions of Act 42 of Geo 3rd chap 90. Their requests have survived for the nicely bureaucratic reason that they were passed to the land tax assessors. To be a major required £400 a year from land, a captaincy £200. There was even a Londoner who claimed rank because he owned land in the county and another because his father was a member of parliament. An ensign needed £100.[55] Patronage was also exerted by the Lord Lieutenant of the county, who had to approve commissions, in this case George Herbert, 11th Earl of Pembroke. Since William's name does not appear in any of the clerks' declarations it is not known how he came to be accepted.

William made this change at the very time when Eden was researching the rural situation. The constantly rising cost of living must have been forcefully brought home to him both by the cost of maintaining his own multiplying family and by the humiliating dependence on the parish of the families of Devizes men who had been embodied into full time service as Militia soldiers. As far back as 1780, order forms had been issued with which the Churchwardens and Overseers of the Poor were to authorize paying the dependants of any Militia soldier who was 'a Volunteer in actual Service in the said Militia'.[56]

James Upjohn's money can plausibly explain how William had been able both to join the Militia and buy a house, albeit an old and poky one. Upjohn's wide business contacts probably put William in touch with would-be purchasers of handsome longcase clocks and of watches. But Upjohn died in 1795. Rebecca had five surviving brothers.[57] With so many brothers, she was most unlikely to have received a large inheritance, since she had a husband to support her, while any income from her father surely ended on his death, along with his business introductions. The market for high quality clocks in the area of Devizes would have been limited. A 1791 directory lists only 39 people as 'Gentry' there, headed by the local MP and Speaker of the House of Commons, Henry Addington, and including one lady, a Mrs Long (but not William). Business contacts in the metropolis, to which buyers from all over the country resorted, must have been invaluable.

William's joining the regular army in the same year that his father-in-law died could be a coincidence, but most probably was not. However, joining the regular army, quite apart from it being held in low esteem before the Napoleonic Wars, did not represent financial salvation for a married officer. It was considered impossible to support a family on less than a captain's pay. The erratic progress of William's short army career in England looks very like a constant search for more money. The couple's first son, William Jnr, had been born on 13 November 1789, James a year later on 1 November 1790, Charles on 13 December 1792, but not baptized until 5 November the following year. George was born on 18 February 1794 and baptized on 14 March. During those years of the 1790s Rebecca was fully occupied with child bearing and rearing, wherever they were living.

After only six months in the 117th Regiment, William transferred to the 68th, which had been raised in Durham in 1758 and to which city he is likely to have been posted, although the history of the regiment at this time is confused. Having been stationed in Gibraltar, it was moved to the West Indies in 1793, when its complement included 369 rank and file soldiers. In Grenada it fought a virtual army of local brigands, while disease out there 'exacted a terrible toll ... the main causes being malaria and yellow fever'. The 32nd Foot lost 32 officers.[58] The 68th was so denuded of men that when it returned home in March 1796 all its remaining rank and file were transferred to the 63rd. It was at around this time, on 20 January 1796, that William transferred to the 68th, in which John Macarthur had served earlier.

The 68th had begun an intensive recruiting campaign in various counties in November 1796 and for some of the time the headquarters was in Leeds. Officers were rewarded financially for obtaining recruits.

A War Office circular of 14 March 1795, aimed at discouraging 'a set of People' who had not been in the army from profiting from recruitments, set the rate at 'Fifteen Guineas on account of a Recruit enlisted for General Service, and Ten guineas on account of Recruit for the Fencibles [reserves]'.[59] On 17 February 1797 William was promoted to lieutenant. However, in that February the regiment was posted to Ireland, where it remained at Malahide for about a year. Although he is briefly mentioned in regimental records, whether he went to Malahide is not clear. What is likely is that he had made welcome bonus from the recruiting, since he was always good with men. What is certain is that the couple were away from Wiltshire when their sons Henry and Frederick were born, in March 1796 and June 1797 respectively, because they were christened together at Devizes on 2 February 1798.[60]

While the 68th was in Ireland, William transferred again, this time to the New South Wales Corps, as a lieutenant, on 28 September 1797 (with his rank in the army dating back to 17 February 1797). Although he had now achieved some promotion, to climb in the officer corps, except very slowly, required purchase and he could not have afforded it. Lachlan Macquarie once commented bitterly that it had taken him 32 years to reach the rank of colonel.

The transfer to the New South Wales Corps seems to have been purely for the financial opportunities it offered and the hope of a new life.[61] In family terms, emigration would not have been a problem for either husband or wife. Both their fathers were now dead, both had siblings who could look after their mothers. The Corps is claimed to have had a low reputation and that a high proportion of the rank and file were the dregs of the army and had been taken from the Savoy Military Prison.[62] This

William Cox as a young officer (Courtesy of Christopher Cox)

is challenged by the military historian Geoffrey Grey, who points out 'that in fact the overall quality of the regiment was not demonstrably worse than that pertaining elsewhere in the British army of the day'. Ex-Savoy recruits never reached 10 percent of the strength, while other regiments had been brought up to strength with men from county gaols and Irish deserters from other regiments.[63] So, as regiments went, the Corps was just about acceptable and had yet to acquire its nickname of 'the Rum Corps', as the result of its officers' extensive trading in spirits. As to the clockmaking, William appears to have abandoned it on joining the regular army, and in Sydney there were already clockmakers, advertising in the *Sydney Gazette* newspaper. In any case, as his actions showed, his objective was to acquire land and farm.

According to a family letter written a century later, in 1903, William sailed out to New South Wales on a convict ship in 1797, two years before he arrived officially on the *Minerva* in January 1800.[64] If he did, he might have arranged to buy a farm from John Macarthur well in advance of his official arrival, which is implied in the *Memoirs* of Joseph Holt, the Irish rebel who travelled into exile on the *Minerva*. On arrival at Port Jackson William almost immediately offered Holt a job as farm manager, for a property 'he had in prospect'.[65]

This possibility of a 1797 visit is difficult to substantiate, although the Army List shows that he had been on half pay in June 1798. A further son, Francis Edmund, was recorded by the surgeon of the *Minerva* transport as having been born at the Cove of Cork on 17 March 1799, when the couple were waiting for the ship to sail.[66] Although this birth is unknown to family historians and is not mentioned elsewhere, the surgeon's record is precise, down to details of the post-natal illness suffered by Rebecca and its treatment. This means that the baby had been conceived around June 1798. The family had been back in Devizes for the double christening at the parish church of St John the previous February, although William might not have been there himself. The baptismal record simply names him as the father. Did he make the 1797 trip?

This is one of those timeline problems which can be so difficult to resolve. William only joined the New South Wales Corps on 28 September 1997. He must have been with Rebecca in England in June 1798. The family kept the house at 4 St John's Alley in Devizes until it was sold at some time before July 1798.[67] William would have to have been there to sign the agreement. This allows a space of nine months for him to have made the journey to and from the colony. The fastest sailing of a convict transport on record had been that of the *Matilda* in August to October 1791, which took 127 days. A more normal voyage took five months, if all went well, but could be much longer. William's voyage back on the *Buffalo* in 1807 took nine months.

Unfortunately, whilst convict records are well documented, sailings of passengers on transports often are not. That William might have gone out before is also suggested by his having been sufficiently knowledgeable to take a stock of cheap goods with him on the *Minerva* to trade profitably in Rio de Janeiro when he did go officially. His familiarity with watchmaking would have helped him in choosing cheap watches to sell. The only possible, but improbable, explanation is that he was enabled to go out before he was officially gazetted to the Corps, which would explain his having been on half pay. It comes down to a question of the couples' motivation.

The *Minerva* had been scheduled to sail in August 1798. It would have been essential to either sell or rent out the Devizes house before then. That the couple chose to sell provides further evidence that they were intending to start a new life. There was then a great delay over the embarkation of Irish prisoners, of whom William was to be in charge. The Coxes did not even arrive at the Cove of Cork until February 1799, having joined the ship in England.[68] They left their two eldest sons, William and James, at the grammar school in Salisbury, spending holidays in the care of a Mr and Mrs Dawe at Ditcheat Manor in Somerset.[69]

As the crow flies, the village of Ditcheat is 32 miles from Salisbury. By road today it is well over 40 miles. In 1800 that would have been a full day's journey. The Dawes were a well-known county family, with strong army connections. Charles Richard Dawe had been High Sheriff for Somerset in 1725. His son, Hill Dawe, succeeded him in 1769 and was a captain in the Somerset Militia. One of Hill's sons, Charles, was born 1789, making him the same age as William Cox Jnr, both nine-year-olds when the boys first stayed at Ditcheat. It is probable that Hill Dawe, although nearly 30 years older than William Snr, would have met him through Militia activities and taken an almost fatherly interest.[70] Even so, the Dawes were accepting a considerable responsibility, especially bearing in mind that William and James were with them from 1798 to the end of 1803 and that the boys had, at the end of that time, to be got on board a ship for the voyage to the colony. Yet there is no mention of the Dawe family in William's letters. When he wrote to his friend John Piper on 28 July 1804, telling him about the boys' arrival, he said nothing about where they had been, only that they were 'safe and well'.[71]

A feature of military life throughout the ages has been waiting for orders. In the end the *Minerva* was a year late sailing, during which time Rebecca gave birth to that other son at the Cove on 17 March.[72] They finally sailed on 24 August 1799. The voyage provided William with his first direct experience of managing convicts and established his early reputation for humane treatment of them. It also revealed a lack of scruple in his commercial dealings en route at Rio de Janeiro, described in the next chapter, although financial manipulations were generally characteristic of the officer class at the time and of the New South Wales Corps in particular.

Of his future military duties, William does not seem to have spoken. This again prompts the question of why he chose to emigrate as an officer to a penal colony, when more lucrative openings were available. But simply making money does not seem to have been his objective.[73] He was looking for a new life and for land and may, in his mind's eye, have anticipated the slightly later colonial existence, of which Douglas Woodruff writes: 'Australia was slowly discovered by the upper and middle classes as a new country where gentlemen might live the free country life which had always been the English ideal … men who were attracted by the idea of a life to be spent largely on horseback, overseeing a vast property'.[74] This was a dream that William and his sons eventually came to live.

Irrespective of whether he did go out in 1797, William would have known from others before he left that John Macarthur, Quartermaster Laycock and other officers had already acquired substantial landholdings.[75] It explains his apparent lack of interest in a military career – a paymastership was not an obvious route to command, though it was to making profits. When he exploited that path in trying to achieve landed status he did so with perilous imprudence. Meanwhile, he and his family had to face the more immediate dangers of the journey out to Port Jackson. It was a voyage which proved to incorporate three of the worst perils the master of a convict ship feared: a mutiny, interception by hostile warships and appalling weather. Once those were past, William and Rebecca were able to start a new life, unaware that they were to meet defeat through William's own risk taking.

2   Emigration – Hostile Ships, Storms and Mutinies

If William and Rebecca had a dream when they emigrated, which there is every reason to believe they did, that dream of a new life in the colony had to endure elements of a savage nightmare en route to its realization. Mutiny, hostile ships and storms plagued the long first sector of the voyage via Rio de Janeiro, not to mention the entertainments of 16 informal 'marriages' between female convicts and crewmen.

It is fortunate that two men on board recorded what happened during this near-epic 139 day voyage. Many of the convict transports suffered from storms and plots. What their voyages usually lacked were such accounts as those of the young Irish ship's surgeon John Washington Price, who was 21 when appointed, and the Irish rebel 'General' Joseph Holt gave of the *Minerva*'s journey. Although this voyage established William Cox's early reputation for humane treatment of convicts, and also some of his own hopes for the future, he himself appears to have left no notes about it, so his actions are seen only through the other's men's eyes and his thinking has to be deduced from his actions.

Joseph Holt, the Irish rebel 'General' who became William's farm manager

Holt had his wife and two children with him. His *Memoirs* were not collated and edited until 39 years later and are more than a little self-serving, while memory is not always an accurate tool.[1] Price described him somewhat scornfully as 'a quite illiterate man, but possessed of a deal of natural courage and abilities' who had 'made himself remarkable in this country [Ireland] for his disloyalty and villainy'.[2] He was not a convict, having negotiated a deal with the governor at Dublin to go into exile with his wife and children, instead of being tried for treason. His trial and probable execution would have caused more unrest than it was worth. He eventually left the colony in 1817, so could have had little ulterior motive for praising William Cox's humanity 20 years later, which he also did in recounting his four years as William's farm manager after they arrived. Holt has understandably been much quoted by historians, though seldom on the voyage.

Price's detailed, neatly penned, not always daily, log had various accomplished watercolour illustrations pasted in and was amusingly idiosyncratic. 'I do not mean to keep an exact daily journal,' he wrote soon after he started it in December 1798, 'but will give an account of all occurrences that are striking, remarkable or will be hereafter entertaining to my friends; in this facts will be related simply as they happen.'[3] How they would be conveyed to his friends he did not explain. Of some 600 surgeons' logs which have survived, few can be of such immediacy.[4] An excerpt will give the flavour of his entries, which usually followed notes on the weather and the sick list. On 1 April 1799, long before they sailed, a convict named Kennedy died of fever. Price wrote 'he was sentenced to transportation for life, but evaded that by escaping to eternity'.[5]

The surgeon had arrived by coach from Dublin in May 1798, only surviving an ambush by highwaymen when a troop of Dragoons chanced by and rescued him. This was after both sides had discharged their firearms and missed! He had also, mildly comically, though not for the woman concerned, got married when chafing at the delays in the *Minerva*'s sailing. 'In the meantime,' he recorded, 'I took care not to disappoint myself, having got married [on] July 24th [1798] to a lady at Corke, with whom I am convinced I shall be happy in whatever situation fortune places me'. Sadly for her, that did not include sailing to Port Jackson. 'Indeed,' he explained to his log, 'when I got married I did not intend going this voyage, but the Minerva arriving so soon after my marriage prevented me from sending in my intended resignation'.[6] In reality the ship had arrived seven months after his marriage, so Price was deceiving only his own journal and its unlikely later readership.

Price and the Coxes were kept waiting by two problems. The *Minerva* had been lying in the Thames while a dispute raged between her owners and the East India Company, to which she was chartered, over her not having had a proper dry dock survey. The Company had a near-monopoly on transport shipping to the colony. This caused the first delays to her sailing. The sentencing of captives from the Irish rebellion of 1798 caused worse ones. She had originally been scheduled to sail to Ireland in August 1798, but the Coxes did not even arrive at the Cove of Cork until February 1799, on board the ship. They had left their two eldest sons, William and James, at the grammar school in Salisbury and in the care of friends as described in the previous chapter. In the end the ship was to be a year late sailing, so the officers took lodgings in Corke, a little distant from the Cove of Corke, and began what would be a long wait, albeit for Rebecca an eventful one. She was heavily pregnant.

On Sunday 17 March 1799 Price wrote: 'I was called to see Mrs Cox and found her in strong labour. At ten past 1 AM she was delivered of her seventh son. Both the mother and child are in good health. The child is to be called Francis Edmund Cox, but ought to have been called Patrick being born on his day, but it seems our titular saint is no favourite with Capt. Cox from the unhappy disturbances … in this country.' All did not stay well for Rebecca after the birth.

On 23 March the surgeon recorded: 'Mrs Cox worse this day than she has done since she lay in, the milk in her left breast having ceased and every symptom of mastodymia appears … I have put her on a strict antiphologistic regimen … the child is in good health'. By 31 March he had to cut open her breast and release 'a very considerable quantity of pus', which made her easier. She was unable to feed the child except on 'pap'.[7] Strangely, there is nothing more recorded about the baby. It is not mentioned in Price's subsequent manifest of all on board, though convict babies are. He only lists Rebecca as 'Captain's wife' with Charles, George, Henry and Frederick.[8] Nothing is said about the child in family records either, but Price was always meticulous about details. The main significance of this birth is that, as suggested in Chapter 1, the child would have to have been conceived the previous July, which undermines the family claims that William first went out to the colony in 1798.

Meanwhile an initial batch of 137 convicts, 19 of them women, had arrived from Dublin on the brig *Lively* on 19 January 1799 in conditions that displayed the worst aspects of convict transportation. Price found them in 'the most wretched, cruel and pitiable condition I ever saw human beings in … they were all lying indiscriminately in the ship's holds on the damp, wet and uneven planks without any sort of covering … half naked some even without the shirt'. He thought that if they deserved death they should have been hung or shot, prior to their departure from Dublin, not treated like this. He immediately had them washed, the men shaved, and provided with clean clothes.[9] Those conditions were just as bad as that to which the slave traders of the first and second fleets condemned their cargos, vividly described by Robert Hughes in *The Fatal Shore*.[10]

Sending criminals to New South Wales (New Holland), America being closed off by Independence, was proposed by Lord Sydney in a letter to the Lords Commissioners of the Treasury dated 10 August 1786.[11] Between 1787 and 1868 transportation to the colonies involved 806 ships.[12] The First Fleet, under Governor Phillip, was well organized, but considered expensive. The more cheaply organized Second Fleet was contracted to professional slave traders. It reached Port Jackson in June 1790, involved great brutality and an appalling death rate of 256 men and 11 women, many of whom had already been weakened by imprisonment on the hulks in the

Thames estuary.[13] Following this, the Home Office paid only for convicts who had been checked and approved on arrival, with a bonus of £4 10s 6d for each convict who arrived safe and sound. Even so the Third Fleet of 11 ships in 1791, organized by the same contractors, saw a toll of 184 dead out of approximately 2000, or 9 percent. Selling the convicts' food was common – Holt noticed that Salkeld sold some of the *Minerva*'s at Rio – as was confining them more closely in order to fit in private cargo to sell in the colony. But no financial reward could eliminate the risk of disease, as befell another ship in the *Minerva*'s small convoy, the *Friendship*, where crew members as well as convicts died.[14]

The brutality declined and the shipboard conditions improved (marginally) after 1801, making most of the later voyages less sensational. In any case, every ship was in some way different, as was every master – however brutal and corrupt – and so was every voyage. Whereas the *Hillsborough*'s in 1798 has had whole books devoted to it,[15] the relatively humane voyage of the *Minerva* is seldom mentioned. Its success has presumably gone against the grain of the 'brutality incarnate' historians. Even in the quite comprehensive *Bound for Botany Bay* published by the British National Archives in London, in which watercolours from the surgeon's log are reproduced, there is not a word about the voyage itself.[16] Yet its extremely low death rate established William's reputation for humanity in dealing with convicts, even though Price was if anything more responsible for alleviating the conditions. The voyage also provided William with his first direct experience of managing convicts, an aptitude he would refine throughout his life.

The *Minerva* eventually sailed on 20 August 1799. On the afternoon of the 19th, Price and William became involved in an incident with some locals ashore which displayed tempestuousness in both of them, as well as physical bravery and a touch of arrogance. 'Captain Cox having spent this afternoon on shore with me, we were insulted by a number of the Cove blackguards and obliged to fight very hard.' Helped by a soldier and a seaman with them, they 'procured some sticks and completely beat off a dozen or more of them from the beach'. Price boasted that the locals would 'remember the Botany Bay men for some time'.[17] As throughout his life, William was a man of action, but in this instance seized a boat which Price admits had 'in some measure created the dispute'. Reading between the lines of Price's account, it sounds suspiciously as though the two of them, aided by the soldiers, had decided to have a final afternoon's amusement. The local men had objected and wanted their boat back. The soldiers' reaction was typical. They gave the locals bloody noses for their cheek.

By contrast, William had not hesitated a few weeks earlier, in June, to go armed aboard a troopship to arrest two deserters. He then exercised a combination of firmness and humanity, Price considering that 'were it not for Captain Cox's exertions, they both would have been severely punished'.[18] Throughout the voyage, William would display an inclination to talk tough, but be lenient in his punishments. Thus he warned the convicts that any attempt 'to contest the command or to force their escape, should be punished with instant death', yet in the event of the attempted mutiny he only gave the offenders six lashes.[19]

The episode with the locals shows that the relationship between William and Price, though amiable, was unstructured. William was an officer. Price was a civilian under contract, not subject to military discipline. In practice this does not appear to have caused problems. It would not be until 1815 that the transport commissioners rectified this by giving the surgeons naval rank as surgeon-superintendents and therefore subservience to the officers.[20]

On the day of their sailing, Price left his new wife behind, not telling her until that very morning. 'With a heavy heart I tore myself away from the arms of my dearest wife.' Only many months later, after the *Minerva* had gone on from Post Jackson to India, did he whimsically send her a message: by attaching one to the neck of a seabird, a tern, which had briefly rested on board.

Between them, the accounts of Price and Holt enable a good picture to be established of William Cox in his role as officer in charge of the convicts.

They reveal something of his character and give indications that he might have already been to the colony and expected to buy a farm, although the conception date of the baby makes this improbable. He is referred to throughout as Captain Cox, and continued to be so-called intermittently after he left the army, to the annoyance of his former fellow officers. This rank is not recorded in the Army Lists.

The most probable explanation is that there was another lieutenant named Maundrell on the ship, junior to William. It would have been logical therefore for William to have been given the local acting rank of captain for the voyage. The absurdly eulogistic *Memoirs* confirm this by saying: 'his commission was really that of Lieutenant, but he had command of the troops'.[21] However, William managed to be known as Captain Cox for the rest of his life, though not by Governor Macquarie. Price incidentally had an exceedingly low opinion of Maundrell, who on 6 May 1799 took some opium, saying he needed sleep. 'But in my opinion he has been asleep since he came on board of this ship,' the surgeon suggested.[22] Indeed when the armed confrontation at sea, described below, took place Maundrell discovered himself to be unwell.

The *Minerva* was a typical three-masted freight ship, built in Bombay in 1773 for charter to the East India Company and not designed as a convict transport.[23] The convicts were held, Price says, in 'a clear airy prison, being eight feet between decks, with a scuttle to each birth [*sic*]' of five men. This deck height was completely exceptional and must have helped to keep the prisoners healthy.[24] The ship had a line of square ports on each side and was armed with eight guns, which she was going to need. In order to avoid extra taxation, she was narrow hulled, which meant she rolled in rough seas.

Although Commissioner Bigge wrote his report on the colony 20 years later, some of his observations about transportation are relevant. In his 'Preface about the Condition and Treatment of Convicts during the Passage to New South Wales' he considered that a berth of 18 inches for each convict was 'sufficient', but that the space allocated to seamen and military guards was 'scarcely adequate to their accommodation for so long a voyage'. He commented on the captains and surgeons being 'much interrupted by commercial speculations of their own' and the 'temptation for a fraudulent abduction of the Government provisions'. Bigge was referring to what captains did with the convicts' food on arrival, rather than their selling it off en route, as Salkeld did. But the principle was the same.[25] There is no indication that Price so profited, in fact he spent his own money on extra food for the prisoners.

When she finally did sail the *Minerva* carried 165 male and 26 female convicts, plus three convict children. Another child was born on the voyage and three men died. This extremely low death rate came at what proved to be a turning point in the death rate from conditions on transport ships. The ship's complement included the Cox family and William's personal servant, a marines detachment of two sergeants, a drummer and 17 privates, 7 soldiers' wives, 6 soldiers' children and several political exiles.[26] Two of the exiles were to figure largely in William's future life. Holt, who has been already been mentioned, had paid for his family's passage – over which the Commander, Joseph Salkeld, attempted to defraud him – and was acutely conscious that he was not a convict. None the less Price listed him as one, with his wife and children as passengers.

A second exile was the Reverend Henry Fulton, with his wife and two children. A clergyman of the established church, Fulton had been accused of political crimes. Once in the colony, where there was a shortage of Protestant clergy, he was quickly appointed to Norfolk Island as chaplain and rehabilitated. William is thought to have later helped to secure him a living at Castlereagh. There was also a Mrs Davis, a returned ex-convict who was, in Price's words, 'now going out again, having got some property in the country'. She was an early example of a convict discovering that life in the colony was more promising than as an ex-convict in England. She and everyone else on the ship is meticulously listed in Price's log.[27]

The *Minerva*'s five-ship convoy sailed in the year before the system of transportation was reviewed in 1801. Her voyage was therefore on the cusp of reform, underlining the ameliorations which William and the surgeon did achieve. It was a period of relatively few sailings. Between the Third Fleet and 1801 only 18 transports sailed and the death rate, despite the *Hillsborough*'s hideous percentage, fell to around 2 percent. Even so *Minerva*'s rate of 1.5 percent was notably low. In fact Price considered that two of the three men who did die would have done so anyway, being elderly and unfit, had they remained on land. This is not to suggest that conditions in the prison were anything other than squalid, despite the eight foot headroom. Convict ships were usually infested with lice and vermin. A stench of rot and excrement rose from the bilges. Yet Holt remembered the *Minerva* as being 'well found and fitted for her voyage. Everything appeared clean, orderly and proper on board.' Salkeld had 'fitted up a little cabin for me, Mrs Holt and my son, off the steerage and we were most comfortable.'[28] Price was less lucky, being once thrown out of his bunk during a storm. The Coxes' cabin was not described.

The August sailing date meant that the hottest season was encountered in the tropics, with all the stifling discomfort which that entailed. On Saturday 8 September Price recorded: 'All the convicts were crying and complaining of the excessive heat in the prison ... those I found most distressed I ordered on deck.'[29] William saw to it that the convicts were allowed up in turns for regular exercise and fresh air on deck, despite Salkeld's opposition on the grounds that there was no quartermaster available to keep watch on them. At William's request, Holt stood in for the quartermaster. It can only have been this fresh air and exercise that did the trick for the men's survival. Even so, later on in the voyage, on 11 October, despite all precautions, a fever began to appear. It was typhus of a 'putrid, malignant tendency', Price wrote. He isolated the victims and had the prison 'cleaned, washed and some parts of it rubbed over with oil of tar.'[30]

Curiously, William thought some convicts were being too leniently treated. When they were two weeks out, at Lat. 30.50N, he ordered the men to be put back into irons, 'as they were all now in good health and spirits.'[31] On 12 September Price recorded, in his neat handwriting: 'We began putting in irons those whom illness and indulgence kept out of them these six months past

… they were now all in good health and spirits, there were a few left without irons and a few in single irons to clean the prison and attend those who should be ill.'[32] This seems, today, a perverse reaction on William's part and is out of character with Holt's descriptions of him. Life was not easy in the prison, with the fit men lying in irons on crowded bunks in sweltering heat. Nonetheless the sick list averaged only 27 to 30 per day, out of the 194, a tribute to Price. Their diet saved most from scurvy.

The women convicts did not lie in irons. Sixteen of the 26 lay with the soldiers or the crew. One area of the ship's life over which neither Salkeld nor William exerted any more than minimal discipline, probably because in practical terms it would have been too difficult, was the sexual relationships of the women. Price wrote on 5 September: 'the sailors were claiming a wife each from amongst the female convicts and in a little time sixteen of the women got husbands for the voyage amongst the sailors and soldiers, on the conditions that for the first offence they would be put down and confined for the remainder of the voyage [presumably on either William's or Salkeld's orders]'. Price continued wryly 'It is singular that in all these matrimonial engagements, they dispensed with the usual ceremonies even to a man, they drank a good quantity of grog on the occasion.'[33] It seems odd that they were able to obtain liquor, presumably from the crew.

Other commanders and Commissioner Bigge (later on) had plenty to say about this sexual activity. Captain Ralph Clark, writing about such conduct during an earlier voyage of the *Friendship*, said 'These damned troublesome whores. I would rather have a hundred men than have a single woman.'[34] Bigge was more analytical, also referring to the *Friendship*, and hitting the nail on the head so far as the *Minerva* was concerned as well: 'No precautions were adopted by the captain or surgeon to prevent an improper intercourse between the crew and the convicts … In consequence of this neglect, a very general intercourse took place between the crew and the female convicts.' Attempts to restore authority were 'opposed by the vicious inclinations of the women themselves.'[35] The worst punishment available was to cut off their hair, although a few were flogged on other voyages.

This said, there is no hint in Price's log that there was any unpleasantness involved. But without doubt, Salkeld, Cox and he never exerted control, or perhaps felt that the crew and soldiers had a right of access to the women. Many years later William's evidence to Bigge showed that he regarded the primary function of women in colonial society was as wives, definitely not as whores.

The historian Joy Damousi has made some interesting points about this, observing that before 1816 women convicts did not have a rigidly supervised and structured routine on board. 'Convict women [then] would certainly have had more opportunity to enter into sexual liaisons with their officers and seaman.'[36] In the *Minerva's* time the ships carried a mix of sexes, while her study is primarily about a later period. However, on female convict ships, 'a concern with order and potential chaos was a concern with the interaction between the "public" and the "private" [space] on ships'. A private space, such as the crew enjoyed, became 'the arena of chaos and disorder … through sexual promiscuity'.[37] This gave the women power. At the same time, 'domesticity was conflated with femininity'. It seems likely that a combination of these factors resulted in the *Minerva's* 'marriages'. But as the log establishes, there is no hint of disorder in Price's account, rather an air of tolerant detachment.

The voyage suffered numerous alarms en route, as already mentioned. On 26 September they had 'repeated information of different plots by convicts to take the ship from us' and kill an informant. The most treacherous were transferred to the strong room. Price commented that the information 'would have hung many of them in a Court of Justice, yet we still wishing to bring them to Botany Bay without flogging any of them'.[38] The actual mutiny attempt came to a head a few days later, curiously triggered by an encounter with hostile warships.

On 30 September they encountered 'two strange sail' at Lat 6.48N, and a charade of flying false colours ensued, in which each side attempted to bluff the other. This was in the same latitude as Recife (Pernambuco) in Brazil although, no longitude being given, it is not clear how far offshore they were. The strange ships apparently assumed the *Minerva* might be worth capturing, while Salkeld was rashly imprudent in preparing to fight, given the relative strengths of their armaments. He hoisted a Danish flag on the *Minerva* and fired a gun, whereupon the strangers ran up English colours and fired back, though at a distance. When within 'gun and a half shot' range Salkeld changed to the English flag and the strange ships took down their English colours and hoisted Portuguese. They were now close enough to each other for the *Minerva*'s crew to see that the two enemy ships were either Spanish or Portuguese and well armed. The larger had 30 guns and the other ship 14.

If they were Spaniards, and enemies, they were too powerful to take on. If they were Portuguese and allies, in Price's phrase: 'we had nothing to do with them'. The *Minerva* therefore made all sail to escape, the enemy's shots fell far short, and 'night coming on we never saw them again'. Price commented: 'we showed more courage then wisdom' and stood to gain nothing, because if the *Minerva* had taken them, she lacked letters of marque to be a privateer and would not have been able to profit.[39] It had been a risky confrontation, probably motivated by Salkeld's greed.

This appears to be the incident related by Holt in his *Memoirs*, when he was requested by the chief mate, Harrison, to man a swivel gun on the poop and asked if he would fight. 'I answered "yes",' said Holt, 'but I answered with mental reservation.' His plan was to turn the gun on the ship's crew, had they been boarded, in the hope of freeing his fellow Irish prisoners. Harrison became suspicious afterwards, but Holt managed to talk his way out of it, even though he had chosen those who should mutiny and 'they knew my mind by a secret signal'.[40]

Holt had a more convoluted character than William may have realized. One of the curiosities of the voyage was the warm relationship which blossomed between them. One of the Irish rebel's numerous tributes to William's humanity was instanced on 8 October when a further conspiracy by nine convicts to seize the ship and murder the officers was discovered by Price. 'We have had very great hopes,' Price wrote, 'that in no instance during the voyage … we should have any occasion to punish these too unfortunate men.' The 'we' can only mean William, at whose discretion convicts would be punished. He ordered four of the plotters to be tied to the capstan and given six lashes each by the boatswain – an extraordinarily modest sentence for actions that might have earned them the yardarm on other ships. Price commented: 'it was but a slight punishment, but we hope it will have the effect.'[41]

With these dangerous events behind them, the *Minerva* reached Rio de Janeiro on 19 October, staying to obtain provisions until 7 November. Here was revealed a commercially exploitative side to William's activities, recorded by Holt but not remarked on by Price. 'Captain Cox brought with him,' Holt says, 'watches, beaver hats, calicoes, shawls, glass of various kinds, cutlery etc.' During the voyage he had had the watches, which were cheap 'London' ones, embellished by a jeweller convict on board. This was a craft William knew all about. He sold the various goods 'at an incredible profit … one day his servant was so loaded with dollars, the produce of Capt Cox's dealings on shore, that it was with difficulty we brought him into the ship'. In this account Holt interjected the caveat 'but this gentleman's traffic was fair and honourable'.[42] It might have been more truthful to say that officers of the New South Wales Corps were renowned for their commercial dealings on the side and that William must have already absorbed the tradition. Whilst in Rio he bought a heifer and a calf to take to the colony. This could be an indication of his farming plans, although it was not an uncommon thing for officers to do.[43]

The purchase could also be held to substantiate the unproven family correspondence, which states that William had visited the colony in 1797. The possibility is supported by such circumstantial evidence as his being sufficiently knowledgeable to take that stock of cheap goods with him on the *Minerva* to trade in Rio de Janeiro, as could the rapidity with which he offered Holt as job as farm manager on their arrival in Port Jackson.[44] Equally, he might have been given a few tips on how to exploit the voyage out by other officers.

Price, on the other hand, bought tea, sugar and portable soup to help keep the sick alive on the second leg of the voyage to Port Jackson – presumably at his own expense. This again emphasizes the 22-year-old surgeon's concern for his convict charges. This second leg was uneventful, apart from stormy weather, which pitched Price out of his berth four times. The third death took place on 2 December, of a 67-year-old of 'decay of nature'. Price had noted on 16 November that 'the old men among the convicts, some of which are 70, 80 and 85 years old continue very weak and languid'.[45]

When they reached Port Jackson on 11 January 1800, after an overall voyage of 139 days, Price's sick return was minimal. No soldiers were ill, one was convalescent, one wife was convalescent. Nine convicts were sick and eight convalescent. Only the three male convicts had died, while one convict child had been born. The eulogistic references to this voyage by William's grand-daughters in the *Memoirs* are justified, which say that the health of the prisoners 'was due beyond a doubt to the influence of Captain William Cox'.[46] The only incident to mar the ship's arrival happened when a small boat came alongside and its occupant, taking no notice of a sentry's warning, was shot through the heart. Interestingly, even though some convicts had plotted to run him through with his own sword in the mutiny, Price had got to know the others well enough to be aware that they expected to get farms and lodgings on arrival. 'I did not distress them, by contradicting them,' he wrote.[47]

Three days after their arrival, William made an offer to Holt. 'The Governor has promised me six men', Holt quotes him as saying, 'and you may be one of them, if you please, not to labour, but to superintend.' Holt angrily rejected the offer, since he was not a convict. He had lodged his family with another Irish exile friend, Maurice Margarot, but rapidly realized that he needed a job and a house or he was likely to be homeless and unemployed. He acquiesced a week later when on 22 January William said he 'was in treaty for the purchase of a farm of one hundred acres from Mr John Macarthur'. Would Holt (who had been a farmer) look it over? [48]

In summary, William had arrived at his chosen destination for a new life. He had successfully brought his wife and children with him. He may have shipped out the family portraits, now at Clarendon, as testimony to his lineage, in the way that a twentieth-century age of settlers shipped their antiques to African colonies when the Great War was over. He had also, though he probably did not yet realize it, made a reputation for himself for both humanity and ability. Next he had to acquire a farm: and from Holt's account, wasted no time doing so, if it was not already arranged.

One of the last New South Wales entries in Price's log, while he was waiting for the *Minerva* to leave again for India, describes a trip to Parramatta and 'the plantations and inclosures [*sic*] belonging to a few houses on each side the river'. Among them was 'a little box belonging to Mr Cox, a small distance from the water'.[49] There can only have been one 'Mr Cox' in Price's mind. This 'box' appears to have been Brush Farm, where the original farmhouse, although some way from Parramatta at Ryde, was close to the river, suggesting that William was already either the owner or the prospective one. Of his future military duties, he does not seem to have spoken. A paymastership was not a career move, but it was a financial one.

3 The Second Largest Landowner in Two Years, Bankrupt in Three

After William bought Brush Farm from John Macarthur in January 1800 he launched into a land buying spree which would make him the second largest landholder New South Wales within two years – and bankrupt him in three. The view he had of Port Jackson when the *Minerva* dropped anchor on 11 January 1800 is worth conjuring up for its differences from the Sydney landscape of today. The Circular Quay did not exist. The Tank Stream flowed down into Sydney Cove with its cargo of detritus, the indigenous vegetation of its valley already gone, while on the right was the jumble of primitive housing on the Rocks, where there was a disregarded midden of the remains of the Eora peoples' fish meals. As Grace Karskens points out, the houses on the Rocks, one- or two-roomed huts of wattle and clay with thatched roofs, were possibly introduced by rural convicts in a vernacular style. 'Convicts and soldiers chose sites in their respective zones, built houses and soon regarded them as their own.'[1] The main street was the High Street (later George Street). Governor Macquarie's regimented town planning was more than a decade ahead.

William and his family, one may assume, were met and probably taken direct by boat to Parramatta. The river was the preferred means of getting to the settlement, partly because of the danger of attacks by Aborigines, partly because of dangers from gangs of escaped convicts. The entrance to the Parramatta River passed the tip of the Rocks and the Dawes Point

John Macarthur, the previous paymaster from whom William bought Brush Farm in 1800 (Dixson Galleries, State Library of NSW [DG 242])

battery, where the harbour bridge spans it today. A painting of the landing place as it was in 1809, now in the Mitchell Library, helps to give an idea of the landscape. Major Grose had built a store on the south bank and there were early houses on the right. The mangroves which now line so much of the river bank had not yet grown. At Parramatta itself the Corps had a barracks, close by the original military redoubt, where Macarthur had established the paymaster's office. Parramatta was an Aboriginal word meaning

Port Jackson as seen by the surgeon of the *Minerva* in January 1800 (British Library Mss 13880)

'head of a river', which Governor Phillip had adopted after he recognized it was a more promising place for a settlement than Sydney Cove.

By November 1791 Phillip had abandoned agricultural efforts at Sydney in favour of the fertile land round Parramatta and established a farm at what he named Rose Hill. He then decided to lay down a township west of the redoubt, between it and Government House, first constructed by him in 1793 as a very simple building. Only later did it become the elegant building which still overlooks the centre of the conurbation. Parramatta being situated 24 kilometres from Sydney by land, further by river, it was never the seat of the Governor's main residence, nor of the New South Wales Corps' principal barracks. Those were in Sydney, between what Macquarie named George Street and York Street, bounded at one end of King Street. Today's Wynyard Square occupies part of the substantial site and the short Barrack Street led to it. It was from there that Major Johnston marched his men overnight to deal with the Castle Hill (or Vinegar Hill) convict uprising in 1804.

In terms of the acquisition of land by officers, Parramatta was far more important than anywhere else in the early days. On 25 February 1793 acting Governor Grose gave John Macarthur, who was administering the settlement there, a grant of 100 acres and a further 100 a year later. This became Elizabeth Farm, named after John's wife. The house is still there today, on land running down to the river. Gradually officers obtained plots of land in the developing town, or near it. William's purchase of Brush Farm fitted into a regimental pattern at the settlement, although it was further out in what is now Ryde. The name Brush Farm derived from the patches of local rainforest, or 'brush', surrounding the upper areas of The Ponds. The present day Brush Farm house was not where William and Rebecca lived. It was originally Joseph Holt's house, greatly extended and glorified by Gregory Blaxland, who owned it from 1807.[2] If the surgeon Price's watercolour of Mr Cox's 'box' is correct, William's own house was much closer to the water. From here he would have ridden on horseback to the paymaster's office in the barracks. The family evidently rode, since

A woman of New South Wales and an officer of the NSW Corps at Parramatta when William was there (Juan Ravenet, published Paris 1824)

Holt described how in 1803 he found Rebecca had no horse at her disposal after the bankruptcy, when they were still living at Brush Farm.

A map drawn in 1804 by the colonial surveyor, George Evans, shows how Parramatta was laid out. The eastern end of the High Street, now George Street, was the barracks, originally called the Redoubt. Facing it at the western end was Government House in its domain on a low hill. The gaol stood to away the north and the hospital a little closer in, by the oxbow lake known as the Crescent. Directly between Government House and the barracks, lining the 205 foot wide High Street, were the thatched homes of the officers and officials mentioned earlier, on small rectangular plots of land. Some of their owners were to feature largely in William's future life, notably Captain John Piper, John Brabyn, Edward Abbott and D'Arcy Wentworth. The contrast between how some lived then and how they lived later is seen at an extreme in the case of John Piper, William's particular friend. Piper later made a great deal of money as the Naval Officer at Sydney, collecting customs duties, and in 1822 completed the magnificent mansion Henrietta Villa at Point Piper on the Sydney foreshore, only to be bankrupted in 1827.

The historian Michael Roe comments that 'The oldest established [gentry] could trace their colonial roots to the first twenty years of Australian history – to the officers of the military establishment ... or the civil establishment'.[3] Among the civilians was that unusual character, the chaplain Samuel Marsden, the sturdy son of a Yorkshire blacksmith who became notorious for devoting as much time to his four-legged flock as to his parochial one. The pumpkin-faced Marsden resided close to the simple church at Parramatta which is today St John's Cathedral, where William's second marriage took place in 1821. He later had a grandiose Georgian rectory built for himself.

Samuel Marsden, chaplain, pastoralist and magistrate, conducted William's second marriage (Alexander Turnbull Library, New Zealand)

Parramatta was thus the focal point of William Cox's first years in the colony. Early sketches show the convicts' huts, cultivated fields, farm carts, Aborigines and women walking down the High Street. It was small community where everyone – excluding the convicts – knew everyone else and where William rapidly became prominent. His experiences illustrate the strong position the New South Wales Corps' officers held in acquiring estates in the 1790s and 1800s (a strength totally demolished when Governor Macquarie was ordered to send the regiment home in 1810). As John Macarthur's wife, Elizabeth, had told a friend back in 1790 – only two years after the landing of the First Fleet – 'This country offers numerous advantages to persons holding appointments under government.'[4] That also presaged the ways by which William, and such of his contemporaries as John Macarthur, acquired grazing land on a large scale and created great estates. It can bear repeating that they had brought with them the overriding lesson from late eighteenth-century England that the ownership of land spelt wealth and power. They relatively quickly turned themselves into a dominant class of landed gentry in the colony, roughly between the governorates of King and Bourke.

Since Elizabeth Macarthur was telling friends about the opportunities in the colony eight years before William transferred into the Corps it is reasonable to assume that he knew all about them in advance, even if he may not have made the 1797 visit. As it was, the early years were for him a sorry saga of the eighteenth-century style chicanery thought acceptable at the time – ambition, opportunism and a quite extraordinary degree of naiveté. The opportunism is illustrated by William unhesitatingly using regimental funds to buy land, as recorded by Joseph Holt and eventually realized by the army authorities at home.

Although the Colonial Secretary's correspondence and the *Historical Records of Australia* yield bare facts about William's acquisitions, while the *Sydney Gazette* published sale notices, most of the knowledge of the early days at Brush Farm derives from Holt's *Memoirs*. At the outset, on 22 January 1800, William had told him: 'I have money, and you are possessed of considerable knowledge in agricultural pursuits; suppose we join them together, I think we should easily make a fortune'.[5] Given that William's main civilian experience was of clockmaking, and Holt had been a successful farmer in Ireland, this was a prudent move.[6] The terms of the deal were not instantly agreed. Holt refused a salary on the grounds that he had been a master all his life and had 'great reluctance to become a servant'. In the end they had no written arrangement, Holt being satisfied that he would receive a fair remuneration, which William called 'a hard bargain'.[7]

Holt continued to work as William's farm manager through to April 1804, long after the bankruptcy, and continued to keep in touch with William, as a letter from William to Governor King of 24 December 1804 shows. In this letter William recounted how Holt had warned him of a planned uprising by English convicts, including some of his own workers.[8] Holt and William also had their quarrels. One such occasion was in October 1800 when Holt, who as a former Irish rebel was held under constant suspicion by officials, was not – in his view – adequately defended by Cox against accusations. After they had made things up, Holt and his wife went home and 'had scarcely got into our house before the servant arrived with a basket, and a note from Mrs Cox; in the basket were two gallons of wine and two of rum, which the good lady begged us to accept'. This is one of the few recorded examples of Rebecca's actions in running the Cox household and illustrates her practicality in immediately making amends for her husband's mistakes plus an instinctive generosity.[9]

Macarthur sold Brush Farm at Dundas because he was thinking of returning to England. William is highly likely to have known this, not least because he was taking over the job which Macarthur previously held. Holt described it vividly: 'I had never seen such mould as it was, for it resembled an old churchyard; loose black rank looking earth'. However, the ground was 'very well situated and I gave my opinion very much in favour of the purchase'. Holt moved his family there on 1 February 1800 and immediately 'prepared sixty acres to be sown in with wheat'. He relates how Macarthur cheated William by selling him 'a large flock of sheep … They were old rotten ewes of the Bengal breed; he paid three pounds each for them and one hundred and fifty pounds for a brood mare.' Given that William had been a clockmaker, it is hardly surprising that he was fooled. Holt later described Macarthur as a 'very overbearing and tyrannical man'.[10]

By contrast to Macarthur, who he condemned, Holt considered 'Captain Cox was a man of strict integrity … But whatever Mr McArthur thought, he [i.e., Macarthur] did not act in this affair in a gentleman like manner'.[11] This is an interesting reflection, given the nature of Cox's land dealings and of Macarthur becoming pre-eminent among the colonial landed gentry. It incidentally shows that William must have had considerable sums of cash with him when he arrived, at least partly from his dealings in Rio, and probably also from having sold the Devizes house.

Whether his first flock was rotten or not, by November 1802 the Agricultural Returns for the colony show Cox as owning 1440 acres and 1100 sheep – as many as Macarthur, who had now left the army. The officers often took over small acreages from ex-soldiers, persuading them to exchange their land for goods or for spirits. The practice was bemoaned by Governor King, who castigated the 'few monopolizing traders … not failing to ruin those they marked for their prey by the baneful lure of spirits'.[12] King regarded the practice as morally dubious, despite the lax standards of such actions of his own as later exchanging grants of land with his successor, Bligh.

Although William Cox was not guilty of such trading, his attempts to build an agricultural empire in a hurry seem to have been rooted in an eighteenth-century view of the perquisites of office. There was a huge advantage in being able to offer bills drawn on the regimental agents, as they were payable in sterling, which did not circulate in the colony and was much sought after. Most payments were made with promissory notes. Looked at from almost any perspective, two aspects of the colony's initial planning were extraordinary. One was that the authorities did not envisage the need for a form of legal currency. The other was that they do not seem to have appreciated how by bringing out female convicts along with men, they were guaranteeing a next generation of free-born British citizens. The effect of this will be seen in later chapters.

Once he had bought Brush Farm, William quickly went on to acquire a highly productive fruit farm adjoining it. This was the 600 acre Canterbury Farm, belonging to the Reverend Richard Johnson, a Church of England clergyman who had brought orange seeds from Rio de Janeiro and also grew nectarines, peaches and apricots, as well as having planted two acres of vines. Having made his fortune he was leaving the colony. William promptly built a road connecting the two farms, along the line of the Kissing Point road, started to build a 'large dwelling house' and continued to expand his holdings.[13] Holt lists a considerable number of other small land purchases from individuals, a selection of which illustrate how the 1440 acres were accumulated in an almost ravenous way.

Holt comments on his own astuteness when he 'made a good bargain for Mr Cox, clearing for him above £1,000 in one year by these purchases'.[14] Two such were of 30 acres from Thomas Higgins for £35 and of 50 acres from Mr Hume for £45. They bought John Ramsey's farm of 75 acres for £60, Berrington's 25 acres for £100, and 100 acres from Captain McKellar 'for £50 and ten gallons of rum', as well as smaller properties which may have belonged to ex-soldiers. Holt again records, with a note of triumph, how they acquired a 100 acre farm from a Dr Thompson, with 124 sheep and paid £500 for it, as usual with bills drawn on the regimental agents. The accompanying stock was, in the words quoted at the head of the Foreword, 'worth twenty five percent more than the purchase money ... Mr Cox paid him with bills on the regimental agents.'

This particular deal had a less than happy ending for the seller, but provides a description of Cox's farms. Dr Thompson's wife deserted him for an officer on the French ship on which they left, taking the bills of exchange with her. The ship was one of two corvettes (*Le Geographe* and *Le Naturaliste*) sent out by Napoleon Buonaparte to survey the coast of Australia. The French naturalist, Peron, who travelled with them, visited Brush Farm in 1802 and was highly complimentary about it. His subsequent book described the farm in a way no one else did:

> Often on the summit of a picturesque hillock may be a discerned a large and elegant mansion, surrounded by more considerable cultivated lands and covered by greater numbers of flocks and labourers ... The one in question belonged to Mr Cox ... As soon as he perceived M. Bellefin and me, he got into a boat belonging to his farm and, coming to our vessel invited us in so pressing a manner to pass the night at his house that we could not resist his friendly solicitations ... On a second voyage which I made to his estate [with Colonel Paterson and Mr Laycock] Mr Cox took us all to dinner to another farm, still more rich and elegant ... more inland on the side of Castle Hill ... The road which leads from one to the other of these farms is so wide and convenient that we went over it in a carriage. It is between six and seven miles in length and to make it immense loads of rubbish were necessary. The whole of Mr Cox's land amounts to 860 acres ... [with] 800 sheep of the finest breeds.[15]

The second farm was clearly Canterbury, the inclusion of which in the estate increased Holt's daily ride of inspection to about 12 miles along the line of the Kissing Point road. The house, which so impressed Peron, must have been 'the handsome place' which Holt describes William as having wished to build. Perhaps the most telling point in Peron's narrative is that he was taken to see Cox's properties by Colonel Paterson (the commanding officer of the New South Wales Corps) and his lady. Paterson was evidently showing off how advanced the colony had become to this French naturalist. He would later be criticized for condoning Cox's venality.

Holt and Cox bought stock again from Macarthur despite the rotten ewes, including 'one hundred head of cattle, bulls and cows' and 69 pigs. Holt cannily 'advised Mr Cox to take a bottle or two of wine with him, and then to make the bargain after dinner'. The Irishman had a great belief in using liquor to facilitate dealings, as he later showed when the bankruptcy sales took place. Whether because of the alcoholic influence or not, William only had to pay £500 down for the cattle, on the basis that the stock would later be divided. When that happened they had so multiplied that Holt cleared a £1200 profit for William on the deal. 'So,' Holt recorded with satisfaction, 'we made up the loss he had sustained by the manoeuvres of the first bargain.' There was an attractive deviousness about Holt. Not all their offers were successful, however. On 14 May 1802 William made a credit offer for Major Foveaux's farm and stock, but was outbid by a Lieutenant Rowley's cash offer of £700. In 1800 Foveaux had been the largest landowner in the colony, was an important officer in the Corps and may have been wary of William's land deals, yet not willing – like Paterson – to denounce the use of bills drawn on the regimental agents. The officers were almost endemically corrupt.[16]

Holt also describes how he set about planting William's land. At the outset, in February 1800, he had prepared 60 acres to be planted with wheat and began sowing the seed on 24 March, finishing on 3 June. In October he planted Indian corn.[17] This was all done by hoeing between the tree stumps, which in the early days were not dug up when the ground was cleared, making it impractical to use ploughs (although Macarthur had imported the first iron plough in 1794). All farming involved the employment of assigned convicts. In the same year of 1800 Holt was appalled when forced to witness the flogging of an Irish convict named Fitzgerald at Toongabbie, who had been sentenced to 300 lashes. During this often quoted incident, Holt wrote that the 'flesh and skin blew off my face as they shook off the cats [cat o' nine tails]'. He commented that this flogging took place although 'it was against the law to flog a man past fifty lashes without a doctor'.[18] Holt then had a seven pound hoe made, which he required labourers working for him to use, instead of being flogged, and called it his personal flogger, also a much quoted remark. On William seeing it 'Mr Cox said "this is a terrible tool"'.[19]

The background to any agricultural enterprise was always that settlers had to learn how to farm in completely unfamiliar territory with strange vegetation, where land could, in Holt's words 'require labour and manure as much as the mountains of Wicklow; but [with the benefit that] every district yields two crops a year'.[20] Even so, the climate was often hostile. Drought could alternate with flood, and army worm could devastate crops almost overnight. Thus on 14 October of William's first year a hailstorm destroyed every acre of the wheat Holt had so laboriously planted. A worse disaster struck on 21 October 1803, when their harvest was attacked by the blight known as rust. The *Memoirs* say that 266 acres of his wheat were completely lost in three days and the produce of those acres was not worth £20.[21] Farming would also involve a problem that Holt did not have to encounter, but which William later did on the Hawkesbury in 1816 and at Bathurst in 1824, namely the increasing displacement of Aboriginal people, with resultant violent conflict.

The way in which William built up this estate needs to be set in the context of the widespread misuse of regimental funds. The military historian Anthony Clayton, reviewing officers' public morals at that time, writes that from the seventeenth century onward 'Officers were all as much preoccupied with the business side of their lives as the professional'. This did not cease until the Victorian era. In William's time the essential corruption of the whole system continued to enable officers both at home and overseas to supplement their income in such dubious, but usually legal, ways as 'managing regimental funds'.[22] The New South Wales Corps officers were particularly adept at this. Between 1792 and 1798 they had invested £36,844 of regimental funds in their own enterprises.[23] Even the relatively more scrupulous Macquarie, when a newly married captain, paid to take on the army paymastership in Bombay in 1795 so that he could draw the regiment's pay three to five months in advance and invest it short-term with Arab money lenders.[24] William's mistake was to invest in the illiquid asset of land.

In parallel with this, William was taking a serious risk by disregarding new official regulations rescinding permission for officers to farm actively, ordered by the Commander in Chief, HRH the Duke of York, the brother of George III, in 1802. This was done at the urging of the Duke of Portland, who had become aware that in 1800 Macarthur owned 1300 acres, in spite of being a serving officer.[25] Macarthur escaped the ban, because he had been sent home for court martial by Governor King in 1801, after fighting a duel with Lieutenant Colonel Paterson (the trial was aborted for lack of evidence) and was allowed to leave the army. But William was caught by the prohibition. As a result, his first appointment as a magistrate (at Parramatta), made on 6 January 1802, was cancelled on 5 October that same year by King, who as a naval officer neither could nor would tolerate the disobedience of orders. Cox rashly continued to disregard the prohibition and the whole question of failure to obey orders eventually became a more serious disciplinary matter than the 'malversation' of the regimental funds.

The historical backdrop to the acquisition of land by officers went back almost to the first days of the colony. Originally Governor Phillip had made few land grants. Samuel Bennett remarks that whereas at the time of his departure not much more than 3000 acres had been allotted, in a short period afterwards the officers secured 15,000 acres for themselves.[26] This was thanks to Major Francis Grose. When serving as lieutenant governor in 1792–95, after Phillip's departure, Grose freely gave land grants to his officers. Another commentator remarks that under Grose 'the spirit of commercialism and the desire to obtain landed estates became the principal motives in life with many officers of the New South Wales Corps.[27] It was no coincidence that in the early 1800s the largest landowner was Quartermaster Laycock with 1470 acres. He and William were the two officers best placed to profit from their official positions.

This heyday of the officers in obtaining land ended with the Bligh Rebellion and the arrival of Macquarie as governor, although during that period of army rule Lieutenant Colonel Paterson made grants of some 67,000 acres, a small one being at Mulgoa to Rebecca Cox for her four-year-old son, Edward – a grant which she later had to ask Macquarie to ratify.[28] Not that the officers had been alone in acquiring land. On a lower level the first free emigrants who arrived on 16 January 1793 on the *Bellona* were given free passages and land grants, tools, two years' provisions and convict labour by government.[29] However, during that decade the landed interests of the officer class – including officials – became paramount.

A considerable change in official policy took place during the first decade of the new century, benefiting only a few gentleman settlers, but allocating much larger acreages to them. The idea originated from the surgeon William Balmain, a friend of Governor Hunter, who suggested to Lord Camden, the Secretary of State, that he should send out gentlemen settlers who could form an élite. The first beneficiaries were John Macarthur (5000 acres) and Walter Davidson the son of the Prince Regent's physician (2000 acres). Their grants were on the Cowpastures, an area of excellent grazing on the south-west of the Cumberland Plain, where a herd of cattle had long before strayed, gone wild and greatly multiplied. It was hoped, ultimately in vain, that the herd could be domesticated again. The grants of were to be 'fit for the pasture of sheep … in perpetuity, with the usual reserve of quit rent to the Crown'. Macarthur was also to be 'indulged with a reasonable number of convicts … for the purpose of attending to his sheep'. He would pay for their maintenance and so 'a saving will accrue to the Government'.[30]

Governor King was opposed to this plan, avowedly because of the hope of domesticating the wild cattle. Additionally, the serving governor had an interest in the herd because he had a share in it.[31] King intensely disliked Macarthur, whom he had called 'The Great Perturbator' on account of the trouble he had caused. But an order from the Colonial Secretary could not be refused. Whilst acknowledging the value to the colony of Macarthur's sheep breeding, King managed to delay the grant's execution. Nonetheless, in the end the whole area became Macarthur's Camden Park.

Lord Camden's instruction was an historic turning point in the rise of the pastoralists. The 5000 acres was the largest grant ever given in the colony. Thereafter, directions were given to governors by secretaries of state to make land grants to favoured settlers, to allocate them convict labour and, to a lesser extent, to give them cattle. In 1806 grants totalling 12,000 acres were ordered by William Windham, as Secretary of State, for two gentleman farmers from Kent, John and Gregory Blaxland, who were selling up to emigrate.[32] King expressed disappointment that, although the brothers had brought out seed, they claimed it had rotted on the voyage and refused to attempt planting it, insisting instead that they should buy 1700 breeding stock from the government herds.[33] Cattle rearing on broad acres would have looked more like a gentleman's occupation than growing crops. King himself was realistically concerned about having sufficient agricultural production to feed the growing population, but had to obey. Thus 1806 can be set as a date for the recognition of the landed gentry in New South Wales. By this time William Cox was bankrupt and waiting to be sent home for trial.[34]

William's whole edifice of debt had collapsed when, in January 1803, he had a quarrel with Dr Jamison, the Surgeon General, to whom he owed £200. 'In February Dr Jamison pressed him for the money,' Holt records. 'The sum itself was a trifle to pay; but the doctor had circulated a report that Mr Cox had failed, which made everyone who had the slightest demand upon him press forward with their claims at once … they made no less a sum than twenty two thousand pounds.'[35] Ironically, this doctor was the father of Sir John Jamison, with whom William was to have a close political and cultural relationship in the 1820s. In spite of maintaining that his debtors owed him enough to cover his position, William was unable to stall the creditors, who foreclosed.

The exact wording of these bills of exchange issued by William is shown by one he gave to Robert Campbell, a leading Sydney merchant and trader, in the same month that the creditors foreclosed. It read:

> Ninety days after sight Pay this my First Bill of Exchange, Second and Third same Tenor and Date unpaid unto Robert Campbell Esq for one thousand pounds and place the same to the Acct of the pay of the New South Wales Corps without or without advice from, Gentlemen, Wm Cox Paymaster

It was addressed to Messrs Cox (no relation) and Greenwood, Craig's Court, Charing Cross. This particular bill had been presented numerous times and was 'protested' on 28 July 1804 by a notary 'In Testimonium Veritatis, Thomas Bonnet, Notr Pub', as others had been by another notary named Venn. Bonnet eventually spoke to a clerk who said the bill would not be paid.[36]

Since any bill had to be sent to London to be presented, it could be nine months at least before its beneficiary learnt that it had not been honoured and could take action through a London agent, in this case Bonnet, taking the time of a further voyage. Meanwhile, of course, William enjoyed the use of the thousand pounds. Between October 1801 and January 1803 William issued a total of six bills to Campbell,

Miniature of Robert Campbell (Courtesy of Elizabeth Forbes)

totalling £4717. Campbell, who then did very well out of William's best farms, was appointed treasurer to William's estate.

The first sale was held on 15 April 1803 at Campbell's order. On 26 May the 900 acres of Canterbury Farm were auctioned, as well as two other farms of 100 acres at Prospect Hill, a third of 94 acres 'adjoining' the town of Parramatta and also 1700 sheep 'part of which are of Spanish breed'. The auctioneer was Simeon Lord (an ex-convict trader, later to become both a magistrate and a pastoralist). Holt helpfully gave everyone there plenty of rum to stimulate the bidding. But the individual plots of land fetched far less than William had paid for them. D'Arcy Wentworth, who bought five, paid only 108 guineas for 100 acres, Samuel Marsden gave 56 guineas for the Barrington (or Berrington) property which Holt had bought for William for £100.[37] On 6 July household goods were sold, including 'linens, curtains, calicos, shoes, leather, soap, tobacco, ironmongery'.[38] It must have been intensely distressing for Rebecca. On 10 May 1803 Holt

records 'I found that Mrs Cox had no horse at her command. I asked if she would accept of my mare … after a pause Mrs Cox said she would accept of my very friendly offer and expressed herself greatly obliged to me. She was a complete gentlewoman.'[39] Rebecca evidently displayed great fortitude, as she did again when her husband was sent home for trial and was receiving no pay.

Simeon Lord, the ex-convict trader who auctioned William's property in 1803 (Mitchell Library, State Library of NSW [MIN 92])

On 11 November 1803, 'a quantity of wheat and about 50 pigs' were sold.[40] Holt began to collect the debts due to the estate, but they were nothing like enough. From Governor King's point of view William's disaster had a silver lining. He reported home, on 17 September 1803, that 'not a few [settlers] have profitted [sic] by the division of the Paymaster's of the New South Wales Corps large stock of cattle, horses and sheep, which he had been monopolizing until he was compelled to sell them to satisfy the great debts he had accumulated in and out of the colony'.[41] King was a realist and William's disaster would have helped his aim of bringing about a wider ownership of property. His comments illustrate how significant a landowner William had become.

For whatever reason, the Governor began helping William in various practical ways. On 3 February 1804 he agreed to accept £1500 from the sale of £2000 of 3 percent stock and also to take £2949 8s 2¼d worth of Cox's wheat into the Commissary, both of these to help liquidate the debt owed to the army agents, which it halved. There followed what seems to have been a curious manoeuvre by King to help even more, when the trustees, headed by Robert Campbell, asked if they could pay another eight to ten thousand bushels of wheat into the Commissary. This wheat had remained in store in William's ownership, despite the forced sales. On 1 March 1804 King informed the trustees that 'The stores are now, and will continue open for the receipt of wheat in payment of debts due to the Crown'. He emphasized that every cultivator would have an 'equal chance' to dispose of wheat. Since no public notification of this opportunity appeared in the *Sydney Gazette* in either February or March, the equal chance appears to have been deliberately non-existent, although the colony and the newspaper were much preoccupied at the time with the Castle Hill convict riots of 4 March. Even better, King gave the trustees a complete indemnity for any damages resulting from the arrangement, which he need hardly have done.[42]

King's assistance had its political side. The Hawkesbury had been settled by Grose in 1794 to accommodate former soldiers and ex-convicts. King wanted to see the settlement improved, populated as it now was mainly by ex-convict smallholders, the soldiers often having been persuaded to sell their plots, usually in exchange for spirits. At the same time King was sympathetic to William, possibly because he was himself in a more or less permanent stand-off conflict with the New South Wales Corps and might have seen Cox in some way as a victim. The Governor had known when he arrived in 1800 that he would have to fight the officers and, in the words of the *Australian Dictionary of Biography*, 'was faced with frequent disobedience and insolence' from them, after he refused to allow a cargo of spirits to be landed (spirits being the great trading asset of the officers).

Court martial records, not often quoted, show how King was constantly frustrated in his efforts to bring the officers to heel. He ordered the trials of a succession of officers for offences as blatant as looting a wrecked ship.

The court martial records show that in at least four cases the accused men's brother officers acquitted him. Each time King appealed to the monarch against the verdict without result.[43] Additionally, officers circulated libellous 'pipes' (doggerel attacks) against him. One, written by Captain Anthony Fenn-Kemp, for which King accused him of sedition, read in part:

Governor Philip Gidley King, who befriended Cox (State Library of New South Wales)

On Monday keep shop
In two hours, time to stop
To relax from such KINGLY fatigue
And rob Government more
Than a host of good theives [*sic*] by intrigue.

The Board of Officers felt the satire acceptable rather then seditious and honourably acquitted the captain. Whether the officers were aware of it or not, these pipes were little different to the cartoons which constantly lampooned the Prince Regent at home in England.

In the end the officers defeated King and when he eventually left in 1807 he was a sick man. But for all his faults, including what we would see today as corruption, King warmed to and befriended the young circumnavigator of Australia, Matthew Flinders, in 1802, and seems similarly to have liked

William. He also gave semi-official appointments to Barrallier and Harris, officers disciplined by Paterson. He sardonically appointed Barrallier 'King of the Mountains', before sending him on an expedition now forgotten to explore the Blue Mountains.

On 16 July 1804 King went further by granting William and his second son James, jointly, 200 acres at Mulgrave Place, near Windsor.[44] This dovetailed conveniently with the founding of the Richmond Hill District as part of Mulgrave Place. It included what were to become the Macquarie towns of Richmond and Windsor (known originally as Green Hills), Pitt Town and Wilberforce. The precise location of the Coxes' grant has been identified as having been on the south side of the Hawkesbury (Nepean) river between South Creek and Yarramundi Lagoon.[45] The importance of this grant to the family, with its eight assigned convicts, can hardly be overstated. William was to call it Clarendon and the estate became the focal point of his life. Nor is 'estate' the wrong word. He instantly expanded the family holdings there, as is explained in an extraordinary letter from Parramatta to his friend and fellow officer John Piper at Norfolk Island on 28 July 1804.

> By the *Experiment* was received our two dearest sons safe & well … I got them sent out as settlers (to save expence) & have got 250 acres of ground for them with 4 men, tools etc etc as other settlers have, this with my spare time assisting them will soon get them a farm, they are likewise on the store … I have no doubts of being able to get a living out of the Regiment, as well as in it.

William also said, 'Charles is still left in England, Capt Nelson [?] of the Royal Admiral objected to his coming and said if I could not maintain him then he would [be liable]'.[46]

This part of the letter is not only hard to read, it is inexplicable. Charles was the third son, born in 1792, he was clearly recorded in Price's manifest as having travelled out on the *Minerva* and no other mention of his staying in England was made, although the details of where William and James spent their time is known. They had been left behind at the grammar school in Salisbury and with the Dawe family.

It was James with whom William had just been given a joint grant by King, perhaps before the boy had actually arrived. William evidently also obtained one for William Jnr, these new grants adding 500 acres to the first 200, illustrating how exploitative William could be. In the 1820s he claimed that his youngest son, Edward, who had been born in the colony, was a new arrival when he returned from training in Yorkshire.

Even more oddly, the letter to Piper shows that, in spite of having been suspended as paymaster when bankrupted, and having disobeyed the C-in-C's prohibition on farming, William expected to be able both to continue farming and remain in the army. Nor was he being paid, since the National Archives records show that in 1809 a Mr Merry, at the Office for War, was calculating what he was owed since 1803. During the intervening six years the family must have lived either off what money they had managed to keep, if any, or more probably what farm produce they could get to market. In 1809 Rebecca was obliged to ask for rations from the government store on three occasions, in February, March and July 1809.

The forced sales continued to the end of 1804, with a sale of household effects reported in the *Sydney Gazette* of 6 January 1805.[47] Brush Farm itself was not sold until 14 January 1805, when Simeon Lord acquired it for £546 (he sold it on to Gregory Blaxland in 1807). This meant that the family were able to remain there until they established themselves on the Hawkesbury grant. The delay in putting Brush Farm on the market suggests that William was being enabled to avoid homelessness. The sale advertisement described it as being situated in the Field of Mars and 'one of the most eligible situations for a family in this colony'. On 31 March 1805 a further dividend to creditors was announced, making a total of 75 percent.

Yet, when the sales were all over, William still owed the Army Agents £7898 16s 4½d. Furthermore, although he had paid a dividend to Robert Campbell, he was to be pursued for debt by him until 1831. In spite of having appeals rejected by first the Governor and then the Privy Council in London, Campbell persisted, refusing to recognize that by accepting the 'dividend' from William many years before he had invalidated his action. It was settled in William's favour by W. C. Wentworth, whose hastily scrawled opinion was preserved in the family papers and is now in the Mitchell Library. Wentworth wrote:

> It appears to me notwithstanding the decision of the former Supreme Court of Judicature in this Colony and the confirmation of that decision both by the Court of Appeal and the Privy Council in England that Mr Campbell first by receiving a divided of 15/- in the £ and next by constituting an action against Mr Cox for the recovery of the balance … on the merits of the case Mr Cox could not fail to obtain a verdict.[48]

This was to say William won, for which Wentworth charged five guineas. The fee was worth roughly 21 acres of farmland, at the going price of 5s per acre. Quite extraordinarily, Campbell had much earlier lost the actions when he tried to obtain payment for three other bills owed to Scott and co., of £700, £500 and £1000, on which William had paid a 15s in the pound dividend on 30 July 1809, when he was still in England. Long before Campbell's final attempt William had paid 27s 6d in the pound on some debts. There was no explanation for Campbell's vindictiveness, but the effect it had on William was obvious enough: he never gave up seeking the government construction contracts which gave him an income independently of farming.

By 1804 William ought to have been in a trough of despair, despite his confident letter to Piper. Most of his land had been sold, his household possessions had been sold, and his house inevitably would be. But he did have King's 200 acre joint grants. With Rebecca's support he began again, with the same determination which a decade later would characterize his road building through the Blue Mountains. The move represented both the nadir of his land ownership and a fresh start. From this small beginning the farm which he named Clarendon developed over the years into a major estate, although the choice of its name is a minor mystery. As was explained in Chapter 1, the Royal Park of Clarendon near Salisbury had only the most tenuous conncection to the family ancestry.

When his other sons had prospered enough to build their own grand houses in the 1830s, they too called them after family-connected places in Dorset, such as Fernhill and Winbourne.[49] Their father must have coached them in these antecedents. Indeed the use of the Dorset names suggests that William was consciously trying to recreate the family's long-lost status in his new home, having lacked the money and influence to do so in England. James Cox also gave the name Clarendon to his great mansion near Launceston, in Van Diemen's Land, in 1834.

However, all this was for the future. In the present time of 1804 what must have preyed on William's mind was the action to be taken against him by the army. A curious light is shed on this by a letter written on 9 November 1803 by John Macarthur, now out of the army and in England, to John Piper:

> Orders are issued to try Cox by a Court Martial, and a reference has been made by the Secretary at War to the Commander in Chief on the propriety of bringing [Colonel] Paterson forward as a party, and as abetter of Cox – the general opinion is he will be broken or be obliged to retire on half pay as a matter of favor. I have seen the Secretary at War's letters to the Duke [of York] and to be sure it is a most severe one.[50]

This letter suggests a deal of intrigue over the case. There may have been someone else in the Corps who coveted the lucrative office of paymaster, and alerted the War Office. Or possibly a staff officer in London noticed both William's past record and that courts martial in the colony never seemed to convict the panel members' brother officers (and brothers they may well have doubly been, in the sense of being Freemasons, too).[51]

At all events, the Duke of York finally did order Lieutenant Colonel Paterson 'to send Mr Cox, the Paymaster of the Corps, home for "malversation".[52] The office copy of a letter from the Deputy Secretary at

War, Francis Moore, to a Colonel Clinton, who drafted the Duke of York's letters, makes it clear that William's prosecution was being demanded at a high level. Moore wrote:

> To acquaint you for the information of H R H the C in C that for the sake of example it seems expedient that Mr Cox should be tried by a General Court Martial for malversation in the office of Paymaster; and if such trial cannot conveniently take place in New South Wales Mr Bragge [the Secretary at War] would advise that Mr Cox should be sent home to be tried … [there is] sufficient evidence of his having disobeyed the orders contained in His Majesty's regulations, by drawing far greater sums than the services of the Corps actually required.

Ironically the Secretary of State, Charles Bragge, MP, later (in 1809) successfully pursued the Duke himself for corruption in having sold army commissions through his mistress in 1806, forcing him to resign, although the Duke managed to get himself reinstated a few years after. To achieve this against the King's own brother illustrates the change in public morality which was gradually taking place and which William largely ignored throughout his life.

Clinton's letter shows that disobeying orders was a greater offence than the malversation. It had concluded by saying that any evidence which would counter a plea of necessity on Cox's part 'might be useful': such 'necessity' might have been the difficulty any junior officer experienced in supporting a family on his pay. The wording of the letter implies that the trial being held in England was to avoid William being acquitted by his brother officers in Sydney. On the other hand, the incriminating evidence of the regimental agents, Cox (no relation) and Greenwood, was in London. An earlier letter of 7 December 1803 attributed some blame to Paterson for not 'discontinuing Mr Cox', but this was not followed up. The overriding impression given is that the War Office could no longer tolerate the venal behaviour of the New South Wales Corps officers. The marker that this set down has passed historically unnoticed because of the great furore created a few years after over the trial of Major Johnston for his part in the Bligh rebellion of 1808.

Although Moore's letter had been written in January 1804, it was August 1806 before William boarded the *Buffalo* at Port Jackson 'under arrest', leaving his family behind. The new governor, Bligh, recorded William's recall dispassionately, informing Secretary of State Windham, 'In consequence of orders which Colonel Paterson received ... Mr Cox ... [returns] in the *Buffalo* to answer such charges as will be brought against him'. This was the ship on which Governor King was returning. Due to his illness she did not sail until 10 February 1807 and then suffered great delays. Rounding Cape Horn on 15 March she was struck by lightning and only left Rio, after repairs, on 12 August, reaching Falmouth on 5 November. The voyage had taken nine months.

Major Abbott wrote to Piper on 28 May 1808 remarking that had the ship arrived earlier 'then there was a chance of Cox being able to state his affairs'. That dim hope collapsed, since William was 'dismissed the service' on 9 April 1808, presumably after a trial.[53] A detailed search of the fragile courts martial records at the British National Archives has failed to locate the record, although D'Arcy Wentworth's and other proceedings are there. Normally the date of dismissal would have been the date of the verdict. William was described as 'Paymaster', which is how he was listed in the Army List. As mentioned earlier, his subsequent use of the rank of captain annoyed his former fellow officers. Family memoirs claim that William returned because his sister Anne had died. She had indeed, in 1807, but after he had sailed. The statement was part of the veil of respectability determinedly thrown over the less creditable aspects of his career by his descendants.

William had received no pay since his suspension as paymaster in 1803. He had still not received any by December 1808, even though one-third of the pay due had been authorized.[54] Government departments were notoriously slow in making payments, from which both King and Macquarie suffered. This explains why he was so long in returning to the colony. He does not seem to have lodged with his brothers-in-law at Red Lion Street, since War Office letters were sent to him at 7 Roberts Row. He did not receive the arrears of pay until the summer and only arrived back in the colony on 17 January 1810, on the *Albion*, via the Derwent, continuing from there on the *Union*, as reported by the *Sydney Gazette* on 21 January 1810. Meanwhile Rebecca was still being promised supplies from the government store in January 1810, when William was back. She was obviously on the margins as far feeding her family was concerned.[55] For all that he returned to family holdings on the Hawkesbury, William must have felt his future was in serious doubt.

Port Jackson as seen in 1817 by James Taylor (Mitchell Library, State Library of NSW [XVI/ ca. 1817/1])

4   Rehabilitated as Macquarie's Protégé

There had been an unanticipated silver lining to William's long absence from New South Wales. He was away throughout the interregnum of the officers' revolt against Governor Bligh, when he could not have avoided taking sides. Happily, too, Rebecca and her sons had been leading signatories of loyal addresses from the Hawkesbury people thanking Bligh for his help after the 1807 floods. One address, led by James Cox (then 17 years old) attracted 546 signatures at a time when the entire population of free settlers was only 703 (although one must assume that many signatories were in fact emancipated convicts).[1] These family actions in support of the legitimate authority, albeit before the officers' *coup d'état*, may well have helped William to re-establish himself, just when the privileges of the corps he had belonged to were being overthrown by the new governor, Colonel Lachlan Macquarie.

A tumult of governmental orders followed Macquarie's arrival. January 1810 was a month few free people in the colony were likely to forget. The Governor immediately asserted his authority. Officers of the New South Wales Corps, now renamed the 102nd Regiment of Foot, were replaced by officers of the 73rd, which Macquarie had brought with him, both in military roles and as magistrates. Thus the detachment at Parramatta changed hands on 7 January. Officials dismissed by the rebels were reinstated, as when the merchant Robert Campbell was appointed a magistrate in Sydney and restored as a member of the Orphan School and Gaol Fund Committee. Lieutenant Colonel Paterson was ordered to

CLARENDON AND THE FIVE MACQUARIE TOWNS

close the accounts for his time in charge of the colony (which included his land grant to young Edward Cox). Bligh was to be reinstated as governor for 24 hours and then to hand over formally to Macquarie.[2] Annoyingly for the new governor, this well-intentioned move backfired, because Bligh then embarked on a supply ship, the *Porpoise*, pulled rank as a commodore to take command and, after sailing to Hobart and back, went through a charade of investing Sydney harbour before finally being persuaded to leave. By late February Macquarie was inveighing against the evils of 'illegal co-habitation' in a lengthy proclamation – an ineffective argument, because ex-convict women were well aware that marriage would cost them all their rights, including those to property.[3]

Against this memorably tumultuous background, William wasted little time in rebuilding both his local standing and developing the businesses of private farming and a new one as a government contractor. These were figuratively three corners of the same triangle. To take farming first, he and his sons started to buy farm tools and to acquire stock, although they did not seem to have done this significantly until the following year, perhaps because the rebuilding of his status mattered more, even though Clarendon became the foundation stone of everything he did. Thus on 12 February 1811 he acquired nine of the late Andrew Thompson's shoemakers' knives for 9s each, while his son George bought a foal and a young colt for £60. On 14 February William bought 25 sheep and on the 25th he paid £6 for a cask of gunpowder and James bought 20 sail needles for 3s. In March William disposed of 100 sheep and goats for £83 5s.

These activities were among other unrecorded moves which set Clarendon on the way to becoming a self-sustaining community and in which William's lifelong aide, the ex-sergeant James King, must have participated. Holt recorded that King had been 'the clerk or steward over the stores' at Brush Farm ten years before.[4] Presumably King had stayed loyal to the family throughout their travails. Although William's purchases cannot be dated easily, it is clear from his will that he bought even the smallest parcels of land, if they became available, while the development of estates beyond the mountains as part of a family enterprise eventually followed and was an integral part of the way in which he established a family dynasty.

Here a comment from a historian of the nineteenth-century English squirearchy is unexpectedly applicable to New South Wales, fitting the pattern of William's and his contemporaries' lives: 'the landed gentry came in a bewildering variety of size and shapes ... but they formed a reasonably homogenous group ... they were the untitled aristocracy'.[5] The exclusives of the colony included John Macarthur, the son of a hosier in Plymouth, Samuel Marsden, the son of a blacksmith, John Piper, the son of a doctor, Sir John Jamison, William Lawson, an army officer trained as a surveyor, John and his younger brother Gregory Blaxland, middle-class landowners from Kent with considerable social pretensions and, of course, William Cox himself, heir to armorial bearings and little else.

Disparate as these settlers' origins were, they came to form an identifiable group, to which the ex-convict traders Simeon Lord and Samuel Terry, despite becoming major landowners, could never truly belong. Apart from their being emancipists, this was also due to the interminable quarrels about what constituted a 'gentleman'. One instance of this was the supposition that since in England a squire was a gentleman and so qualified to be a JP, in the colony the reverse must be true and therefore a JP was by definition a gentleman – except that Lord, despite being appointed to the bench by Macquarie, was not.

This question of gentlemanly status was implicit in William's rehabilitation. Disgraced or not, he was still 'an officer and a gentleman' and it seems that the expansion of Clarendon only got going after William had firmly established this status among the Hawkesbury's inhabitants. He may well have been short of money, despite selling produce. Advertisements in the *Sydney Gazette* show him acting as a collector of the debts of the failed business of a Mr Lyons on 17 February and as the intermediary in letting a farm at Richmond Hill on 7 April 1810, as he was over selling a farm at South Creek on 13 October and again in March 1812. On 8 March 1810 he was the foreman of the jury at an inquest.[6] On 1 August he was a joint signatory of a convict's request for a document of emancipation, a move likely to gain him support from local emancipist smallholders.[7]

Less happily, at this time the trader Robert Campbell had taken advantage of the return of legal authority (with Macquarie) to warn that debts due to Messrs Campbell were to be 'immediately liquidated' and, so that settlers on the Hawkesbury and Nepean should have no excuse, he would accept payment in wheat to a representative at the Green Hills.[8] William would have been prominent among such debtors, despite having paid a 75 percent dividend. As was seen in Chapter 3, Campbell finally lost his case in 1831. But in 1810 the generalized warning must have reminded William that he needed a stable income. It came in an unexpected way.

The first major step in William's rehabilitation came on 27 October 1810, following the death of the emancipist magistrate Andrew Thompson, when Macquarie appointed him to the bench on the Hawkesbury with a salary of £50 a year.[9] It is extremely unlikely that the Governor would have done this had he considered there to be any stain on William's character. As explained in an earlier chapter, Macquarie himself had profited from the 'management' of regimental funds when he was paymaster in Bombay in 1795. His character and enthusiasms proved crucial to William's career, although at times inhibiting. As a colonel and later major general he often viewed what were intended to be constructive criticism or proposals as disobeying orders. He kept a near-relentless grip on everything that happened in the colony but ended – as his last portrait reveals – a broken man (a farewell portrait commissioned by William on behalf of the

Hawkesbury residents has never been traced).

Macquarie had come up the hard way. He came from an impoverished minor Scottish clan and in 1777 had obtained an ensigncy in the second battalion of the 84th Regiment, or Royal Highland Emigrants, commanded by a cousin. This taught him the value of patronage, connections and money. Through most of his army career he lacked them and was short of cash. He is said to have remarked that Arthur Wellesley (later Duke of Wellington), who possessed all three advantages,

Macquarie in 1822, 'the Old Viceroy' but a broken man (Mitchell Library, State Library of NSW [ML 36])

reached the rank of colonel in nine years, whereas it had taken him thirty. His beloved first wife, Jane Jarvis, died in India in 1796. He was married again, to a cousin, Elizabeth Campbell, in 1807, who was to be a considerable force in New South Wales, not least in her classical architectural taste.

Macquarie's becoming governor was accidental. He was the lieutenant colonel of the 73rd Regiment when its commander, a major general, was chosen to replace Bligh as governor, ending the short tradition of appointing naval post captains. The general turned the appointment down. Macquarie wrote to Lord Castlereagh asking to go instead and, after chancing on Castlereagh walking through London's Berkeley Square, was given the job. His instructions from the Secretary of State emphasized improving the morals of the colonists, encouraging marriage, providing for education, prohibiting the use of 'spirituous liquors' and increasing the agriculture and stock of the colony.[10] What the instructions did not cover, but which came to concern Macquarie greatly, was the layout of towns and the erection of handsome public buildings, over the expense of which he frequently dissembled to the

Secretary of State. These improvements regularly involved William Cox as a contractor, helping to create William's fortune. But what was seen in London as their extravagance was part of the reason for Commissioner Bigge being sent to the colony in 1819 to find out what was going on.

When Macquarie appointed William as magistrate, the residents sent an address thanking him for this appointment of 'a gentleman who for many years has resided amongst us, possessing our esteem and confidence', effectively a tribute to Rebecca's leadership in the small community, given her husband's long absence.[11] The Colonial Secretary's formal letter of appointment indicated that the office carried wide powers locally. William would be 'Superintendent of the Government labourers and cattle and of the Public Works in the District of the Hawkesbury'.[12] He was to report on both of the latter. Reinforced by the prestige and the £50 annual stipend, William now set about further widening his interests, in the community and commercially, whilst gradually increasing the size of his Clarendon estate.

The *Sydney Gazette* noted William's social progress in various reports, and his official actions are largely in the *Historical Records of Australia*. His exertions for the community during a flood in March 1811 were praised. In May he was appointed treasurer of a committee to build a schoolhouse at Richmond, for which he drew up a plan. After Macquarie ordered the setting up of the five towns, described below, in October 1811, the constables were ordered to make a return to William of the farms liable to be flooded – Macquarie was particularly worried about the dangers of floods, which indeed in 1819 took Rebecca Cox's life.[13] Come January 1812 Cox was organizing and signing an address from the residents to Macquarie, congratulating him on his safe return from a voyage. In July he subscribed five guineas towards a new schoolhouse at Richmond (which he might well have hoped to build).

The social peak of this activity was reached when he acted as vice president at a dinner to celebrate the anniversary of Macquarie's arrival in the colony. The vice president at a military dinner sat at one end of the table and when asked by the president, at the top end, to propose a toast,

This early watercolour, c. 1809, shows the Green Hills settlement (Windsor) from across the Hawkesbury (Mitchell Library, State Library of NSW [PXD 388 Vol. 3 no. 7])

The street going down to the river from Thompson Square at Windsor (Author's photo)

would rise and do so. On this occasion the tables to seat so many people were set in a semi-circle. The *Sydney Gazette*'s fulsome description of the dinner, attended by 'nearly 150 persons, among whom were many Gentlemen of the first respectability' will bear quoting, as it describes formal colonial hospitality of the time at its peak. There were, of course, no ladies present:

> [In] the apprehension that a *fête champêtre* would be better adapted to the warmth of the season, a spacious tent was erected in the front garden of Mr Hubert Jenkins, one of the stewards, and fancifully decorated with various ensigns, together with a variety of shrubs and boughs, formed into festoons … on the outside of the tent the British Colours were displayed … At six the company sat down to an excellent dinner, during which the full band of the 73rd Regiment … played a number of appropriate airs.
>
> William Gore, Esq, President, and William Cox, Esq, Vice President, were each supported by a Clergyman on the right … and the rest of the Company placed themselves promiscuously without respect to rank … and the challenge to '*hob or nob*' was proffered and accepted with a cordiality that was truly gratifying … After dinner succeeded the Toasts, all of which were followed by well adapted airs.

There were a dozen toasts and it was 'near eleven when the last toast was drunk … the company retiring highly gratified'. It was hoped for the occasion to be repeated.[14]

William thus honoured not only Macquarie's anniversary, but implicitly his patronage. However, there were other aspects to the Hawkesbury with which William had to cope as a magistrate and which made it vital for him to be respected. Grace Karskens explains that the popular culture there 'was seen as notoriously "riotous" and "disorderly" because it was beyond the pale of administration'.[15] Andrew Thompson, William's predecessor, so mourned by Macquarie, had been the constable there as a trusted convict ten years earlier. He had both established some degree of order and become wealthy as a trader, proving that an emancipist did not have to end up impoverished. He would be 'a hard act to follow'. Finally, the Hawkesbury had been the scene of early clashes over land with the Aborigines, and would be again in 1816, with which William had to deal.

Socially, the Hawkesbury was a tremendous step down from the Parramatta area. By contrast Sir John Jamison, whose father had instigated William's bankruptcy, but who became a close associate, had his estate of Regentville on the Nepean River near what became Penrith, much more of a gentleman's location. This underlines Rebecca's shrewdness in getting her grant for Edward at Mulgoa, a few miles beyond Penrith. Whether William was responding to both local realities and his own by building his house at Clarendon unpretentiously, or whether he was so inclined anyway, is not clear. Possibly it was a bit of both. People's aspirations, both men and women, are often expressed architecturally, Mrs Macquarie being a good example, as were William's sons. They built themselves grand houses for the continuance of dynasties. Unlike them, their father seems to have had little ambition over his houses.

Clarendon is described as having been 'a large irregular bungalow built about 1810', to which he only added a formal dining room a decade later.[16] His grand-daughters, who knew what remained of the house at the end of the century, confirm its rambling character. Although in 1824 William built a much more classically elegant house in Sydney, on the corner of Bent and O'Connell Streets, his correspondence shows that it was intended only for rental to the government. Four years before his death he built another house called Fairfield at Richmond, safe from the floods, where he eventually died. It was later greatly enlarged and is now a hotel, so that it is had to tell what it originally looked like.

Day to day life on the Hawkesbury involved a continual interaction both with his own convict employees and with ex-convict small settlers, in which undue pretensions would have served William poorly. A most important aspect of his life in the Macquarie years was that he fully endorsed and practised his patron's belief in the rehabilitation of convicts,

once their term was expired or they were given tickets of leave to work on
their own account. Macquarie had explained his views to the Secretary of
State within four months of his arrival, telling Castlereagh:

> I have taken on myself to adopt a new Line of Conduct, Conceiving
> that Emancipation, when united with Rectitude and long tried good
> Conduct, should lead a Man back to that Rank in Society, which he had
> forfeited and do away, in so far as the Case will admit, All Retrospect of
> former Bad Conduct.[17]

However, Macquarie named only four men who he had 'admitted to his
table'. They were D'Arcy Wentworth, the Assistant Surgeon, William
Redfern, Andrew Thompson, the magistrate, and Simeon Lord, the trader.
None had been common criminals, while D'Arcy had never been a convict,
and all were men with whom William would have many dealings, both
professionally and, in Wentworth's case, socially.

In fact Macquarie's statement is curious in two ways. For him to refer to
Wentworth in that way was incorrect. D'Arcy was a former volunteer officer
and medical practitioner, related to the Earls Fitzwilliam, who had gone
into exile to become the colony's assistant surgeon after three times being
acquitted of highway robbery. Although court martialled in 1809 on the
grounds that, when in charge of the hospital, where sick convicts had to be fed
by their employers for the first 14 days, he had not returned the sick to their
employers, he had been acquitted. The Judge Advocate had remarked that he
had known D'Arcy for 17 years and he had 'Conducted himself … with the
most propriety'.[18] He was described as being 'a handsome tall man with blue
eyes … popular with all classes and both sexes'. He was married to a convict
woman and fathered William Charles Wentworth of the 1813 Blue Mountains
crossing. The younger Wentworth trained in London as a lawyer and later
became a prominent politician, whose path crossed William's often from the
1820s, as well as acting as his counsel over the action by Campbell.

Macquarie did not mention the Reverend Henry Fulton, the Protestant
Irish clergyman who had travelled out as a convict on the *Minerva*

under William's supervision. Fulton had been conditionally pardoned in November 1800 and fully pardoned in 1805, when a Crown chaplain. He had supported Bligh and been suspended by the rebels, but restored to office by Macquarie in January 1810. He eventually founded a school at Castlereagh, which may have been attended by two sons of William's second marriage.

Other convicted professional men who came to play a large part in the colony's development, and with whom William had dealings, included Francis Greenway, who was appointed as the civil architect in 1816 by Macquarie and was subsequently pardoned after building the Female Factory at Parramatta in 1820. He designed various public buildings, the most notable being St Matthew's church at Windsor, although it has been much altered since, and the court house, still preserved as William

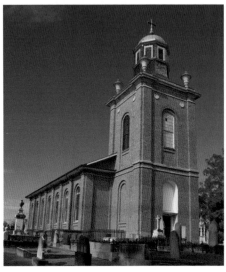

St Matthew's church, Windsor, which William helped to build and where he is buried (Author's photo)

The impressive interior of St Matthew's church, Windsor (Author's photo)

The tomb of William and Rebecca stands in the St Matthew's churchyard at Windsor (Author's photo)

built it. What might be called Macquarie's 'fit to dine with me' qualification was odd at the best and very few men qualified for it. Although a great many working-class convicts became emancipated, Macquarie's readmission to society does not seem to have worked except for a few former professionals. Indeed Macquarie's position had been officially disagreed with back in 1817, when the Secretary of State wrote that he had been 'compelled to conclude

The Rectory at Windsor, built by William at Marsden's direction

that most of the emancipists elevated to positions of trust were unfit for such preferment' and urged restraint on the Governor. [19] Overall the way in which Macquarie viewed criminals had progressed from the classicist 'crime-is-in-the-blood' school of the late eighteenth century towards the ideal of rehabilitation, anticipating aspects of the Positivist approach of the 1820s in England. The historian J. M. Bennett considers that 'In Macquarie's personality … were mixed a broad sense of justice and a humanity far ahead of Georgian concepts'. Acting as a magistrate William shared this outlook. His recorded judgments show that common sense tempered them, for example when on two occasions he met an unreasonable complaint from a master by simply transferring the 'offending' convict to another employer. His sentencing – he was the chairman of three justices sitting together and the others opinions are not known – became tougher after Commissioner Bigge's visit, although he always maintained that harsh penalties (such as severe floggings) only hardened the criminal.

A subsidiary part of the magisterial role was that convicts were sent up from Sydney to be allocated to employers by the local JPs, the supervision of government labourers being part of the job. Initially there were too few convicts available for private assignment and on 24 December 1810 the Colonial Secretary, John Campbell, referring to the arrival of the transport *Indian*, instructed that convicts being sent to the Hawkesbury should be distributed 'free of favour or affection to the most deserving'.[20] A letter dated 7 March 1811 from William to Campbell spoke of problems he had in allocating convicts to employers, particularly ex-convicts who now wanted convicts assigned to them. William wrote:

> I have been careful to prevent Prisoner settlers being set down for servants and has [sic] rejected many who have not the means of maintaining themselves, but still the claimants are numerous (170) … there are others still in the list who are very unworthy of Indulgence from the Crown, being bad members of society … also I am of opinion many of the Settlers has [sic] set down more acres in hand than they ever had in cultivation altogether.[21]

Although initially he allocated himself few men, throughout his magisterial tenure, that is to say for the rest of his life, William considered himself to be one of 'the most deserving'. He gradually accumulated a substantial number, which reached 128 by 1822 and included many 'mechanics' (skilled men). This was later bitterly complained about to Bigge by other settlers, as is detailed in Chapter 8, although he was not alone among JPs in the practice and it was just as true that he always believed in the potential rehabilitation of convicts and helped them towards it.

After Macquarie left, and Commissioner Bigge's report was acted upon, the ideal of rehabilitation faltered and the aims of punishment reverted to the old view, expressed by the Duke of Portland when he had told Governor Hunter that 'crimes of a more heinous nature … can only be repressed by a sense of the certainty of punishment that awaits them'.[22] This has been explained by the authors of a work on criminology as showing less concern with understanding the nature of the 'criminal' and more with developing rational and systematic means of delivering justice.[23]

Whilst William's role as a magistrate rapidly widened his knowledge of the community he lived in and was serving, only Macquarie's personal writings underline the role which William played in developing the five 'Macquarie towns' on the Hawkesbury, the area on which most of his life was centred. These were Richmond, Windsor, Pitt Town, Castlereagh and Wilberforce. The Governor's 'Journal of a Tour of Inspection 1810–1811' describes how he called first at the Coxes' former farm 'the Brush' on 10 November 1810, which Gregory Blaxland had acquired in 1807 and Macquarie found to be a 'a very snug and good farm and very like an English one in point of comfort'. On 18 November he went out with Mrs Macarthur into the foothills of the Blue Mountains. He next inspected farms granted 'by the late usurped government' and on 30 November, a Friday, visited the owners of a chain of farms along the Nepean where 'we were joined by Mr Wm Cox the magistrate of these districts' to 'view the confluence of the Nepean and Grose rivers … from the confluence [where] the Hawkesbury commences'. When they camped that night 'Mr Cox took his leave of us to go home'.[24]

They then began a series of surveys to lay out possible towns, with William among Macquarie's advisers. On 1 December, after 'visiting the Government House – or more properly speaking the Government Cottage at the Green Hills', they rode to the Richmond Hill accompanied by Evans the surveyor and William. They found Richmond Hill very steep and covered in brush and wild raspberries, though there was a terrace running parallel with the Hawkesbury River for about three miles. Similarly there was a terrace or ridge at the Green Hills, which was where Windsor would be laid out, overlooking the river. On Sunday 2 December they all went to church, lamenting the loss of the deceased Andrew Thompson's 'good sound sense and judicious advice'. Macquarie recorded: 'Mr Cox and Dr Mileham [also a JP] dined with us today'. On the next day William accompanied them again around the Green Hills farms, Macquarie noting that they 'yield in this present time very fine crops, but the houses and habitations of the settlers are miserably bad … and liable to be flooded on any inundation … The Revd Cartwright, his wife, Mr Cox and Dr Mileham dined with us.'

William continued accompanying the Governor almost daily, as he identified 'safe and convenient' situations for townships, away from potential flooding, sometimes by boat, more often on horseback. Mrs Macquarie also rode on horseback, as well as in a carriage, and met Rebecca and William's family. By 6 December the Governor had decided upon names for the new towns. Windsor was to be in the Green Hills district 'from the similarity of this situation to that of the same name in England'. Richmond was named for the same reason, while Castlereagh honoured the Lord Viscount, Pitt Town 'the late great William Pitt' and Wilberforce 'the good and virtuous Wm Wilberforce Esq. MP'. Wilberforce had long taken a keen interest in the affairs of the colony and been responsible for Samuel Marsden going out as chaplain many years before. Macquarie recommended those gentlemen with him to urge the settlers to lose no time in removing their 'Habitations, Flocks and Herds to these places of safety and security'. The advice had little effect. William himself continued to live on low ground at Clarendon, with fatal results for Rebecca.

Macquarie returned to Sydney for Christmas, but was back in January to mark out the townships. His descriptions show quite vividly how his plans were literally breaking fresh ground. On Thursday 10 January he set out from Windsor 'attended by family, the Surveyor, the Revd Mr Cartwright, Mr Cox and several other gentlemen' to view the site of Castlereagh. The future great square in the centre had been marked out and 'the name of it – Castlereagh – painted on a Board was nailed to a high strong Post and erected in the Centre of the Square'. The same was done in Richmond. On 12 January William went with Macquarie to examine Windsor and Macquarie wrote: 'The Revd Mr and Mrs Cartwright, Mr Cox, Dr Mileham and Mrs Fitzgerald dined with us this day … and we again drank success and prosperity to the new Townships'. On 13 January 'Mr Cox and his wife and family dined with us today previous to our return to Sydney'.[25] It is fair to say that the Governor's writings display William as a trusted adviser and official, though not as a personal friend in the way that Sir John Jamison on the Nepean became. Both Macquarie and more particularly his wife Elizabeth, who had an animated social circle around her, appreciated the social boundaries of patronage.

Again the *Gazette* records some of William's projects around the Macquarie towns, following the Governor's tour of inspection, as does the Colonial Secretary's correspondence. On 26 October 1811 he received payment for fencing the burial ground at Windsor. In 1812 he fulfilled a much larger project in the shape of a new gaol there, plus a house for the gaoler and a wall round it, for which the part payment in October was £350, with a similar payment in October 1813. In that year he also began the Glebe House (parsonage) at Castlereagh, for which he earned a total of £500. This immediately preceded the commission to build the Blue Mountains road.

Meanwhile in July 1813 he had begun to collect subscriptions for a new court house at Windsor. Given that he also supervised the building of local roads, his career as a contractor kept him both busy and remunerated. He never had to face a bankruptcy again. He continued this work throughout

The court house of 1822 at Windsor, built by William (Author's photo)

his life, despite his growing success as pastoralist. In 1820 he built a new schoolhouse at Castlereagh for the government. One of his most distinguished buildings is the court house, which he completed in 1821. It was designed by Francis Greenway and is the least altered of the architect's many public buildings. Overall, William was an extremely energetic and a good organizer, which was what Macquarie meant when he later called him a man 'of great arrangement'.

Macquarie's references to miserable living conditions on the Hawkesbury were nothing new at the time and were to be repeated by other visitors for many years to come. Grose had written, when he settled 22 convicts whose sentences were expiring there in April 1794, that the fertile alluvial soil was 'particularly rich', although he did not visit the area himself.26 By 1804 – when William and James were given their joint grants by King – it was becoming the prime agricultural area of the Cumberland Plain, even though in 1800 Governor Hunter had reported that the settlers were 'more in debt than in any other district' (a direct result of the officers' trade monopoly and payment in spirits) and the houses were of a very poor standard, usually only of two rooms with earthen floors. Half the colony's smallholdings were there.27 Worse, as William would tell Commissioner Bigge in 1820, when these ex-convict settlers were allotted a convict labourer, the pair would often cooperate in petty crime, the unexpressed fear in William's letter to Campbell of 1811.

A more recent historian of the Hawkesbury, Jan Barkley-Jack, disputes the poverty, arguing that many of the smallholders were successful (William subsequently admitted to Bigge that some were).[28] However, John Blaxland told Sir Joseph Banks in October 1807 that 'a large portion of the farms [were] deserted, the buildings down or tumbling down, the poor creatures almost naked and many of them [with] nothing but maize to eat'.[29] Even in 1820 Bigge found the occupiers in a state of abject poverty.[30] The disparity between these accounts and Barkley-Jack's is easily explained. Her account relates basically to the period before 1802, whereas Blaxland and Bigge both visited in the aftermath of disastrous floods which were the cause of Macquarie urging settlers to move to higher ground when he laid out his five towns.

Over the years the Hawkesbury's fertility gradually became exhausted. When the Coxes moved there in 1804 this was not yet so. True, the soil was relatively fragile and was being overcropped by settlers who had no money for any kind of fertilizer, if they did not own cattle. Nor was it only on the Hawkesbury that this happened. Much of the entire Cumberland Plain was affected, while plagues of caterpillars (army worm) sometimes devastated crops. This was why Gregory Blaxland, William Lawson and the young W. C. Wentworth made their iconic expedition across the Blue Mountains to find new land in May 1813, for which they were rewarded, although in fact they did not cross the main range. A decade before Governor King had sent his Lieutenant, Francis Barrallier, to try to cross but he failed, as did Bass. George Caley, the botanist, penetrated 100 miles from Nattai with a party of four soldiers and five convicts in November 1804, but failed to cross the Great Dividing Range, being stopped by a huge waterfall. This was the most significant of the attempts. There is a cairn of stones supposedly marking 'Caley's Repulse', and so-called by Macquarie, but not erected by Caley.

The first European to find the entire way across the mountains to the plains beyond was the assistant land surveyor, G. W. Evans, who did so in seven weeks from November 1813. Macquarie heaped praise on him in an order of 14 February 1814, reporting that the land he had passed through was 'beautiful and fertile with a rapid stream running through it [Coxs River]' at the point where he reached 'the termination of the tour made by Messrs G. Blaxland, W. C. Wentworth and Lieutenant Lawson.' The three had, of course, not crossed the top of the mountains, but gone around the side of them towards what is now Hartley. Evans progressed as far as the Macquarie River, 42 miles (68 km) beyond the future site of Bathurst.

Macquarie rewarded Evans with £100 and 1000 acres on the Coal River in Van Diemens's Land, where he was to be deputy surveyor of lands. He reported the achievement to Earl Bathurst in a letter of 28 April and proposed calling the new country, punningly, *West-more-land*. He told Bathurst that 'For the purpose of rendering this new tract beneficial to the Settlers' he intended to have a cart road constructed across the mountains.[31] This would be a very different matter to crossing on foot, as Evans had with his small party. A road would have to tackle precipitous ridges, rising to 3483 feet (1061 metres) at Mount York and higher elsewhere.

Bearing in mind the distances and communications involved, events moved quite fast and it was only a matter of a few months before William met Macquarie in Sydney to discuss the road project. On 14 July 1814 Macquarie sent a letter detailing his requirements. They were exacting ones. The road had to be 12 feet wide to permit two carts to pass each other 'with ease', although he preferred it to be 16 feet wide 'where it can with ease and convenience be done'. In forest and brush ground the timber had to be cleared away to 20 feet. It was to run from the Emu Plains, on the Nepean River, to a 'centrical part' of the Bathurst plains, following a track laid down on Evans' map. Depots were to be established en route.

For this task William was to be provided with 30 artificers and labourers and a guard of eight soldiers 'you have already yourself selected'. They were to be fully provisioned with food and tools. The reward for the convicts was to be emancipation. Evans had reckoned optimistically that the job could be done in three months with 50 men. When William did it in just under six months with far fewer men he was widely praised. As is clear from Macquarie's letter, all this had been pre-arranged before his letter was sent. He told Bathurst that William had 'Very Kindly volunteered his services … he is particularly Well adapted for such a business, being Active and very Intelligent in the Conduct of Such Affairs'.[32] By the time Bathurst received the despatch the road was complete and William had already accomplished the dangerous and exhausting commission which made his name.

5   The Challenge of the Blue Mountains

William Cox kept a journal of almost all the six months spent building the mountain road. It is a small volume, about seven inches by five, bound in brown leather and was given to the Mitchell Library with other family papers in 1965. He must have kept it protectively in a pocket or other covering throughout. In terms of personal papers it is all but unique, since every entry is in William's own handwriting, expressing his own thoughts, as opposed to his more carefully considered official letters. Although it is unlikely that he wrote it for others to read, it has often been published, including in an online version.[1] The entries end before the road was finished, possibly because he kept a record of expenses starting at the back and going forwards, so there were only two pages left blank at the time he stopped. Or, more probably, he felt the road had progressed so far that his presence was no longer needed, that his supervisors could complete the job of reaching 'the centrical part' of the Bathurst plains, and he wanted to get on with other contracts. Certainly, on 15 January 1815, the day after the road was finished, he was back at Clarendon, busy submitting estimates to the government for road and bridge building at Windsor.

In fact, had he been less determined and resourceful, William might have failed in the project, since he made one near fatal mistake. This was to follow the line of the ridges, not the valleys, an error which was to bring the project close to catastrophe at Mount York. Not that he could be blamed for that. As the *Oxford Companion to Australian History* observes, '[Gregory] Blaxland was regarded as the originator of the plan of following the ridges as a means of crossing this barrier.' And as the last chapter notes, Blaxland had not in reality got across the mountains at all.

When William had succeeded in his task, Macquarie expressed, in a generously worded letter drafted by his secretary, John Campbell, 'astonishment and regret that amongst so large a population no-one appeared within the first 25 years of the establishment of this settlement possessed of sufficient energy of mind fully to explore a passage over these mountains'.[2] But this was *after* the Governor had traversed the route on a tour of inspection in April and May 1815 and he gave no recognition to the efforts of Barrallier in 1802 or Caley in 1804. Indeed when he wrote that the road promised to be 'of the greatest public utility, by opening a new source of wealth to the industrious and enterprising', he was also disregarding the reality of other roads, some of which were little better than tracks.

In January 1789 Governor Phillip had led a party of woodcutters to mark out a line of road from Sydney to Parramatta. However, the road towards the mountains did not go that way. The road from Parramatta to the Hawkesbury ran west to Richmond and Windsor, whereas William's new one would start further south, crossing the Nepean River at a ford near present day Penrith. Today the Great Western Highway largely still follows Cox's line as far as Mount Victoria and in some sections is not a great deal wider than Macquarie's specification. It was first realigned in 1823, with a major change passing Mount Blaxland, so that that today's route is much further north than William's. It has been altered at intervals ever since.[3]

The Governor had decreed that the expedition would receive 'provisions, stores, tools, utensils, arms, ammunition, slops [work clothing] and other necessaries'. These would be sent from Sydney to a depot to be established by William on the Emu Plains by 'two separate conveyances or convoys' one immediately, the other two weeks later 'which you will be pleased to receive and take charge of on their arrival there, placing such a guard over them as you may deem expedient, the sergeant commanding the guard of soldiers being instructed to receive all his orders from you for the guidance of himself and party and for their [the stores'] distribution'.

To meet these ideals, the labour gang William assembled was a much less ill-kempt bunch than was usual. A typical road gang depicted around 1815 in the bush near Sydney (the drawing is in the National Library in Canberra) were clothed in ragged trousers, often patched at the knees, wearing an assortment of rough jackets and smocks, and headgear of all kinds from flat caps to battered high hats for protection against the sun. Their guard of soldiers in high plumed shakos, shouldering muskets with bayonets, was dominating them.

William's men were very much better fitted up and motivated. They had volunteered their services, in Macquarie's words, 'on the Condition of receiving emancipation for their extra Labor on the conclusion of it. This is the only remuneration they receive, except their rations.'[4] He might have added that they would be provided with clothing, which William replaced as necessary. It has been observed that back in Governor Phillip's time convicts responded much better to the indulgences and incentives which the military offered than to other employers' inducements.[5] William had been an officer and gave continual minor incentives to the men, whilst at the back of their minds must always have been the eventual reward of freedom. His diary states that the 30 men were issued with a 'suit of slops and a blanket to each man'. We know that slops included shoes and trousers, because a few were found to have been stolen. The blankets were for the cold of the high ridges awaiting them and later more were issued, as well as 'strong shoes' for the rugged terrain.

This was not the only respect in which the gang was different from normal. The word 'convict' is nowhere mentioned. William referred to the men by their names and trades as 'workmen' or 'quarrymen' or 'carpenters', while Macquarie had called them 'artificers and labourers'. Not being labelled convicts must have been mentally invigorating for them. Furthermore, although William had the detachment of eight soldiers with him, the troops were directed towards safeguarding the stores and provisions, not supervising the work.

There were several supervisors, the chief being Richard Lewis, who had that role at Clarendon, assisted by Hobby and Tye, whilst a fourth named Burne was to prove less satisfactory. The following June Macquarie made Lewis a superintendent 'in the new discovered country to the westward of the Blue Mountains', under William's orders, with a salary of '£50 per annum and the usual indulgences'.[6] William's 20-year-old son Henry assisted at the depots. The soldiers – on Macquarie's orders – also prevented curious sightseers from intruding on the project. 'I have deemed it advisable,' Macquarie wrote to William, 'to issue a Government and general order prohibiting such idlers from visiting you, without a pass signed by me.' He sent copies of this order to be displayed in conspicuous places and directed William to 'give the necessary order to your guard and to your constable to see it strictly enforced'. This restriction on access was maintained after the road was completed, presumably to prevent convicts escaping up the road, which Macquarie feared might happen.[7]

When the expedition set out on 18 July 1814 the men shared one defining aim: to finish the job and gain their reward, for which they were prepared to work waist deep in rivers and be wet and cold for weeks on end, apart from the sheer physical effort demanded of them. Seven years later Commissioner Bigge, who had a sniffer dog's nose for wrongdoing and strong views about not freeing convicts early, attacked abuses of the project, of which alleged abuses William seems to have been unaware. These might have included Macquarie's subsequently giving the supervisor Lewis the official job at Bathurst. In his all-embracing 1822 report into the state of the colony, Bigge specifically referred to the road. He commented that Governor Macquarie's policy had been to bestow pardons and indulgences as 'rewards for any particular labour or enterprise' and 'The men who were employed in working upon the Bathurst road ... and those who contributed to that operation by the loan of their own carts and horses, obtained pardons, emancipations and tickets of leave.' He named one convict, Tindall, of having only lent a cart, when Tindall had been a labourer throughout, and asserted that 'the nature of the services, and the manner in which some of them were recommended, excited much surprise in the colony, as well as great suspicion of the channels through which the recommendations passed.'[8] There is no evidence of such reactions in the Colonial Secretary's correspondence relating to the road.

Happily, the Commissioner did not criticize William personally (though he did on other matters), merely mentioning that those who were employed were selected by Mr Cox and Richard Lewis and that 'The first principle was capacity for labour and it is stated by some of the free persons, who assisted in it, that the men worked hard and that they were excited to exertion by the hope of receiving emancipations'. This is exactly the impression which William's journal gives.

Augustus Earle's painting of a distant view of the Blue Mountains from Cox's road in the 1820s (Nan Kivell collection, NLA)

William was unworried by the possible problems and had arranged everything a week before Macquarie wrote to him on 14 July 1814. The first entry of his journal is dated 7 July and reads: 'After holding conversation with His Excellency the Governor at Sydney relative to the expedition, I took leave of him this day'. With the help of Lewis he had already assembled the team of 30 trusted convicts. On 11 July he began 'converting a cart to a caravan to sleep in, as well as to take my own personal luggage.' This was completed on the 16th. The next day he left Clarendon at 9 am for Captain Woodruff's farm, carts and provisions arrived from Sydney and he 'mustered the people', not calling them convicts. They were issued with slops. The man in charge of the stores was called Gorman and would feature unhappily in William's later life at Bathurst.

The next morning they started to make a pass, or ford, across the Nepean. The party found the river banks very steep, as most that they were to encounter were. The Nepean was already notorious for flooding, as William well knew because he had been warmly commended for rescuing a woman caught in the flood of 1806 on the Hawkesbury, previous ones having been recorded in 1795 and 1799. Whatever 'pass' he built would need to be flood-resistant. The existing one was merely an improvement on the ford and suffered from flooding. A bridge was only built much later. July 18 and 19 also brought the first of what would become very repetitive observations. The weather was 'fine, clear and frosty', some items of slops had been purloined, there were complaints, the first of many, about the food, the pork being deficient. It proved to be underweight. William 'wrote to His Excellency the Governor for additional bullocks and some small articles of tools'. By the end the Governor's secretary must have had a small library of such requests, but they were invariably met. In order to speed up re-provisioning, William often obtained supplies from his own estate at Clarendon, while problems with the bullocks used as draught animals to haul supply carts lasted throughout the project.

The next need was for axes, which the blacksmith fashioned from iron and steel provided by William, but 'the timber being hard, they all turned. Kept the grindstone constantly going.' These, with hoes, spades, picks, sledgehammers and a small amount of gunpowder, were all the tools they had. On 23 July a hut was fitted up on the left (the further) bank of the Nepean to store provisions and William wrote to the Governor for pit saws, iron and steel, then went ahead to plot the next stage from the Emu Plains, which would cross a creek and 'begin ascending the mountain'. On

24 July he noted that 'The workmen exerted themselves during the week, much to my satisfaction'. By way of reward he gave them 'a lot of cabbage', which he had exchanged for a pound of tobacco. By 26 July they had made a 'complete crossing place' from the end of the Emu Plains to the foot of the mountain, although the ascent was steep and 'the soil very rough and stony; the timber chiefly ironbark'. The trees were not so named without reason, but the expedition was now well under way, after little more than a week.

There had been various personal disadvantages for William regarding this enterprise. One was being absent from his own farm for a long period. A Cox family memoir suggests that 'Clarendon still had growing pains' and asks, in relation to the building of the mountain road, 'Was the absence from home and family justifiable?' Macquarie recognized the same point, remarking that 'Mr Cox voluntarily relinquished the comforts of his own house and the society of his numerous family and exposed himself to much personal fatigue, with only such covering as a bark hut could afford from the inclemency of the weather'.[9] As far as organization was concerned, Rebecca had managed Clarendon perfectly well during her husband's three-year absence from 1806 to 1809, assisted by James King, and William brushed such disincentives aside. He had grown into an extremely determined man and the Governor was correct in admiring his qualities of leadership and personal courage.

Nonetheless, one disincentive was inescapable. Come December, William would reach his fiftieth birthday and would attain that age high up on the mountains in bitter weather. True, he was at the peak of his abilities, but the half century is a moment when any man has to start looking after himself physically. The roughness of the mountains would often mean that the improvised caravan was unable to be manoeuvred up slopes and had to be laboriously taken ahead. Addendums to his diary refer to William sleeping in bark huts, while later diary entries reveal that on several occasions he was 'completely knocked up' by his exertions.

The road progressed fast. A resting place subsequently named

Springwood was created 12 miles from the ford, beyond the first depot. Secretary Campbell, in his account of the Governor's tour of inspection in May 1815, described the 12 miles from the Emu ford to the first depot as passing through 'a very handsome open forest of lofty trees, and much more practicable and easy than was expected'.[10] His detailed account of that journey is very helpful in establishing how far exactly William's party had reached at various times.

Soon the going became tougher and the obstacles more evident. William noted that 'The ascent is steep; the soil rough and stony; the timber chiefly ironbark'. A superintendent was sent ahead to mark the next five miles through the bush from the depot to the next forest ground. The blacksmith's forge was brought up and a chimney built for it. The soldiers were moved from the river to the depot.

Confusingly, by comparison with the distances later quoted by Campbell, William recorded, 'Removed my caravan from the river to the depot on the mountain, a distance of five and three quarter miles and slept there the first night'. The depot was, as William makes clear, not far from the river and was certainly not on the mountain in any real sense. On 28 July he returned home to Clarendon for a brief stay, leaving Richard Lewis in charge, coming back on 1 August when he 'found the road completed to the said depot, much to my satisfaction'.

In effect they were progressing in a leapfrogging way, as they would throughout the expedition, with William himself at the centre and the advance party ahead, while behind them provisions were moved slowly forward to new locations for the depot. 'The workmen go with much cheerfulness and do their work well,' he wrote on 2 August. 'Gave them a quantity of cabbage as a present.' Cabbages became a frequent gift to the men and must have been welcome to enliven the carefully counted pieces of pork from the barrels. Green vegetables also ward off scurvy, which did affect one man later.

Despite this good start, 2 August was soured by the fourth supervisor, Burne, refusing to take orders via Richard Lewis, saying he would only obey any from William. The response must have taken Burne aback. 'I told him I should send any orders I should give to him by whom I pleased,' William declared roundly. Eventually the supervisor said he would leave. On this William ordered the constable who was accompanying them to receive Burne's gun and ammunition, he was struck off the stores and the party was informed that 'he had nothing more to do with me or them'. Permitting such insubordination could have been potentially fatal to driving the project on.

On the following day two working gangs were sent two miles ahead and on 4 August the depot was 'removed to seven and a half miles forward, as also the corporal and three privates'. The soldiers were there partly for protection against the 'natives' some of whom had been heard chattering in the distance after a single gunshot the day before. Nevertheless on 8 August 'two natives from Richmond joined us; one shot a kangaroo'. It emerged later that William employed them as guides. Later he employed Aborigines, one from Mulgoa and the other from Richmond, at both of which places he owned estates.

The 'natives' were very minor nuisances compared to the thick scrub and brush which blocked the road builders' path for days on end. William complained about it continually: 'Very thick troublesome brush ... Timber both thick and heavy with a very strong brush ... brush very thick and heavy from the ninth to the tenth mile' (8 August). A further hindrance was that good water might be a mile or more from the path of the road. They were briefly visited by G. W. Evans, the deputy surveyor who had established the route but whose track would later prove impossible to follow. Always ahead of them lay the enticing prospect of 'good forest ground down in the valley'. The problem was to be getting to it, or rather to a series of forest grounds, from the precipitous slopes of the long ridges which collectively constituted the massif of the mountains.

They ran out of food on 12 August. Gorman reported there were only 14 pieces of meat left and no sugar. At daylight next day William 'sent Lewis to the depot with a letter to Mrs Cox to send me out immediately

300lb of beef'. Obtaining supplies from Clarendon, rather than from the Commissariat further off in Sydney, would become a relatively frequent occurrence. However, that 13th day of the month, far from being unlucky, although one of the soldiers became ill, saw them out of the brush ground. 'Gave orders to all hands to remove forward tomorrow morning to the forest ground, about half-a-mile ahead of our work'. On 14 August William: 'sent Lewis with a letter for the Governor, informing him we were without meat or sugar'. Happily, the next morning 'at 9.00 a.m. arrived a cart from Clarendon with a side of beef 386lb, 60 cabbages, two bags of corn, etc, for the men'. He does not say what the men felt, but it would have been extraordinary if their loyalty had not been bolstered by these supplies coming from their employer's own farm. As a young army officer, this author was told, 'always make sure your men eat before you do'. William knew how important this can be for morale.

They now set off along a 12 mile ridge, as Blaxland had so unfortunately advised. The going through the forest was as bad as through the brush. The trees were gigantic. William noted on 17 August: 'The timber … very tall and thick. Measured a dead tree which we felled that was 81ft to the first branch and a blood tree 15ft 6in in circumference'. Inevitably there were casualties during the tree felling, typically from long splinters, while both the men's gear and the tools were wearing out. On 18 August Rebecca Cox came to the rescue again. 'Got 2lb of shoemakers' thread from Clarendon and put Headman, one of our men, to repair shoes during the week" The blacksmith was employed repairing tools and making nails for the men's shoes in an improvised forge, for which a primitive chimney had to be built. The evening was stormy, a precursor of bad weather to come, 'but the wind blew off the rain'. The stonemason went forward to examine a rocky ridge about three miles ahead, the aim being to level it. The roughness of the terrain is unchanged today and adventurous tourists can, and do, become perilously lost in it.

William returned to Clarendon for a week on 19 August, leaving Lewis and Hobby in charge. There must have been a great deal to attend to at home by now, what with up to 100 employees and the lands around Mulgoa as well, where Rebecca had first obtained a grant for Edward in 1804. Around 1811 William had built 'The Cottage' there for the boys until such time as they married. When he returned to the road building on 26 August he brought with him his son Henry, who had helped earlier at the depot. He records Henry helping to count what proved to be a satisfactory 75 pieces of pork in a cask at the first depot, but does not mention him again.

There was a minor drama that day: 'At 10 a.m. arrived at Martin's, where I found the sergeant of the party, he having died the day before. Sent to Windsor for the sergeant commanding there for a coffin and party to bury him at Castlereagh (the Reverend Henry Fulton's parish), but Sergeant Ray sent for the corpse to bring it to Windsor. Wrote to the Governor for another sergeant.' It is all very laconically told, in the unemotional terms with which William would have been instructed to log events as an officer, a world away from the artificially elegant prose of the Governor's secretary. He finally reached the working party at 2 pm, finding the road finished thus far, although Lewis had left 'very ill of a sore throat'. This was a precursor of things to come. Continual rain and cold on the mountain would make many of the workmen ill. Meanwhile William recorded of the men tersely: 'Done well'.

By 28 August William had 'removed, with all the people, to a little forward of the 16th mile'. Lewis was back and two more natives, Joe from Mulgoa and Coley from Richmond had joined them – promising to remain. But the mountain was proving a formidable obstacle. In the ensuing days they had to remove 'an immense quantity of rock, both going up the mountain and to the pass leading to the bluff on the west of it'. William decided to make a road off the bluff, instead of winding round it, and had timber cut to 'frame the road on to the rock to the ridge below it, about 20ft in depth': not an easy procedure.

When William eventually reached it on 3 September he recorded unemotionally: 'The road finished to Caley's heap of stones, 17¾ miles'. This was near present day Linden. It had taken from 7 August to construct nine miles of road. The next day he clambered up to Evans' cave and got 'a view of the country from north west round to south west as far as the eye can carry you'. He could even see Windsor. It must have been truly inspiring, because William was not given to praising the scenery. On the Governor's tour Campbell recorded the country here as becoming 'altogether mountainous and extremely rugged'. The pile of stones attracted his attention; 'it is close to the line of road on top of a rugged and abrupt ascent, and is supposed to have been placed by Mr Caley'. The Governor named it Caley's Repulse.[11] As mentioned earlier, the cairn had not been created by Caley at all. Today this is part of an excitingly 'wild' Blue Mountains Drive for tourists, but two centuries ago the landscape was menacingly hard to negotiate. Fortunately the one hazard the forests did not conceal was dangerous predators. Australia has none, except crocodiles.

At the same time construction of a bridge had been started further on, over a river between Linden and what is now Wentworth Falls, employing 10 men. There was no water for stock by the bridge, the nearest being in a 'tremendous' gulley nearly a mile away. Nor was there a blade of grass. The bullocks helping with traction were soon to be more of a hindrance than a help. On 8 September the wind was high and cold and 'blew a perfect hurricane': again a precursor of future conditions, totally different to those they had left on the Cumberland Plain. They would have liked to shoot kangaroos for meat, but saw none, only bagging three pheasants.

On Sunday 11 September – they could not spare the time to observe the Sabbath – William went three miles forward along the road with Hobby and Lewis over two or three small passes to Caley's pile again. He wrote: 'From thence, at least two miles further, the mountain is nearly a solid rock. At places high broken rocks; at others very hanging or shelving, which makes it impossible to make a level good road.' On 12 September the long bridge, the first of many, was completed, except for the handrails and battening the planks. It had taken the labour of 12 men for three weeks, 'which time they worked very hard and cheerful'. Its dimensions were impressive. 'The bridge we have completed is 80ft. long, 15ft. wide at one end and 12ft. at the other'. On the approach to the bridge there was a rough stone wall about 100 feet long, while from the top of the mountain to the lower end was about 400 feet. It was, William considered, with evident pride, 'a strong, solid bridge, and will, I have no doubt, be reckoned a good-looking one by travellers that pass through the mountain'. He must have been mortified when Campbell's account made no mention of it. He issued a pair of strong shoes to each man, an indication of the tough going.

William continued to move forward ahead of the road construction, 'as far as the firemakers had finished' (burning away the scrub and brush) and keeping 'a strong party at the grub hoe'. The stone in the rocky ground was too hard to break with sledgehammers and was having to be levered up. There could hardly have been a more basic way of clearing a road. He also observed various birds, like a 'quite mottled' cockatoo. The brightly coloured mature cockatoos remain a feature of the forests around Mount Victoria.

On 25 September, a Sunday, while working out ways to conquer a 'steep mountain', William noticed a river below running east, the banks of which 'are so high and steep it is not possible to get down'. This was the river which Macquarie named after him, which empties into the Wollondilly. He now chose the site for his second depot 'close to a stream of excellent water' with 'the grass tree and other coarse food, which the bullocks eat and fill themselves pretty well'. By 2 October the store building, 17 feet by 12, had been weatherboarded, with gable ends. It was to enter local history when it became the Weatherboard Inn, for many years giving its name to the settlement now called Wentworth Falls. This establishes exactly how far the expedition had reached. William reckoned it to be 28 miles from Emu Ford, but unknown to him it was only a little more than a quarter of the way to the 'centrical point' of the Bathurst plains. He now returned to Clarendon, handing over control to his supervisors.

William had observed earlier that the country to the north was 'extremely hilly, with nothing but timber and rocks'. This was the area through which Bell's Line of Road would eventually run, and spectacular it certainly is. Range upon range of hills, with steep and often sheer escarpments, are bisected by long valleys. Campbell described:

> a succession of steep and rugged hills, some of which are so abrupt as to
> deny a passage altogether, but at this place a considerable extensive plain
> is arrived at, which constitutes the summit of the Western mountains
> and from thence a most extensive and beautiful prospect presents itself
> on all sides to the eye.

It was easy for the secretary to observe all this when travelling in the comfort, if somewhat bumpy, of a carriage. For William, relying on his compass and the muscular brawn of his team, wielding tools that were often damaged and with men falling ill, it was very different. He was trying to avoid using his limited supply of gunpowder if he could. Meanwhile the wind tore at them savagely. 'The wind has been very high and cold from the west since Sunday last,' he had written back on 8 September and it had continued, 'last night it blew a perfect hurricane … but we got scarcely any rain.' The next several weeks were tiring and frustrating for everyone.

On 3 October they achieved 'a very handsome long reach [of road], quite straight', which he called after Hobby. They were still on the top of the mountain. There were many large anthills around. One he measured was 6 feet high and 20 feet around the bottom. In the evening his servant arrived from Clarendon with horses and William left for home the next morning, writing to the Governor 'stating to him my arrangements'. He would be away until the 23rd, dealing with the sheep and the harvest at both Clarendon and Mulgoa, as well as attending Macquarie at a muster. On that date, close to three weeks after he had returned home to deal with what must have become pressing affairs – especially the ensuing harvest – William was again confronting 'the mountain'; or rather the next mountain, since he found he was dealing with a series of ridges. During his absence nine more miles of road had been laboriously constructed. He sent Hobby back in his postchaise to the Nepean for a week and also sent back his own saddle horse, which he could not keep 'for want of grass'.

Richard Lewis returned on this Sunday evening, 23 October, 'from the end of the mountain, about ten miles forward, having been with three men to examine the mountain that leads to the forest ground. His report is that the descent is near half a mile down … that it is scarcely possible to make a road down; and that we cannot get off the mountain to the north to make a road … much more difficult than he was before aware of'. William responded to this bad news by setting all hands to road-making the next day, 'being extremely anxious to get forward and ascertain if we can descend the mountain to the south before we get to the end of the ridge'. He wrote to the Governor for a further supply of gunpowder.

A few days later, on 30 October, he recorded seeing to the east north-east 'a table rock seen by us from the rocks near Coley's [sic] pile to our right'. This can only have been the Pulpit Rock, which places their position at the end of October at present day Blackheath. From there it would not have been possible to descend the mountain to the south. The Great Western Highway of today veers west north-west after Mount Victoria and goes steeply down the side of the ridge. William sent three men to search for a way down, unsuccessfully. It rained a lot and the 'blankets belong to the men were very wet and uncomfortable'. On some days they could not work at all. The changeability of the weather was defined by the Governor, when he made his tour of inspection in May 1815, writing that it did not rain, there was very little water in the Macquarie River at Bathurst and the Nepean at Emu Ford was only six inches deep.

William was not in the mood to pen a panegyric about the scenery, but again the Governor's secretary subsequently did, giving a much clearer description of what William simply saw as a cold, wet and challenging landscape. 'The majestic grandeur of the situation, Campbell wrote, 'induced the Governor to give it the appellation of the King's Table Land … on the south west side the mountain terminates in abrupt precipices of immense depth, at the bottom of which is seen a glen [the forest ground: Macquarie was a Scot], as romantically beautiful as can be imagined, bounded on the further side by mountains of great magnitude … the whole thickly covered with timber.' This is what Richard Lewis had reported, more prosaically, to William on 23 October. Macquarie later bestowed endless politically deferential names, now mostly forgotten, on various features, such as the Prince Regent's Glen and the Pitt Amphitheatre (after Prime Minister William Pitt).

On 2 November William decided to survey it himself 'as a road must be made to get off the mountain'. The next day, having started off at 6 am with Lewis, Tye and a soldier, he found the descent 'much worse than I expected … The whole front of the mountain is covered with loose rock … the hill is so very steep about half a mile down that it is not possible to make a good road … without going to a very great expense.' Never prepared to accept defeat, he therefore 'made up my mind to make such a road as a cart can go down empty or a very light load without a possibility of its being able to return with any sort of load whatever'. In carriage or wagon transport terms this was tantamount to defeat, although 'such a road would answer to drive stock down to the forest ground'. In his estimation only fat bullocks or sheep would be able to be brought up and the sheep would have to be shorn at the top.

This scene is just as spectacular today. The long forested ridges are bounded by sheer dolerite escarpments, in places eroded into craggy pinnacles and other weird shapes, and with lone trees clinging to their sides, below which lie forested valleys interspersed with grassy plains. Evans had described how on 24 November 1813 he had come 'to the very end of the Range from which the Prospect is extensive … the descent is rugged and steep'. Having got down it he found a valley that was 'beautiful and fertile with a rapid stream running through it [Coxs River]' and then reached the place where the Blaxland, Wentworth and Lawson expedition had terminated, west of present day Hartley, and had named a prominent sugarloaf hill as Mount Blaxland.[12] The attractions of this forest ground far below were tantalizingly visible to William. When he managed to get down there on foot he found 'Grass of a good quality … Timber thin and kangaroos – plenty'. But 'in returning back we had to clamber up the mountain, and it completely knocked me up'. He was now close to his fiftieth birthday.

Despite the fatigue of middle age, William did not give up. He removed all hands further along, to 45½ miles from the Emu ford, and gave them a gill (140 ml) of spirits each to cheer them along. Ever persistent, on 4 November he 'sent three men to examine all the ridges and gullies to the north, offering a reward if they found a better way down. All returned unsuccessful.' He decided to get the bullock herds down to the pastures below, since many were suffering from 'lameness or poverty' of feed, remarking that they had 'not carried a single load of anything for me since Sunday week last'. He must have been feeling deeply frustrated, although he did not say so. He was remarkably restrained about his own feelings and health.

The whole group was now forced to camp at the top of the escarpment. Whether William had the caravan with him at this stage is not stated, but the Governor later praised him for having shared his men's discomforts in a bark hut. There are still two small waterholes near the track to Mount York (named by Macquarie), close to which his men slept in those huts. They are to be found a few metres to the side of the road, quite small, and in soil thick with leaf mould. The overhanging rock ledges where others sheltered are easily identified, too. William described them as 'so lofty and undermined that the men will be able to sleep dry'.

Some leaders would have accepted this situation as a stalemate and turned back, as earlier expeditions had. Instead, William ordered the blacksmith to make eight pikes for defence against hostile natives, and sent yet another party to find an alternative route down the mountain – which again failed. There were saplings here like white thorn, which grew tall and straight and could be easily bent, and William resolved to send some to Clarendon, an interesting reflection on his lifelong quest for agricultural improvements, even when facing potential disaster. He wrote to Sydney for more gunpowder and spirits and on 7 November 'went forward with 10 men to commence operations for a road down the mount'. A historian of the mountains, Chris Cunningham, calls the eventual achievement 'perhaps the most noble of all the stories involved in crossing the Blue Mountains'. But William and his men were not there yet.

The Weatherboard hut at Wentworth Falls was a supply depot during the road building and was painted by John Lewin in 1815. It became the Weatherboard Inn (Mitchell Library, State Library of NSW [PXE 888 no. 3])

Augustus Earle's painting of convicts repairing Cox's road, c. 1826 (Nan Kivell Collection, National Library of Australia)

6   Mount York Defeated

On Saturday 5 November 1814, two days before he began the operations 'for a road down the mount,' William had 'Examined the big mountain, and fixed on the spot where to begin on Monday, having given up all thoughts of attempting it elsewhere. J. Manning sprained his ankle in bringing up a keg of water from the rocks below'. These entries in his journal encapsulate the problems William was now facing. Somehow or other the road had to be got down from the ridge to the forest ground below, in spite of the precipitous descent, illnesses and injuries, and miserable weather. When he achieved the objective it was, in Macquarie's subsequent admiring words, 'with incredible labour and perseverance [which] does him infinite honor'.[1] A tribute indeed.

If you go to Mount York today, not far from an obelisk commemorating Cox's achievement, you will see a short section of the road his men made, which has been restored by the Blue Mountains Council. When the track reaches the lip of the mountain it plunges down, twisting between gigantic boulders, which it was impossible to shift, in places swerving past the very edge of cliffs. The descent was only achieved in a series of semi-circular bends, like a sailboat tacking. The Governor's secretary, John Campbell, in his account of Macquarie's tour of inspection in May 1815, described this three quarters of a mile as 'a rugged and tremendous descent in all its windings'.[2] Even when it was finished, horses harnessed to carriages had be taken down backwards because they became terrified. Great logs were attached to the rear of wagons to slow them – and created a pile of discards at the bottom. When Macquarie's entourage went down in May 1815 their descent took from 11 am to 2 pm – three hours – and when you look down there you can see why.

That was in the future. Now, when William went forward with his 10 men, there were 'Light rain and heavy fogs'. In the mountains the climate hardly feels like the Australian summer of the plains below, let alone that there was a drought in the country they were striving to reach. The next day he 'Employed the same hands in the same manner. Light rain as before. The men very wet and uncomfortable, their clothes and bedding being also wet.' But at least they were still on fairly level ground, grubbing out trees and creating the track that runs near to the monument. Not far back there is a signpost pointing to the various explorers' routes across the ridge and a slightly confusing map on a noticeboard.

On 9 November, with his team levelling the ground on top of the ridge quite briskly, William 'removed to the extreme end of the mountain with the whole of the party', although the road had not reached there yet. He was glad that 'The rocks here are so lofty and undermined that the men will be able to sleep dry, and keep their little clothing dry also, which is what they have been unable to do this last fortnight'. This was just as well because there was 'cold rain' that day, and on the next and on 11 November again, after a fine working day and a starlit evening previously, 'Rain commenced before daylight and continued the whole day. Wind S and very cold.'

Three men were ill, one man called Raddock (Roddicks) so much so that he had to be sent back to Windsor. The other two who were laid up included a carpenter with 'a cold and swollen face'. The sick list was going to mount dramatically in the next few days. Food was a problem too. On this same day, 11 November, William sent two carts back to the second depot for a re-supply of provisions, though they were managing to kill a kangaroo a day for meat. Infuriatingly, having brought the bullocks to provide haulage, trouble was the only thing they were providing. All the beasts had achieved in the past two weeks was to bring one (presumably very large) bag of biscuits the 43 miles from the first depot on the Emu Plains. One bullock had gone blind, wandered into a gully and had to be extricated. William ordered them all down to the forest ground, where they could recover 'until we remove forward to the Fish river'. In just under four months his men had constructed only 43 miles of road. By 12 November, mercifully a 'very fine day' though cold, the road had been completed 'to the beginning of the large mountain [Mount York], which we have to descend to the forest ground … Continued to clear away the timber and rubbish through the large rocks, and to the beginning of the bluff end of the mountain. Two men on the sick list.'

Again Campbell's account gives a clearer view of what William faced than he was able to describe himself, when in the thick of tackling the descent. The secretary wrote:

> The road continues for the space of 17 miles, on the ridge of the mountain which forms one side of the Prince Regent's Glen, and then it suddenly terminates in nearly a perpendicular precipice of 676ft. high, as ascertained by measurement. The road constructed by Mr Cox down this rugged and tremendous descent, through all its windings, is no less than three-quarters of a mile in length, and has been executed with skill and stability, and reflects much credit on him … In order to perpetuate the memory of Mr Cox's services, the Governor deemed it a tribute justly due to him to give his name to this grand and extraordinary pass.

Campbell went on to identify, without apparently intending to, the expensive error in the Blaxland strategy. 'Although the present pass is the only practicable point yet discovered for descending by, yet the mountain is much higher than those on either side of it … it has the appearance of a very high distinct hill, although it is in fact only the abrupt termination of a ridge.'[3]

After he began the descent William's activities became relatively complicated, since with characteristic energy he was both supervising the road building at the top and exploring the potential of the forest ground below. On 13 November he went down there and 'from thence to the rivulet, and traced it to the river, about five miles'. Having found the river, which Macquarie later named after him, he went one mile down stream, reckoning it must 'empty itself into the Nepean River', then 'came back on the high lands, exploring the best ground for a road'. This may sound easy but it cannot have been at all so, even though they gratifyingly found the timber was only thin and the grass 'would be very good pasture for sheep'. But within a week William had to admit that he was overdoing the physical exertion, as he had before.

When he got back up to the work site he found that the horse carts had arrived from the second depot, but had only brought 'very small loads indeed'. He was irritated and ordered two of them to leave next day for the first depot and return 'on Sunday next, loaded'. As a result of this disappointment he had to cut the rations. Evidently the men were eating in small groups. He 'Ordered Gorman to issue 4 lbs. biscuits and 3 lbs. flour for each mess, instead of 6 lbs. each, the biscuits running short, and being also too bulky to bring so far, being 90 miles from head-quarters'. The next day he did note, however, that the men were getting fresh kangaroo at least three times a week, which should improve their health. 'So many men sick,' he noted. At noon there was thunder, with rain and hail, a cold east wind and rain all evening.

Any relief was short-lived. That next day, 14 November, also brought worse sickness problems, so that the plaudits William later received at not losing a single man on the enterprise were well deserved. The sick list speaks for itself. 'F. Dwyer, cold, pains in limbs; S. Freeman, cold and swelled face; S. Crook, cold, bad eyes; V. Hanragan, cold, pains in limbs; S. Walters, hurt by bullock. The extreme wet weather we had for a fortnight before we arrived here has given most of the men colds, but as they are now dry lodged … it is to be hoped they will soon recover.'

What is *not* said in this record is quite as important as what *is* said. There is no suggestion that any of the sick men were malingering. Nor did William make any complaint about his own condition; and he must have been every bit as wet and cold as his men. Nonetheless, on 14 November they did get on with a bridge at 'the beginning of the descent off the mountain, and blowing up the rocks that are in the line of our intended road down to the forest. Find is [*sic*] difficult work and it will cost us much labour.' This was generally referred to as the first bridge and was on top of the Mount York ridge. On 15 November the men 'Fixed two trees as side pieces [to the road] ... one 45, the other 50ft. long'.

The need to blow up rocks would also have made William glad that he had been so careful to conserve his small supply of gunpowder. Looking at those rocks today makes one realize that he needed skilled quarrymen. On 16 November 'the rocks cut [were] extremely hard'. On 17 November the men 'Worked on the front of the mountain. The ground extremely hard, and very large rocks as we dig into it. Some we blow up, but the greater part we turn out with long levers and crowbars. Kept six men cutting and blowing up rocks, two splitting posts and rails, and it is as much as the 'smith can do to keep their tools in order.'

Happily 18 November saw an inspired piece of innovation. 'W. Appledon [a former sailor] fixed the blocks and tackle to trees, and got a most capital purchase to turn out an immense large rock at the side of the mountain in the way of our road ... two men received slight hurts in doing it by one of the purchases slipping. This rock would have cost me at least 5lb. of powder to have blown it up.' One can imagine the dislodged monster tumbling down the mountain, crushing undergrowth and small trees on its way to the forest ground below and terrifying any kangaroos that were there.

It was now a full four months since William and his party had set out from the Emu Plains and, if their progress was fast, given the problems, it had a continuing human cost. On 19 November the sick list numbered six and a further six out of the 30 had to be discharged from the mountain work. In the evening they all endured two hours of heavy thunder, hail and rain. Possibly the continuance of the bad weather, the sheer hard work and the constant obstacles tried William's patience. At all events, on Sunday 20 November he set off early with Hobby, Lewis and Tye to go down the mountain himself. This foray was to leave him soaked to the skin after a near-disaster and uncomfortably aware of his age.

Meanwhile, preparations for bridging the first river on the forest ground below had continued laboriously. The aim was 'to examine the rivulet, river and ground as far as Blaxland's mountain, to find out the best passage across the water, as also to mark the road to it'. Evans had described this as a stream going south and joined with one from the west 'forming a considerable rapid riverlett', where Campbell recorded that the Governor was 'much gratified by the appearance of good pasture land and soil fit for cultivation'. Macquarie named it the Vale of Clwyd

> in consequence of the strong resemblances it bore to the vale of that name in North Wales … a rivulet of fine water runs along it from the eastward, which unites itself at the western extremity with another rivulet containing still more water. The junction of these two streams forms a very handsome river, now called by the Governor Cox's River … which empties itself into the River Nepean, near Mulgoa.

Since the Cox River was 56 miles from the Emu ford, according to Campbell, and William had reckoned the top of the mountain was 45½ miles from there, this first bridge down below must have been over the Coxs River, were there are still traces of one today. But, as maps show, there were a number of rivulets. What is now marked as the River Lett appears to be Evans' 'riverlett'.

Campbell's account explains the problems which William encountered, both here and beyond. The combined rivulets were too large to cross when they became one river and the terrain beyond was tricky. On Sunday 20 November, William may well have been swearing under his breath as he tried to establish a route across either the river or the rivulets, although he was probably too self-controlled to swear out loud in front of his men. It was a bad day for him. First of all, after crossing a small swamp, 'my horse got stuck in a bog, and plunged until he fell. I received no hurt, but got wet through.' He then did the only sensible thing, given that they were all short of clothing: 'Pulled off my clothes, wrung them and left them in the sun an hour, when they were tolerably dry'. It was just as well that it wasn't raining. Evidently he had acquired a saddle horse.

Shortly after this, when crossing the lower rivulet, close to the junction, 'Mr Hobby's horse stumbled and threw him into the water, which from the last heavy rains was quite rapid'. After all that, despite finding 'the sort of grass fit for cattle and sheep', William was further frustrated by the crossing places on the river being so encumbered with rock, and the sides so steep, that 'I did not fix on a crossing place on it, but intend having both rivulets well examined the ensuing week'. He was just about done for, himself. 'Came back at 6 p.m., completely knocked up from fatigue.' It really was a game for younger men. Evans had been only 33 when he embarked on his expedition. To cap it all, that evening they again experienced violent winds and three or four hours of the interminable rain.

This soaking, dispiriting weather persisted all week. William only noted the days which were Sundays, perhaps in obeisance to what ought to have been times of rest. On 21 November thunder and rain began at 10 am 'and continued the whole day, at times very heavy. Only four hours work done.' He issued all hands a gill of spirits each. The next day was a bit better and the men continued despite light rain and heavy fogs. They turned out a great many rocks, blowing up one in descending the mountain. 'The ground as we dig discovers many more rocks than we expected.' November 23 brought 'a very cold wind, east south east', though the weather did clear up. William tackled his re-supply problems by sending 'two carts to Emu Plains, with three horses, and the sergeant and two men to bring a load of flour from Martin's. Sent Gorman with them, and he took six weeks provisions for two of the soldiers that are to be left at the first depot.'

That same day the supervisor Tye was sent with a soldier and a labourer 'to re-mark the trees from the second rivulet to the Fish River, a distance of 20 miles [32 km] from hence' to the west and given directions to return by a ridge of high land 'that bears as we suppose, from within three miles of the Fish River back to Mount Blaxland, it being my wish to make the road on that line, if practicable'. From the river to Mount Blaxland was ten miles. That this relatively minor exploration was not going to be easy is underlined by the men being given a week's rations.

When they returned on the evening of 27 November they brought rock cod that they had caught with them, but it rained constantly and the river waters were so high that they had been unable to follow the ridge. They had to come back the way had gone, through hilly country considered unsuitable for a road, although that had to be the route eventually taken, passing just to the south of Blaxland's mountain. Confusingly, William's journal entry for 3 December also has Tye and the soldier returning on that day and reporting that 'we cannot go on either of the ridges pointed out, and that we must cross the valley by Blaxland's mountain'. Possibly Tye, who made a series of probing expeditions for William, had been sent a second time.

During Tye's absence work had continued on the rocky descent from Mount York, as did the rain. 'It mizzled,' William recorded, using an evocative Middle English word for drizzle which has sadly fallen out of use. The men were turning out 'an immense quantity of rock, which was very handsomely veined, very like marble'. They were issued with more shoes and trousers. The bullocks disappeared and had to be searched for. Although work was progressing further ahead at the river bridge down below, progress on the descent of Mount York was slow.

On 26 November William wrote that: 'We have been fortunate in turning out very large solid rocks 2ft. thick without breaking them, and we have used but little powder this week'. To add to this annoyance the bullocks had 'not been seen these 10 days. Sent Lewis after them and found them up a valley three miles away'. But at least the carpenter had 'got 100 posts split and 200 rails for fencing the road down the mountain'. William certainly made his free men supervisors work, for which they were well rewarded at the end with grants of land. The next day a team of the errant bullocks was sent off to bring provisions from Emu Plains, after their harnesses had been repaired. A man named Finch, who was very ill, travelled as a passenger in the cart.

The labour force was still divided between the road down the mountain and the first river bridge, with greater progress around the bridge, albeit at the cost of much effort. On 28 November two very welcome 336 pound casks of flour arrived from Emu Ford and a good day's work was done. The stonemason completed the rock work a little below the bridge. 'It has cost us 10 blasts of powder and great labour to get rid of it.' On 29 November the bridge approach was reinforced with a tree trunk so massive that its mere size was a major challenge. 'Got a tree,' William wrote, '55 ft. long and 9 ft. in circumference by the men in the woods into his [sic] place as a side piece below the bridge … Men stuck very hard picking and grubbing the rocks and forming the road.' The next day four were on the sick list. On 1 December Hobby and Lewis 'again examined the river to find a proper place for a [second] bridge that can be got at from the main ridge we discovered about two miles from the valley below. They found two places and marked back the best one.'

A week earlier William had been intensely aggravated when the government teams bringing supplies reached Emu Ford but refused to swim the bullocks across, because of the height of the river, unless they had a written order from himself. One can imagine him fuming, especially when, after searching for a government horse, his men were unable to find one and on 3 December he had to send the long-suffering Gorman on foot for the 50 miles to Emu Ford with the order. That same Saturday he had the men working hard on what he called the 'second circle' down the mountain (as explained above, the steepness of the descent forced the road to be made in a serious of half-circles). The sick list included a man with scurvy, probably for fear of which William had earlier given them cabbages.

On 4 December they were close to success with the mountain road. William recorded that his caravan was taken down the mountain 'by men, the road not being finished sufficient for horses or cattle to draw on it'. Once down there again himself – and doubtless very relieved to have the caravan available – he 'removed about two miles to where there is water. The bullock cart took the provisions etc forward [how the cart was got there is not explained]. Went on to the river and fixed on the spot to make the first bridge.' He had noticed 'a most beautiful ridge, near three miles long, that leads direct to the spot [on the Coxs River]', although he could not see any timber fit for it. There was also second lesser river, the River Lett, as an obstruction.

The horses 'were brought back by Sullivan and two others, who were given the promised reward – half a pint of spirits'. William also issued a gill of spirits each to all hands. It rained all night. 5 December was no better with sleet, hail, thunder and lightning. But 6 December dawned clear and he removed after breakfast with the caravan, horse and bullock cart to the junction of the two rivers (where the River Lett flowed into the Cox) and decided that the obstacles to making one bridge were so great that he would make a bridge over each.

So, on 8 December, after dealing briskly with a variety of logistical problems of transport and provisions, William 'Left 12 men to finish the road down the mountain, under charge of R. Lewis', while another 12 laboured on the section between the mountain and the river, which they finished that evening. That day William also made a momentous decision in terms of marking his progress. He changed his point of reference for calculating distances, making reconciling them with his account difficult. Presumably he reckoned that he was roughly halfway. 'Measured down the mountain to the valley to the fiftieth mile from the ford,' he wrote. 'Here I drop this reckoning and commence from the 50th mile to [towards] the west.' His quoted distances are further confused by references both to rivulets and the River Lett. However, Campbell's observations make it evident that, having got down the mountain at about 45 miles from Emu Ford, the next major bridge was over the Cox River, some 10 miles of track across hill and vale further on, as already mentioned.

The journal's descriptions of these various rivers, which as yet had no names except for the Fish River, are confusing. The first major bridge was near the top of the mountain, whereas the next bridges and the two rivulets – where William's horse had become stuck in a bog on 20 November and he got wet through – were below on the forest ground. He 'fixed on a spot over each [rivulet] as being less trouble and more convenient than making one bridge over the river'. Furthermore the ascent from the possible single bridging place was 'much steeper and worse ground for a road'. By the time the road was finished 12 bridges had been laboriously constructed.

Again the Governor's secretary was later able to give the route a perspective denied to William. The route of the road ran past the junction of the River Lett and Coxs River, close to present day Glenroy, then just south of Mount Blaxland and westward to cross the Fish River, eventually turning north to Bathurst. Campbell wrote: 'A range of very lofty hills and narrow valleys alternately form the tract of country from Cox's river, for a distance of 16 miles, until the Fish River is arrived at; and the stage between these rivers is consequently very severe and oppressive on the cattle'. This route had been thought unsuitable at first. Macquarie described it as having 'numerous steep ascents and Descents the whole way'. It ran quite a long way south of the present Great Western Highway and was to be frequently realigned, the first notable change being in 1823, taking it north of Mount Blaxland, with a major change in 1832. But as yet, on 9 December, William had not crossed the river that Macquarie named after him.

During that day of 9 December, the men had laboured intensively before breakfast on a bridge across the River Lett. At 9 am William 'took all hands to the second bridge, and before dinner got one of the side pieces, 45 ft. long fixed in its place without accident'. The other side piece was created by felling a tree across the river, 'about 60 ft. long'. Shifting such timber on a river bank would have involved intense effort and several of the men seemed to be inclined to give in and shirk work, 'the greater part of whom, in my opinion, are quite as well as myself'. William gave them a 'reproof in earnest', expecting it to 'make them all well by tomorrow'. In the army a reproof in earnest meant having a cat-o-nine tails hung outside the offender's tent, a salutary reminder of possible punishment. No such sanction existed here, but the reproof worked, since the men had their freedom at stake.

The trouble seems to have begun with an act of kindness to a convict. On 5 December William wrote to the Reverend Cartwright on the Emu Plains asking him to 'send two of the gaol gang to cut and house Tindall's wheat at the Nepean. He has a large family and it is his all.' This was the same Tindall who Bigge later claimed had not laboured on the road at all. Now he 'could not allow himself to go in, as many others would fancy they were entitled to the same indulgence'. Nonetheless it may have caused resentment. Possibly as a result, in the ensuing days William quite frequently dispensed practical rewards in the shape of half pints or else gills of spirits, as when men had been labouring half the day in the water of the river. He often became very fatigued himself, which was hardly surprising. He was like a circus ringmaster trying to control two arenas at the same time: the recalcitrant road down the mountain and the perilous approaches to the river that later bore his name.

On 11 December William sent six men back to complete the mountain road and ten forward to camp at Blaxland's mountain, while he set out on horseback with Lewis and Hobby 'to examine the ground for a road' as far as the Fish River, 16 miles beyond the Coxs River, through which they must have waded. They found that after passing the distinctive sugarloaf hill of Mount Blaxland on their right they had to ascend a high and rising ridge which was 'very unfavourable for a road'. William then tried to return via Evans' route and found it 'impracticable even for a horse'. He noted that 'the hills to the west, north and south are extremely high and difficult of access'. In the end he was forced to make his road past Blaxland's hill. He got back at sunset, 'much fatigued and disappointed'.

Encouragingly, William found the land here was favourable for grazing, but 'hills to the west, north and south are extremely high and difficult of access'. Along this section to the Fish River Macquarie later named three hills as Mount Blaxland (already called that by Evans), Wentworth's Sugar Loaf and Lawson's Sugar Loaf, honouring the hardships of their expedition, 'the severity of which labour had seriously affected their healths'. It affected William's too. Those explorations may sound blundering to a modern traveller. But in such a tangle of virgin scrub and timber William often had a job literally to see where he was heading, even with the aid of a compass.

William's 'reproof in earnest' of 9 December was effective. The next day the men had 'finished the bridge over the east branch [i.e., rivulet], 22 ft. long, 13 ft. wide. Carpenters etc, made a good strong job of it.' In the days through to 14 December work on the bridges continued, despite thunderstorms and some men having to work standing in the water, for which they were again rewarded with a gill of spirits. At the same time, William was all too aware of the uncompleted job of the road down the mountain. At 6 am on 11 December, another Sunday in the long march of working weekends, his order was carried out for 'six married men to go back to the mountain to finish the road down it to the valley. When done they are to be discharged.' The six included Tindall, who had been so anxious about his harvest on the Nepean. Again this demonstrated William's considerable skills at man management, giving willing workers the immediate reward of discharge, with emancipation sure to follow, and so re-motivating the rest, although he risked causing resentment.

The next two days saw six men working 'nearly all day' in the river. William gave the men a gill of spirits each after they had 'Got a good day's work done'. In the evening of 12 December there was 'a violent thunderstorm, with wind, lightning and heavy rain, which lasted until 9 o'clock'. The men can hardly have been much drier in their bark shelters than in the river. The contrast with the dry weather and drought when Macquarie made his tour of inspection barely five months later was extraordinary.

Further efforts were made to bring supplies forward from the mountain, while work was well ahead in working the road around Blaxland's mountain. Then, on 15 December came the moment William had so long been waiting for. 'At 1 p.m. one of the party at the mountain came to report they had finished their task. Sent Lewis back to examine it, and found it completed.' There is no hint of celebration in the diary, even though it had taken since 18 July – all but five months – to get there. William simply noted the fulfilment of his promise: 'Gave them their discharge (six men), and sent a cart with them as far as the Nepean, to carry their bedding'. The dismissed men's feelings of relief can be imagined.

With the mountain conquered, the project really could forge ahead. On 16 December a sergeant was sent back to bring the tools used on the mountain, while the bridge across the west branch of the river was finished. Again a massive tree trunk was indispensable as a side piece. It was 'an oak tree, with a girth of 9 ft. at least 6 ft. above where it was fallen, and was [a] good 50 ft. long. I never saw such a tree of that sort before … The carpenter worked remarkably well while at this job.' Next day they broke up their quarters at this bridge and moved forward to where Hobby was superintending work on smaller bridges. William 'selected 14 men to go forward road-making'. There must by now have been a feeling amongst the teams that they were near the end, despite the daily rains and storms.

On the Sunday, 18 December, William enjoyed a pleasant al fresco Sunday lunch with Hobby, Tye and three others, when they 'caught some fish, and dined on the banks of the river'. Here he fixed on a possible line of road 'except going up the hill, which must be avoided, if possible'. This was Blaxland's mountain, on the side of which Hobby's team had been working. Happily the next day William 'Found a way to avoid the high hill … and marked the ground for a road' despite a violent thunderstorm at 3 pm. They returned three hours later to find that Lewis 'had brought the bullocks forward'. The following day was 'extremely clear and hot', with a violent afternoon thunderstorm.

A curious episode now erupted, again perhaps symptomatic of exhaustion, on the Tuesday when William ordered the sergeant (Kelly) to take back a man named J. Allen, who had been very ill for some days. 'To my surprise he made such frivolous objections as I did not like … said neither his horse or himself had shoes; but if he was ordered he must go.' It was an unwise underling who refused orders from William. The Parramatta cart was promptly ordered to take the sick man back to the Nepean and the sergeant was sent off at dawn next day to the first depot to relieve a corporal with written instructions 'for his guidance there'. History does not tell us whether the sergeant was demoted, but it seems likely. William did not take kindly to insubordination.

Christmas was rapidly approaching, and with it more thunderstorms and daily rain, often extremely heavy. It was proving to be an exceptionally wet season, which swelled the waters in a succession of small rivers over which bridges had to be constructed, although there was a drought on the far side of the range. Both bridges (near Glenroy) were completed on 21 December. Two days later William sent a progress report to the Governor, and being without the Parramatta team, had to get timber for the last six bridges cut by the men with him. He recorded 'we are now at 15½ miles' – presumably this was from the 50 mile mark – but on 24 December he quoted the total distance as 90 miles and added: 'Went forward this afternoon to ascertain if I could get my caravan with safety to the Fish River'. He succeeded in doing this on Christmas Day. On 24 December they 'Finished a very good bridge at 1 o'clock. Went on after dinner half a mile, and began another bridge.' One can sense the impetus, even in William's purely factual writing.

On Christmas Day William recorded that they had 'three bridges to make and five miles of road'. Possibly he had now established the line of road for a total of 90 miles, though his subsequent entry for 27 December suggests that he had not. It being Christmas Day, he 'issued to the men a gill of spirits and a new shirt each'. He now fixed on a spot to cross the Fish River, though the timber 'appears to be bad and scarce about here. Cannot find any for sawing.'

On 26 December William sent back to Clarendon 'for a good cart horse, to prevent delay after we cross the river'. The forge was erected 'to repair the tools, they being much out of order'. The next day, 'At 9.00 a.m. crossed the river for the first time with Mr. Hobby, J. Tye and a soldier … to ascertain the best place for a road'. William noted that 'the grass in this valley was the best and thickest on the ground I have yet seen in this colony'. They 'saw six kangaroos, a flock of 11 emus, wild ducks and pigeons, but for want of dogs killed none. At 6 p.m. returned and reached the river quite tired.' From this description the land beyond the Fish River was a grazier's paradise. The Governor's secretary, Campbell, gave a parallel impression. He wrote that the land beyond the river to the Sidmouth Valley 'abounds with a great variety of herbs and plants, such as would probably interest and gratify the scientific colonist'.

William was now preoccupied with getting across the Fish River, having already built 10 bridges. The Campbell River would be the final obstacle, and he was pursuing a direct line west towards it. However, he did note on 29 December 'A fine morning, which the birds seem most to enjoy on the banks of the river. The shrubs and flowers are also extremely fragrant.' He wrote to the Governor 'with the proceedings down to this period, but shall not send it away until my return from the western excursion'. This 'excursion', though he made it sound as simple as a trip to the seaside, was to be gruelling and the last one he described, in the longest entry of the whole diary.

The next entry was on New Year's Day 1815, a Thursday. William and his party crossed the Fish River at noon, leaving Gorman in charge. They headed for the Campbell, crossing the Emu Valley and then the Sidmouth Valley, 'a most beautiful one', where they found many kangaroos and wild turkeys. On the first evening they crossed the Campbell and camped. The next day, heading north-north-west on their horses, they 'followed the course of the river about three miles across the O'Connell's plains to the point where the Macquarie and Campbell rivers unite, at 11.30, where we sat down for the day'. The Macquarie had been named by Evans in November 1813.

They were now into the lands of which Macquarie had such high hopes. William commented that 'At Sidmouth valley I never saw finer grass, or more on the same quantity of land in a meadow in England'. This was confirmed in the secretary's account.[6] The Governor was highly gratified by the appearance of the country ... gently rising grounds and fertile plains. Judging from the height of its banks and its general width, the Campbell River must be in some parts be of considerable magnitude, but the extraordinary drought which has apparently prevailed ... as throughout the colony for the last three years ...

has reduced this river … [to] a chain of ponds. At the time this must have seemed extraordinary, in view of the torrential weather on the mountains. It also underlines that the hazards of farming have not changed in the two centuries since. Campbell noticed great numbers of 'the water platypus mole' in the river pools.

Thus over three days William's group had crossed the Campbell and ridden the whole length from the Macquarie River back to 'where we are building a bridge in the day' over the Fish. The Fish is the main tributary of the Macquarie, joined by the Campbell. 'The whole of the line, about 20 miles due west, would make most excellent grazing farms,' William wrote, explaining 'This is the south side of the Fish River I am describing. On the north side I have not yet been.' He had been on the south side ever since he crossed the river. When they got back he 'ordered a bullock to be killed for the use of the people, which I had issued to them in lieu of giving them a ration of salt pork … when the men were mustered this morning they were extremely clean, and looked cheerful and hearty'.

On 2 January William sent off letters to the Governor and the Commissary. They were 21 miles beyond the mountain, which by the secretary's account would have been several miles short of the Fish River, and were faced by yet another difficult hill. On 3 January 'the men finished filling in the piers at each end of the bridge.' Some of the logs had to be brought three miles (he had originally noted the lack of local timber for sawing). He further explored the south bank, but found gullies and less good land. Quite apart from the road, he constantly had in mind the future farming settlements it would serve. Next day he went with Hobby to mark the line of road from the Emu Valley to the Sidmouth Valley (both run roughly north to south) and in the evening moved the gang of 12 to the Emu. Sending so many men home had depleted his workforce. To his disappointment, the cart of provisions from Parramatta failed to arrive.

Then on 5 January, quite suddenly, the strain of the long and punishing endeavour overtook William and he fell sick himself, the last of the team to do so. 'About midnight I was taken violently ill with excruciating pains just above my left hip.' Perhaps he had spent too long in the saddle. 'In about two hours it became easier, when I got into a perspiration and slept a little. Was in considerable pain until about 9, when I again dozed, and got up at 11 considerably better.' There was no medical orderly on the expedition, so William had to treat himself. This may be another reason why the diary ended abruptly two days later, after a brief 7 January entry.

Some consolation was that on the day he fell ill the Fish River bridge was completed. No doubt forcing himself to write, William noted that it was 'strong and well built' with stone piers of 25 feet at each end. 'The span across is 25 ft. more, which is planked with split logs. It is altogether 75 ft. long and 16ft. wide.' On 6 January he 'crossed the river over the new bridge with the caravan and two carts, as also our horses, and went as far as Sidmouth Valley'. He marked the road 'from the valley to the next creek, where we have a bridge to build, as also one in the valley'. His final entry, on 7 January, recorded his ordering the men further forward and himself riding to the head of the Sidmouth Valley. 'Returned by the hills, which are very fine. An emu and a kangaroo passed quietly along.' These last words conjure up a vivid picture of William in his paradise, riding in the wilderness. But he was quickly back at work at home. On 15 January 1815 he submitted an estimate to government for the construction of two bridges and the road of Bridge Street at Windsor at a cost of £200. This estimate included details of the number of trees that would be needed and how many logs could be fixed in place in a day – on all of which he was now an expert.[4]

The road was completed at the Bathurst plains on 14 January 1815. When the Governor arrived at these plains on 4 May he 'remained a week, which time he occupied in making excursions in different directions through the adjoining country on both sides of the river'.[5] Macquarie remarked in his own journal on 5 May that the Bathurst plains extended 'on both sides of the Macquarie River for 11 miles and nearly three miles each side'. He was almost ecstatic about the land, which was beautiful and 'very fit for Sheep Walks'. This was where William and his sons were to make their fortunes as pastoralists. On 7 May he fixed on a site for the future town of Bathurst 'in honor of the most noble Earl of that name'.

On several occasions Macquarie met small groups of 'natives'. He observed one such group, whose members showed 'great surprise at seeing so many strangers', to be 'very inoffensive and cleanly in their persons'. On 10 May he gave three men presents of 'slops and tomahawks' and ordered

that they should be given plenty to eat from the public stores. These were members of the Wiradjuri who, only 10 years later, were to be protagonists and losers in the 'Black War' around Bathurst, resulting from the pressure of white settlement on their ancestral lands.

Secretary Campbell's account finished: 'The road constructed by Mr Cox and the party under him commences at Emu Ford ... and is thence carried 101½ miles to the flagstaff at Bathurst'.

Obelisk monument to William on Mount York. The plaque reads: 'The first road over the Blue Mountains was completed in January 1815. The commission to execute this was entrusted by Governor Macquarie to William Cox Esq. J.P. Lieut 102nd Reg of Clarendon, Windsor, died 15.3.1837' (Author's photo)

He continued: 'The Governor cannot conclude this account of his tour without offering his best acknowledgements to William Cox, Esq, for the important service he has rendered to the colony in so short a period of time' and 'shall have great pleasure in recommending his meritorious services on this occasion to the favourable consideration of his Majesty's Ministers'.[6] This Macquarie did, but no honour was gazetted, although William was granted 2000 acres at Bathurst, near the junction of the Macquarie and Cudgegong Rivers. This became Hereford farm, very close to the township.

More formally, Macquarie wrote to Bathurst on 24 June saying, 'The ... road is as good as the Nature of the Mountainous hilly Country, thro' which it is made, Could possibly Admit ... [the road] thus constructed by Mr Cox, does him and the Party, who worked under his direction, Infinite

Credit'. The Governor went on to say 'I therefore beg leave to recommend Mr Cox in the Strongest Manner to the favourable Consideration of your Lordship'. He asked authorization to pay William £300 from colonial funds and give him 'a handsome Grant of Land in the New Country'. He further asked permission to appoint a commandant at Bathurst at a salary of £200 a year and recommended William for the post, 'he being in My Opinion eminently well qualified … Mr Cox is a Sensible, intelligent Man, of great arrangement, and the best agriculturalist in the colony'. Macquarie envisaged the job as only being necessary for two to three years and indeed William Lawson was appointed as superintendent in 1819.[7]

While Macquarie considered that under a normal contract the road would have taken three years, Evans had suggested three months (though with 50 men). William constructed those 101 miles in under six months and without the loss of a single life. Yet settlement on the Bathurst plains did not begin in any numbers until after Macquarie had left in 1821. The Governor had told Bathurst, in his 24 June 1815 despatch, 'I shall not make any Grants of Land in the New Discovered Country, Until such time as I shall be honored with your Lordship's Commands'. He did not want to put the government to the considerable expense of sending settlers there, the only expense at that moment being of six soldiers and six labourers. Other reasons for not settling the area were that he wanted to allocate all the land on the Cumberland Plain first and also feared that convicts sent to Bathurst (as farm workers) would escape. Given Macquarie's earlier astonishment that no one had previously found a passage across the mountains, and that the 1813 expedition had been prompted by the army worm and exhaustion of the soil on the plain, this restraint made little obvious sense.

However, Macquarie was as good as his word over the road workers' reward. Three received free pardons, one a ticket of leave and all the rest were emancipated. The superintendents received land grants and cows. William not only made his name and earned a place in the history of the colony – to this day there many Cox roads in New South Wales – he emerged financially a great deal better off. He now had both the £300 reward and the annual £200 salary at Bathurst on top of his existing £50 a year as a magistrate at Windsor. His career as a government adviser acquired a much greater impetus than just as a contractor: he accompanied the Governor on another tour across the mountains in October 1815, was sent to explore the Lachlan River in 1817, and helped provision Oxley's expedition in 1818.

The price was that for the next three years William's activity was divided between Bathurst and his home at Clarendon on the Hawkesbury, a minimum of five days apart on horseback, more in a carriage. His full career as a pastoralist did not develop until the 1820s, although he had flocks of sheep at Clarendon and could fairly be described as a landed gentleman there. But his becoming one had to wait on these years spent as an official, which themselves throw light both on William and on the way the colony was run, while the administration of Clarendon is a case study in the management of an estate, of its convict labour and of his wife Rebecca's role in that enterprise.

Lake Lyell on Coxs River near Bathurst. Damming the river to provide water for a thermal power station has greatly reduced the river's flow (Author's photo)

7 A Family Enterprise

Having been appointed as commandant at Bathurst, William's life was to be divided for the next three years between the 'New Discovered Country' and his home estate of Clarendon. His activities were therefore more sharply split between his increasing official duties and the development of his own estates than they had been before, or would be again. So the present chapter deals with his estates, their management and to some extent with the continuing emergence of the colonial landed gentry. The next will examine his complicated official life, as magistrate and administrator, which had considerable ups and down and exposed him to much criticism, as well as compliments.

The greatest expansion of the Cox estates, like that of most pastoralists, took place on the Bathurst plains. But in 1815 Bathurst itself was a mere handful of simple thatched houses, as depicted by Lewin, the official artist who accompanied Macquarie on his tour of inspection. Although one might have expected the opening up of the area to have been fairly immediate, in fact it was not. There was a long correspondence between Bathurst and Macquarie about this. On 30 January 1817 Bathurst reminded the Governor that 'You cannot but be aware how much the Length and uncertainty of a voyage to New South Wales must at all times interfere with a very regular communication'.[1] There is a note of aggravation in that all too true remark, foreshadowing the official discontent with Macquarie which culminated with Commissioner Bigge being sent out in 1819 to find out what was really going on.

More immediately, as regards land grants, in July 1818 Bathurst ordered

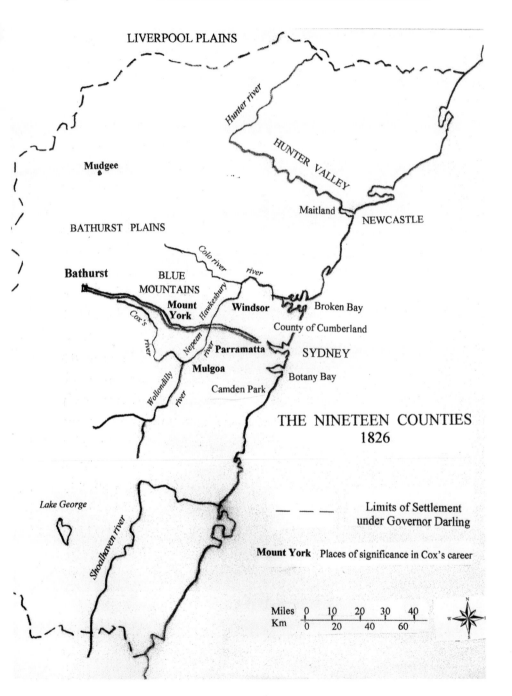

LIVERPOOL PLAINS

Hunter river

HUNTER VALLEY

Mudgee

Maitland

NEWCASTLE

BATHURST PLAINS

Colo river

river

Bathurst

BLUE
MOUNTAINS

Mount
York

Hawkesbury

Windsor

Broken Bay

Cox's

County of Cumberland

river

Nepean river

Parramatta

SYDNEY

Mulgoa

Botany Bay

Wollondilly

river

Camden Park

THE NINETEEN COUNTIES
1826

Lake George

Shoalhaven river

— — —   Limits of Settlement
under Governor Darling

Mount York   Places of significance in Cox's career

Miles 0   10   20   30   40
Km   0   20   40   60

N
W   E
S

that land grants to 'Civil and Military Officers should be altogether discontinued', although such officers as were 'meritorious' and settling in the colony after retirement could be favoured.[2] This crossed with a letter, which Macquarie wrote home in May 1818, about 'poor' settlers being permitted to come out, of whom he said: 'the moment their Indulgences cease, they Contrive in some underhand way to Sell their Farms and take to lawless pursuits, keeping low Public Houses, or becoming itinerant Merchants, Hawkers and Pedlars'. He urged that no more should be allowed out 'for at least three years to come'.

Instead, only settlers who brought out with them 'a Clear Capital of at least Five Hundred Pounds ... [for] ... agricultural pursuits' should be allowed.[3] A few years later Edward Cox asked for land on this basis, supported by his father's guarantees. More immediately, the historian John Ritchie records that 56 men did so in 1818, that in 1819 applicants numbered 133, and in 1820 the number was 237, most of whom 'wished to farm sheep'. But those were applicants. In 1819 Bathurst only approved 24, including one woman.[4] Even so, this helped to increase 'demands that New South Wales should be treated less as a gaol and more as a colony'.[5] Apparently because of that, Lord Liverpool, leading the home administration, caused the move to be restrained, although the long-distance debate continued to the end of Macquarie's rule. On 28 November 1821 he wrote to Bathurst proposing a scale of grants from 100 to a maximum of 2000 acres, however great a prospective settler's capital might be, justifying it by referring to 'the present Scarcity of Land within One Hundred miles of the Capital'.[6] He was obviously not considering land beyond the mountains, for reasons explained below. The expansion westwards, in which William and his sons so vigorously participated, only took place after Macquarie's departure and increased between 1825 and 1830 for a number of reasons.

The Blue Mountains historian, Chris Cunningham, suggests that this was really due to lack of interest, although he takes no account of Macquarie's restrictive attitude. Cunningham writes: 'Despite a further drought in the Sydney region in 1817, there was hardly a rush to take advantage of the western lands. In 1821 there were only 287 people in the Bathurst settlement and most of these were convicts.[7] The colony's entire population, exclusive only of the military, was only 36,968.[8] There may have been a simple lack of demand, although stock was allowed to be pastured temporarily beyond the mountains in 1816 after a drought, but not every potential pastoralist was uninterested. The fortunes of William Cox and William Lawson illustrate this, while expansion formed the background to Cox's three years as commandant.

In any case, Macquarie's illogical caution over settlement was a major restraint. Even though few men were needed to shepherd large flocks, the Governor feared that convicts working on the other side of the mountains might escape. From 1816 he had a military guard posted at Springwood on the mountain road. Another reason for his caution was that not all the Cumberland Plain had been taken up. Macquarie apparently discounted the floods, the caterpillars, and that the fertility of the farming land around Parramatta, based upon shale, was becoming exhausted, which had been the reason for Blaxland, Lawson and Wentworth's 1813 expedition. His reluctance to allow expansion is shown by the 2000 acre grant he gave William for building the road still not having been officially laid out when Bigge went to Bathurst in 1819. In his report Bigge wrote 'Mr Cox occupies a considerable tract of land immediately opposite the station [government buildings] … No grant has been executed upon this land but I understood from Mr Oxley [the surveyor] that it was intended to be conferred on Mr Cox.'[9] This was the farm William named Hereford.

During this decade of 1811–20 William's own holdings on the Cumberland Plain were supplemented in a chequerboard of *ad hoc* acquisitions. Several appear not have been too scrupulous. For example, James Watson, who had worked on the Blue Mountains road, sold 100 acres to him, subsequently telling Bigge, 'He gave me £25 for it.'[10] Samuel Marsden, the chaplain who was more successful as a pastoralist than as a priest, also collected land piece by piece. The complexity of William's holdings was eventually shown by his 18 page will, which lists 29 plots of land.[11]

In fact, this was misleading, since William had worked collectively with his sons in a family enterprise from as early as 1804 and the family's Mudgee holdings alone came to 100,000 acres. As Brian Fletcher says of Macarthur, Marsden and Cox: 'They were enterprising settlers who were constantly seeking to improve their possessions'.[12] Meanwhile, nothing that William recorded up to 1819 about agriculture mentioned the plight of the unfortunate Aborigines, although he had to deal as a magistrate with a particular outbreak on the Hawkesbury in 1816. Conflict with them had begun on the Cumberland Plain from the time of the First Fleet in 1788.

To return to Clarendon, this was where William, in the words of Barrie Dyster, 'created the pattern of an ambitious landholder', as well as on estates at Mulgoa, and west of the mountains. The management of those estates might have had an English inspiration, but was achieved in an 'indigenous' manner which evolved in the colony, yet is often not recognized as having been distinctive.[13] In reality the colonial model owed little to English landed traditions, even though it was the ideal of the English landed gentry which had motivated the pastoralist settlers from the start. The evidence which William gave to Commissioner Bigge on agriculture in 1820, after he had left Bathurst, provides details of his enterprise which would not otherwise be available.

The acquisition of land in the colony was a totally different endeavour to anything which William, or his contemporaries, could have attempted in England in three respects. First, the estates were created with grants or purchases of uncleared land from the government, which was not comparable with the enclosures of common land in England. Second, miserable as the pay and conditions of farm workers at home were, the colonial estates were built on the foundation of actual forced labour, with all the attendant problems of motivation and competence. Third, many were developed as family enterprises, like William Cox's, the Lawsons' and the Macarthurs'.

The family enterprise was possible because the inhibitions of the English primogeniture system were seen to be irrelevant in view of the wide availability of land. Thus the estates of Cox and Lawson were expanded jointly with their sons. William's comparatively small landholdings at Mulgoa adjoined those of his sons Edward and George, and he had built The Cottage there for them around 1811, although Clarendon remained entirely his. There were also problems in educating children, which seldom occurred in England. William himself had been educated at a first-class grammar school, literally around the corner from his mother's house. Tutors were easily available for the children of aristocrats at home. But in the colony all such facilities had to be created from scratch, often depending on convict teachers. Finally, there was the role of women in the management of the estates, wives whose lives were a far cry from Jane Austen's country ladies in that first generation.

There was a further, peculiarly colonial, social dimension to this, directly influencing how estates were run. While Marsden, Bell and others opposed the admission of emancipists to society, William did not. He ran Clarendon personally, as did John Macarthur at Camden Park. But unlike some non-resident landowners, he therefore gained an understanding of convicts' thinking (which Bigge could not really comprehend, either in terms of how the convicts thought or of why William was interested). His first manager, the Irish exile Joseph Holt, in the early days at Brush Farm, recorded that 'His good treatment of the convicts in his service had the happiest effect upon many of those who were so lucky as to get into his service'.[14] William's idea of a desirable relationship between master and servant was encapsulated when, in the later interview on convicts, he told Bigge that 'where the man is capable of performing the task with ease to himself, he pleases his Master who makes his life more comfortable'.[15]

In agricultural terms, William was among the leading settlers. Bigge had been told by Bathurst that 'The Agricultural and Commercial interests of the Colony will further require your Active Consideration'.[16] He responded to this instruction in his Report on Agriculture, saying: 'The estates that are in the best state of cultivation, and exhibit the greatest improvement, are those of Mr Oxley, the Surveyor General, Mr Cox, Sir John Jamison, Mr Hannibal

Macarthur'. He also listed four others and named William, along with 'Mr M'Arthur, Mr Wentworth and Sir John', as owning 'the herds in which the greatest improvements have been made'.[17] These were serious compliments.

The best documented of the estates William owned (after his bankruptcy) were at Clarendon on the Hawkesbury, at Mulgoa on the Nepean, and later at Bathurst, where family cooperation came fully into its own. It is not easy to disentangle his land ownership from that of his sons. A list of his land holdings in 1823 (undated, but probably early January) had him with 5530 acres, out of a total held by the family of 10,690, including 850 at Mulgoa, as shown on a contemporary map.[18] After his return from England he had added progressively to the 800 or so acres which the family collectively owned in 1810. There is relative clarity over the subsequent extensive acquisitions across the mountains, described later.

William's primary estate of Clarendon, close to the river on the Hawkesbury, was a very substantial establishment. He had begun preparing for this self-sustaining community little more than a year after his November 1809 return from England. In 1811 he began buying implements at auction and also trading himself, as described in Chapter 4, in concert with his sons. These were early examples of the family members acing in consort. Well before the time of Bigge's visit Clarendon had become a self-sustaining community. William told the Commissioner:

> We manufacture clothes for Prisoners & frocks from our own wool & boots and shoes from hides tanned upon the estate, we grow our own flax here and make our own harness, we keep a Taylor to make up the cloathing … blacksmiths' forges and a carpenter also a wheelwright when we can get one.[19]

In this interview he referred to himself and his sons jointly employing convicts. Quite apart from this possibly being a device to make his own numbers seem less, it shows how his sons' participation in the enterprise was growing. The second son by William's second marriage, Alfred, recalled Clarendon when he was a boy in the early 1830s, when it was at its height.

In his 'Reminiscences' he wrote:

> The house ... was built of brick and in cottage form, containing many rooms with windows on all sides of it ... There were extensive orchards and gardens on one side of the house. Some 50 to 60 outdoor servants were engaged in various industries. There was a flour mill, a cloth factory, a tannery, meat curing house, blacksmith's forge and buildings in which were to be seen every day at work carpenters, tailors, shoemakers, saddlers, tobacco curers and of necessity butchers and bakers, having quite the appearance of a village.

He remembered a watchman, who had been a convict, and 'in my mind's eye I still see nurses young and old, overseers as they were called, and men over whom they were placed in authority. Our head nurse was in her way a somewhat remarkable woman.'[20] It is notable that women were placed in charge of male convicts.

The character of the house was of importance, both because it reflected the way William looked at life and because it was the focal point of a community. Rather in the manner of Kenyan and Rhodesian settlers a century later, he added rooms as he needed them.[21] Indeed the author Douglas Woodruff has remarked that: 'Australia ... was the Kenya of early Victorian England', because of that colony's opportunities in a largely untouched land.[22] That comparison is particularly meaningful to this author, who lived in Kenya for many years. William only added an 'extraordinarily highly finished' dining room to Clarendon in the 1820s, after his second marriage, presumably to satisfy his new wife's social aspirations.[23]

Sadly Clarendon did not have a happy later history. In 1834, having himself been unwell since 1828 and needing medical attention, William moved the family into a more accessible house called Fairfield, away from the river at Richmond. He would have vividly remembered Rebecca's death in a flood in 1819. He then let the Clarendon house to the auctioneer Laban White.[24] It was inherited by George, but does not appear to have been lived in by him or the family ever again.

Fairfield at Richmond, William's last house and where he died, since extended to be an hotel (Author's photo)

Organizationally, Clarendon could be compared to other estates. Where it differed was in the unquantifiable human terms of the people who ran it. The estate in that form did not survive many years after William's death and it must be questionable whether it could have done so without its original begetter, whereas the estates west of the mountains expanded under his sons. William's great grand-daughters, thought to be the authors of his *Memoirs* of 1901, knew the house. They described it as:

> A large cottage house, built of brick and plaster. It has large handsome rooms, and wooden wainscot runs around the ancient drawing room … But alas in our land woodwork endureth not. We have 'white ants', which eat the inside from solid timbers … as you walk across the once solid floor of native timber it gives way beneath the feet, and the gray dust rises that tells of rot, ruin and decay.

All that the *Memoirs* then say, of around the year 1900, is that 'the levels are all askew … all is wild and uncared for … the trim paths are overgrown with weeds.'[25]

George Cox's letters reveal that he had great difficulties with the estate after inheriting it. He had rented it out and wrote on 2 January 1848, when he was suffering greatly from the financial crash, that he called 'at Clarendon to see the misery there, and made up my mind at once to lose the half of the rents for that place. The whole farm has not produced 150 bushels of wheat, no hay and not the slightest prospect of corn'. Two days later he set to work arranging 'a division of the property ... these money matters do indeed most dreadfully harass me'.[26] He bequeathed what remained of Clarendon to his son Charles, who sold it to a man called Arthur Dight.

Owing to William's lack of pretensions, Clarendon had never been a house for an aspiring gentleman and his sons had no need of it. William had greatly improved Hobartville at Richmond. In 1824 George had built Winbourne at Mulgoa, where Edward built the classical Fernhill, and Henry built Glenmore, while James created the most elegant and classical of all the sons' houses, Clarendon in Tasmania.[27] The rambling old Clarendon would not have suited their decidedly upper class sense of style. Eventually, Dight's executors auctioned 'Clarendon Park, containing 623 acres' in 1909. It was bought for £7500 by a Captain Phillip Charley. On 12 December 1911 the *Daily Telegraph* newspaper reported: 'Part of the old building being a ruin and the rest showed signs of decay, while the century old garden was a wilderness'.[28] It finally fell into complete ruin around 1921. A newer house has been built close by, which has been misidentified on a website biography of William as being Clarendon. What are thought to be the remains of William's detached kitchens still stand, just outside the perimeter fence of the RAAF airfield which now occupies much of the site of the farm.

There was a defined structure of oversight at Clarendon, particularly important during William's absences at Bathurst, although it is clear from the *Memoirs* that Rebecca was emphatically the mistress of the house. The senior assistant to William on the estate was the former New South Wales Corps sergeant, James King, who was described as his secretary and had been with him since shortly after his arrival. Holt called him 'the steward or clerk over the stores' at Brush Farm in October 1800.[29] King was both retainer and friend. The *Memoirs* called him 'a good man and true', which he clearly was. He never married, but was godfather to Edward Cox, to whom he left everything. William made sure he had a plot of land at Mulgoa and obtained him local preferment; for instance putting his name forward on 25 June 1812 as slaughterhouse inspector at Windsor.[30] He must have played an important role in running Clarendon when William was away. He died at Mulgoa on 27 June 1829 and was buried in a grave close to Rebecca's in the Windsor churchyard. The tomb's inscription describes: 'Mr James King … many years a respected friend and faithful assistant to William Cox, Esq. J.P.' He was 'Mr 'whereas William was 'Esq.'[31] His age is not given.

Beneath King came the overseers. The job of an overseer was described by the surveyor Oxley to Bigge: 'On large estates the supply [of ordinary goods] to convicts' is usually made by the overseer who is a sort of storekeeper to the proprietor; he sends to Sydney when anything is wanted for the farm & states to his principal what the articles are.'[32] The overseer's account at Camden shows that he was not only supposed to supervise most of the work on the estate, but that he was often sent to Sydney, mainly for the purchase of supplies and to meet new labouring families'.[33] The structure at Clarendon would have been little different.

James King's tomb at Windsor (Author's photo)

Clarendon's senior overseer was Richard Lewis, a free man, who had been the senior supervisor during the building of the mountain road and was later sent to Bathurst as the government's superintendent. He had proper authority there, as when in July 1818 he certified the abstract of the government establishment at Bathurst.[34] Oxen given to William as payment for road building were delivered through him.[35] As might have been expected, although now a government employee, he continued to look after William's personal interests, as accounts of the 1822 and 1824 troubles with Aborigines reveal.

At Clarendon there were several other overseers. When he was available, William took a personal hand in matters, as is evidenced by the survival of his farming smock, still in family hands (it may well be that when he told Bigge that they made 'frocks' these were in fact traditional smocks). After 1816, his absences made it vital to have a strong support team. Thanks to the distances and time involved in crossing the mountains, he had difficulty reconciling the demands of his various activities. Thus as early as August 1815, soon after the completion of the mountain road, the Colonial Secretary had to order Cartwright and Mileham to alternate as magistrates at Windsor 'during the temporary absence of Mr Cox, who is on Government service elsewhere'.[36] He was actually on another mountain mission with Macquarie and had also been supervising the improvement of the road from Parramatta to the Nepean. In February 1818 he was additionally appointed as magistrate at Bathurst. He was kept more busy than ever he had been.

This official dual capacity ended in August 1819, when Macquarie wrote to William personally informing him that, as Lawson had now been appointed as JP and magistrate at Bathurst, 'there will be no occasion for your acting in a Magisterial capacity in that country in future'. William was asked to return the commission and warrant to Macquarie. It was signed simply with the initials L. M.[37] Macquarie's phrase 'in that country' indicates how distant the Governor felt it to be, as in terms of travel it was. Thereafter William was less frequently at Bathurst and from 1821 left the management of his expanding estates there to George, although sometimes he was physically unable to get away from Clarendon at all. On 15 February 1819 he apologized to Jamison for having to miss one of his many committee meetings in Sydney the next day, because 'the waters are too much out to attempt it from Clarendon upwards'.[38] It was in the following month that Rebecca was drowned in a flood.

All this meant that supervision was vital to the Clarendon enterprise. William's overseers can be presumed to have been instructed to follow his liberal ideas. Certainly Lewis did. William aimed to keep relationships favourable through incentives, culminating with the issuance of tickets of leave, which landed him in such trouble with Bigge. In a personal letter to the Commissioner, previously quoted, William wrote about servants needing small comforts.[39] Richard Waterhouse explains: 'On most properties a task system operated, with servants free to earn extra food, alcohol and money in the time left over once they had completed their prescribed work for the day or week'.[40] William believed in task work to provide an incentive and so get the work done effectively. But this was for a private employer. It was less effective when the men were working for the government.

Rebecca's tomb at Windsor (Author's photo)

By comparison with Cox, John Macarthur was relatively parsimonious and a great deal less understanding, which points up the favourable aspects of William's attitudes and the difference between their styles of management, although Macarthur did give some incentives. When asked by Bigge about feeding his domestic servants, he replied: 'They are fed plentifully … beef, mutton or pork, milk vegetables and fruit and they have Tea and Sugar twice a day'. He did not pay them the £10 a year. 'I clothe them decently, allow them tobacco and occasionally give them a little money … altogether to the value of £15 or £20 per annum, according to their different degrees of usefulness'.

John Macarthur's view of the men's capabilities was also different to William's. The idea that the convicts would one day be the making of the colony would have seemed inconceivable to him. When Bigge asked if comparisons with England were possible, he answered vehemently: 'I will not admit of a comparison ... those [men] brought up labourers have acquired such habits of idleness, that not one in ten can be induced to feel any pride in the performance of his duty'.[41] Quite apart from his notorious arrogance, or perhaps because of it, he lacked William's understanding of how to motivate men, upon which the management of Clarendon so depended. Atkinson records of the next generation that 'The gulf between the Macarthurs and their own convicts ... was carefully kept up by an array of supervisors and upper servants. James Macarthur explained "We find it more convenient not to give orders to the convicts ourselves". Yet the Camden workers were motivated and there was also 'nothing of the constant violence between masters and men which happened in some places'.[42] But then James Macarthur was a thoughtful and considerate man, one of the few exclusives who developed a coherent vision of the colony's future, albeit a strongly patrician one.

In one significant way Camden later came to differ from the Cox estates, although after William's death. When the Molesworth Committee's report of 1838 recommended the complete ending of assignment, the Macarthurs countered the labour problem by following the ideas of Edward Gibbon Wakefield, which had inspired Goderich's reforms, and began obtaining labouring emigrants from Dorset under a government sponsored scheme. These families became small tenant farmers on the 24,000 acre estate, as did locals. The Coxes did not do this until the 1850s at Burrundulla (near Mudgee), when George Cox 'set up a system of tenant farmers, but continued to work most of it himself'. He also sold some of the farms to tenants, presumably to alleviate problems.[43]

The great importance of assigned labour in developing and running estates in the earlier years is emphasized by the sheer size of William Cox's labour force. In 1822 he maintained an unusually large number of assigned convicts, as well as six who were free by servitude and had chosen to remain with him. In addition to agricultural workers, he employed carders, weavers, stable boys, a carter, a horse shoesmith, a gamekeeper and watermen, as Alfred recounted. It is small wonder that these aroused envy from other landowners. Unusually, he also employed a wheelwright, named Kendall, who had been assigned to him on 25 October 1814 but who moved on.[44] In 1820 one of the free men was Richard Kippas, reputedly the 'best fencer and hurdlemaker at the Bathurst settlement, since pardoned'. He appeared on the 1820 Hawkesbury 'Return of Tradesmen' as a wheelwright working for William of his own will.[45] This was the very same Richard Kippas who made complaints to Bigge against William, as will be seen in a later chapter. In his evidence given to Bigge on 29 November 1820, presumably at Windsor, Kippas explained that he had broken his leg and been in hospital at Windsor, after which 'I came out and went to Mr Cox … and am still with him'.[46] William must have been a good person to work for, since any man with Kippas' skills was in demand.

There does, however, appear to have been a deliberate attempt by William to confuse the Colonial Secretary as to the numbers he employed, even allowing for family collaboration. In 1820 he had told Bigge that he and his sons employed about 100 men and 'we manufacture clothes for Prisoners & Frocks from our own wool & boots and shoes from hides tanned upon the estate … we keep a Taylor to make up the clothing'.[47] On 30 March 1823 he wrote to Secretary Goulburn saying that 'on an average of the last five years I have employed jointly with my sons George and Henry Cox of Mulgoa from seventy to one hundred convicts free of Expence to the Crown'. He listed them. Then on 30 April 1823 Edward wrote from Fernhill at Mulgoa, transmitting a list of 'one hundred now in the employ of my Father, self and Brother Henry' and speaking of 'exertions both for my own good and the benefit of the colony'.

The figures they had submitted had evidently been queried by the

Colonial Secretary, because William wrote to his son George on 17 May of that year, asking if he was agreeable to providing a separate list 'of convicts maintained by us during the period of six years'. The aim was 'to shew that we have maintained a considerable number of them more than the Land Regulations require during the last six years as this appears to be what Major Goulburn requires'.[48] Some complicated 'back of the envelope' mathematical calculations followed and the family papers in the Mitchell Library show how he arrived at these 'averages'. There is no record of whether Goulburn was satisfied, but the history of the family collusion suggests that he had been justified in asking.

The overall convict employment by William in 1823 was officially listed as 113.[49] But the figure conflicts with the 1822 Muster, where a careful analysis of the names shows he had 128 assigned convicts. These included a waterman (Clarendon was by the river), shoemakers, shepherds, weavers and a woollen manufacturer.[50] The number had increased rapidly after his second marriage in February 1821, before which they totalled 104.[51]1Subsequently William also benefited from a scheme introduced by Governor Brisbane (and abandoned by Darling), under which government convicts were hired in groups to clear and prepare land for settlers. At the November 1822 Muster he had 15 of these.[52] The accusations made against William over using his position as a magistrate to obtain the best convicts appear never to have stopped him doing so.

Governor Macquarie was concerned for the wellbeing of female convicts. A circular sent by Campbell to magistrates on 24 August 1811 told them that 'a vessel being daily expected with female convicts … His Excellency proposes indenting these females … among settlers … as may require their assistance in the necessary business of a country life'.[53] But William did not share the Governor's view on females being paid. He wrote to Bigge in May 1820, saying that although they were entitled to a wage of £7 a year, he thought they should not be paid at all. 'Their situation is totally different, they do not draw a ration, but live as the family do … get regular meals, have their tea or milk and are not in want of anything. They should be found in decent and proper apparel, but not any wages allowed them.'[54]

The reason for this view, or prejudice, is not entirely clear, beyond that the women were living with the family and were therefore outside the system of incentives which William gave to the male convicts for defined jobs. In England living-in female staff were paid, as well as receiving board and lodging. As long before as 1658 a cook in Hertfordshire had received £2 10s a year and a chambermaid £3.[55] In 1810 at the Duke of Rutland's Belvoir Castle, admittedly a wealthy aristocrat's establishment, housemaids were paid eight to nine guineas (£8 8s to £9 9s), while 'Her Grace's woman' earned 20.[56] Kay Daniels, making a comparison with male convicts, points out: 'Domestic work was not like task work, measurable and discrete … it flowed into the whole day'.[57] In terms of having female convict servants for herself and the house, Rebecca was undemanding, most of the time having only two, as in 1818.[58] Bureaucracy being what it always will be, she was assigned another, Jane Williams, on 27 January 1820, ten months after she had been drowned.[59] Anna had three assigned women, as well as, from her son Alfred's account, the free women who were running the household and would have been paid.

The women on Hawkesbury farms were few. In 1800 less than half the Hawkesbury farms had a woman living on them.[60] Where free settlers were married, the wives were of huge importance in the organization of an estate, especially one relatively so distant from Sydney (Clarendon was three days by river, a day along the 'roads'). The historian John Gascoigne writes that: 'Women agricultural improvers such as Elizabeth Macarthur were valued for the results they achieved rather than criticized for stepping out of their traditional domain. And women were associated with the civilizing virtues … gender roles could work in favour of women.'[61] But the conversation of lady-like women, and their ideas, were wholly overshadowed by those of their men and Elizabeth Macarthur must have been virtually alone in making her voice respected when she arrived in 1790.[62]

Rebecca's unsung farming efforts can be directly compared to the better known and much longer lasting ones of Elizabeth, during John Macarthur's absences between 1801 and 1817, when she was also bringing up young children. It can be assumed that the two women knew each other. It also possible that the reason Rebecca does not seem to have been invited to Mrs King's social occasions for ladies in her new drawing room of 1804 might have been William's disgrace, as well as the distance involved, even though Governor King assisted William materially himself.

Although both wives were propelled by their husbands' circumstances into decision making roles, in Rebecca's case her actions went almost entirely unrecorded. She is described in some family papers as having been 'An early day society woman, whose name was always mentioned at social events. She took part in every good work.'[63] However, this account was written a hundred years later and there is nothing to indicate that she *was* a society woman. Present day descendants emphasize that she was remembered as a very caring person. Holt thought in 1803 that 'She was a complete gentlewoman', despite her hardships.[64] She had signed the Hawkesbury residents' 1807 address of welcome to Bligh and in 1808 was a leading signatory of two petitions thanking the Governor for his help after floods.[65] Atkinson suggests that it was unlikely that many 'of the 244 signatories to the Hawkesbury address understood the fine line between acquiescence and obedience.'[66] Whether that is correct or not, Rebecca displayed leadership in the community.

According to Atkinson, 'Women were conspicuous consumers.'[67] But it can only have been many years after the 1803 bankruptcy that Rebecca might have become one, if ever (unlike Anna). Back in 1803 and 1804 she had been faced with replacing basic household equipment and her principal supply was of fortitude. During William's absence, when he was receiving no pay due to being suspended from office, she had to feed her family. With total family landholdings of about 800 acres, and convict labourers, she would have grown much of what they needed themselves, plus a surplus for sale. But they could not produce everything and basic prices were high, sometimes exorbitant. 'Sugar two and six a pound,' Mrs King, the wife of the Governor, wrote, 'butter four shillings, soap six and tea £4. "The common necessaries of life are far, very far, beyond my reach".'[68]

These prices might be why Mrs King generously lent £300 to William, even though she and the Governor were in straitened circumstances themselves. Wheat had rarely cost more than 10 shillings a bushel, but by August 1806 it was fetching two guineas a bushel and maize £2. Three months later both maize and wheat were selling for £4, thanks to speculators driving up prices.[69] Not that meals were often grandiose, even for the well-off. At Sir John Jamison's, 'they seem to have been fairly simple, rhubarb or pumpkin pie and wholemeal bread baked in dripping were considered luxuries and appeared on Sundays. Fruit certainly was plentiful.'[70]

One of the most challenging aspects of describing William's domestic life is that there is so little known about Rebecca's contribution at Clarendon (slightly more has survived about Anna). With that notable exception of Elizabeth Macarthur and also the remarkable convict midwife on the Hawkesbury, Margaret Catchpole, the domestic lives of women in dairying, provisioning, cooking, washing, dances, courtship and children are completely absent from contemporary accounts. Despite the efforts of recent female historians to reconstruct their roles, there simply are very few contemporary records. The women's activities seem not have been considered central to the lives of men, particularly pastoralists.[71] There is a great contrast here with the wives of the next generation of Coxes, who entertained and wrote letters to friends, some of which correspondence is given in Chapter 13.

That Rebecca was both instinctively practical and generous is shown by her taking the present of wine and rum to the Holts after William's had crossed swords with Joseph Holt in 1800. Only one letter written by her is known to this author and sadly it is a transcript, so nothing can be deduced about her character from the handwriting.[72] But the wording is still revealing. She wrote to Macquarie from 'Clarendon Farm, Hawkesbury' in January 1810, very soon after William's return from England, pleading for confirmation of a land grant 'given to my youngest son [Edward, then aged four] by Colonel Paterson'. This grant had been given during the Bligh interregnum. She enclosed the deeds, trusting that she might be 'deemed worthy of a renewal of the said Grant for my little boy & more particularly for the present use of my stock, which is much in want of fresh pasture, the food on the common they now run being greatly exhausted'.[73] This letter makes it clear that Rebecca actively ran Clarendon while William was awaiting trial in England and that she was reduced to grazing her cattle on common land. More significantly, it shows her displaying remarkable foresight in extending the family estate into a new and promising area.

This grant for Edward was at Mulgoa, on the Nepean River, a good 28 miles (45 km) south-west of Windsor as the crow flies, and further by cart track. It extended the family enterprise into what amounted to a fresh start. Years later, when Edward had completed five years training in sheep farming in Yorkshire, both he and William continued enlarging this landholding.[74] In the end Mulgoa became like a family estate, although the Blaxlands also had land there. William built a dairy and cheese factory, which eventually became the school, and in 1881 George Henry Cox donated land for a new one. Edward donated five acres for St Thomas church, where many generations of Coxes are buried, and established a racehorse stud, with 44 brood mares.[75]

In 1810 Rebecca must still have been very conscious of her husband's disgrace and unlikely to have been in any Sydney social circle. Nor, when he was restored to favour by Macquarie, does she seem to have been in Mrs Macquarie's very active one. Later on, although William accompanied Macquarie on his surveying tours of what would become the five towns in 1816 and dined with him, the Governor did not stay with the Coxes, but camped or stayed in a government cottage.[76] When he embarked on his tour to Bathurst in 1821 he stayed at Jamison's Regentville.[77]

Possibly during Rebecca's time Windsor was simply too far out to make socializing easy, although that did nothing to stop Anna. Where Rebecca does match an overall analysis of settler motivations is that, like Elizabeth Macarthur, she clearly thought of her children as 'future inhabitants of their native country'. When the Macarthur family first came to the colony it had not been 'as a promotional step to somewhere else'.[78] Nor did the Coxes see it that way. This predicated a considerable preoccupation with the children's education, which was also to concern William after his second marriage.

The education of the landed gentry's children was crucial, not only to those children's own futures, but to the future management of the family estate, which William and Rebecca had begun to build up from 1804 onwards. When the couple sailed from England in 1799 they had left their two eldest sons, William and James, at the grammar school in Salisbury, spending their holidays with friends in Somerset.[79] William must therefore have hoped that their education would parallel his own at the Queen Elizabeth I Grammar School in Wimborne; and indeed it was to a standard which enabled William Jnr to be commissioned into the New South Wales Corps in 1808. The two eldest boys were only brought out to the colony in 1804, when they were respectively 15 and 14 years old, as was explained in William's letter of 28 July 1804 to John Piper, quoted in Chapter 3. In that letter he said he had 'got 250 acres of ground for them with four men … as other settlers have'.[80] So their careers as landowners had begun. But for the younger children education was less easy.

A school was run by the Reverend Richard Cartwright, the chaplain on the Hawkesbury. He testified that parents were 'eager to have their children educated … They came to school for unpredictable periods between about four and twelve years old.' This has the sound of emancipist small farmers' offspring, although Bigge found those children 'manageable when treated with kindness'.[81] In any case, by 1811 only Rebecca's last two children, Maria and Edward, were as young as that. Probably Rebecca taught them herself when they were very young.

For the boys of William's second marriage the solution may have lain in a school established later at Castlereagh by the Reverend Henry Fulton, who had travelled out on the *Minerva* with them in January 1800. In June 1814, after involvement in the rebellion against Bligh, who Fulton supported, he became resident chaplain in charge of Castlereagh and Richmond. He is thought to have been helped to this by William and rapidly established a seminary for 'young gentlemen' at his parsonage.[82] W. C. Wentworth described it as it was around 1818. There were: 'Several good private seminaries for the board and education of opulent parents. The best is in the district of Castlereagh and is kept by the clergyman of that district, the Rev. Henry Fulton, a gentleman peculiarly qualified both from his character and acquirements for conducting so important and responsible an undertaking. The boys in this seminary receive a regular classical education.'[83] Time there would have been folowed by terms at the King's School at Parramatta, which Alfred says he attended.

William subsequently built a new Castlereagh schoolhouse for the government. In April 1820, after Rebecca's death, he reported its completion to Macquarie in something of a self-congratulatory tone: 'This new building in the Township is made strong, neat and useful, but expensive … Knowing it was Your Excellency's wish to have this useful building completed without delay I feel much pleasure in thus reporting it'. It would also be used for Divine Service. 'The person Your Excellency sent us as a clerk & schoolmaster will, according to Mr Fulton's opinion, be properly able to perform his duties.'[84] It sounds as though Fulton handed over some of his teaching to the clerk. Nonetheless, William had problems educating his second family, although dynastically they would prove to have little importance, since none of the men remained in New South Wales.[85]

Asking for assignment favours, as ever, William wrote to McLeay on 14 September 1826 from Clarendon:

In the Gazette I have received have observed an English ship is arrived with prisoners, will you have the goodness to cause an application to be made [to His Excellency] for a man fit to teach two of my young children aged three and five years their reading and writing, they are too young to send to a boarding school and we have not a day school near us.

This assignment was ordered on 22 September.[86] Apparently it did not last, because early in 1827 a young immigrant called Alexander Harris, who had been arrested for travelling with no visible means of support, was offered work. Cox intervened, saying, 'I have two children who need a tutor. Would you like the job?' This seems to have been the same Alexander Harris who, 20 years later, in 1847, published *Settlers and Convicts; or recollections of Sixteen Years Labour in the Australian Backwoods*. He had arrived in 1825 and, although an educated young man, was living as a vagrant. William must have seen something worthwhile in Harris, a capacity in keeping with his liberal views. [87]

Alfred makes no mention of Harris, only saying that when he was older: 'The first school that my brother Tom and I were sent to was some 10 or 12 miles from home kept by the Rev. W Wilkinson. He had the reputation of being a fair classical scholar … but when in a passion used to knock about in fine style.' In terms of location this might have been Fulton's school, which was famous. Of Wilkinson's establishment Alfred said, 'we were somewhat proud of him and ready enough to proclaim to the world that he had been our schoolmaster'. He also recorded: 'My brothers and myself were packed off to a public school at a somewhat early age. We had of course no opportunity of riding there, but when our holidays came round, were again quickly in the saddle, to the pride of our father, and somewhat to the concern of our mother.'[88] The two boys were next sent to the King's School at Parramatta, where there was 'a pretty strong contingent of boys not attending the King's School … ever ready to try conclusions with us … we had in our little way "Town and Gown" encounters'. The charges for Board and Tuition were £28 a year. Their minds were 'saturated with Greek' by one of several masters.[89] Alfred made no mention of how his sisters were educated.

Overall, in the management of his estates William appears to have been in pursuit of farming improvements from the start. Even though he had been a clockmaker in Devizes he must have been alert to farming techniques, or was encouraged to be by Holt. He began breeding merino sheep at Brush Farm in the early 1800s. Originally land was cultivated by hoeing around the stumps of trees, in spite of the gain there would have been from grubbing out the stumps. This was because convicts would not perform well enough grubbing stumps to even pay for their rations. Holt recorded that the men were using hoes at Brush Farm in 1800. William is said to have estimated that 15 men with the plough equalled the work of 300 convicts with hoes. The removal of stumps from the ploughlands gradually became more general.[90]

When Commissioner Bigge commended Cox's farming it was not without reason. Improvements were his lifelong concern and even if he might have been unaware of the Enlightenment as an intellectual movement in Europe, what he carried through in practice was certainly enlightened in the best sense. His initiatives took two forms; improving the cropping locally on the Hawkesbury and experimenting with 'artificial grasses' to provide better fodder for grazing animals.

Bigge asked him in 1819 how some farms retained their fertility. He answered: 'A farmer can by raising artificial food such as rape, clover, turnips and English grapes, maintain a flock of sheep and the manure from them will enable him to raise his crops of wheat'.[91] Clover, lucerne and sainfoin were far more nutritious than the indigenous grass for animal fodder. W. C. Wentworth claimed in his description of the colony that: 'The natural grasses are sufficiently good and nutritious at all seasons of the year, for the support of every description of stock, where there is an adequate tract of country for them to range over'. But it seems unlikely that he was right, given the efforts that were made to grow better fodder.[92]

Bigge reported on this subject that: 'These gentleman [Oxley, Cox, Jamison, Hannibal Macarthur, Redfern, John Macarthur, Throsby and Howe] have turned their attention to the culture of the various qualities of artificial grasses; and from the experiments they have already made, there is every reason to expect that the supply of food for sheep and cattle may be greatly augmented'. The improvements took two forms: introducing better farming techniques and the improved breeding of sheep. This reflected the values of an English landed class, which had become convinced of the possibilities of increasing wealth by the application of improving techniques.[93] In line with this belief William became a founder vice chairman of the Agricultural Society in 1822.[94]

At the same time, managing a large estate involved near-continual interaction with the Aborigines, although not necessarily in conflict with them. William employed Aborigines satisfactorily at Mulgoa in 1826. But Mulgoa was also a potential flashpoint. Settler relationships with the two linguistic tribes whose boundary met there, the Dharug and the Gundungurra, had been extremely volatile. Both to them and the settlers the river was of great importance.[95] In 1816 the *Sydney Gazette* had reported an attack at Mulgoa in which a shepherd and 250 sheep were brutally killed, the sheep having their eyes gouged out.[96] This had been during a severe drought, when river water was crucial. By the 1840s the 'Mulgowie', as their remnants became known, no longer led a traditional life. The whole issue of relationships with the Aborigines is dealt with in Chapter 11.

Although that issue is now far more important historically than it was seen to be by either government or settlers at the time, it should not detract from coming to conclusions about William's management of Clarendon in the larger context of the colony and the emergence of its local landed gentry. The early colonial estates, whether pastoral or agricultural, Clarendon being a combination of the two, evolved to suit physical and social circumstances which were barely imaginable in England. This was both in the environment and in the employment of forced convict labour, even though the living conditions and wages of English farm labourers, as William Cobbett pointed out in the 1820s, made them little better off than slaves. The success of those management methods enabled the exclusives to turn themselves into a dominant class.

William's estates were never the largest in the colony, but they were among the most efficiently and humanely run. Ambition was at the core of the early settlers' lives and William did indeed create the pattern of an ambitious landholder. At the same time, his understanding of convicts' thinking and motivations, his basically liberal outlook and his willingness to mix with emancipists added unusual dimensions to the way he worked. This is not to suggest that his attitudes and actions were unique, but they were untypical of his class and not shared by quite a few of the Pure Merinos. It remains greatly regrettable that so little detail is known about Rebecca's central role in establishing what became more and more of a family enterprise after her untimely death in 1819.

8   The Perquisites of Office

A gentleman much distinguished for experience and sagacity [and having] many of the qualities that are essential in a magistrate, who is to administer the law in New South Wales.[1]

John Thomas Bigge in his 1822 Report on the Colony

The life of a magistrate in the colony in the early years was more turbulent than might have been imagined, dealing with many more social problems than simply administering justice. As explained in Chapter 4, William was appointed in October 1810 to be 'Superintendent of the Government labourers and cattle and of the Public Works in the District of the Hawkesbury'. The implications of this were far-reaching, including allocating convicts to masters and dealing with the ensuing problems. He continued in office until his death in 1837, a period little short of 27 of the 37 years he spent in the colony, making his career on the bench a significant part of his life. Additionally, during the period from 1815 to 1819, in spite of his home remaining at Clarendon, he both administered the Bathurst area, where he carried out various exploratory missions for Macquarie, and acted as a magistrate there as well as on the Hawkesbury.

At Bathurst he was responsible for fitting out and supporting the surveyor Oxley's expeditions, to which Macquarie attached great importance. He also conducted expeditions himself, which 'added to the knowledge of the country through the exploration of much of the Lachlan River region'.[2] All this was a considerable burden for a man now in his fifties who had admitted to being 'knocked up' when building the mountain road. Worse, if it brought him credit, it also brought vituperative attacks on his probity. One of his responses has been quoted in the Foreword, when he told Bigge on 4 December 1820, after he had handed over the Bathurst appointment:

> There is not a magistrate in the Colony who has given as much of his time to the business of the Crown & the public these ten years past as myself ... If any man ever laboured amidst a den of thieves and a nest of hornets it is myself.[3]

Although criticizing William for giving too many tickets of leave to convicts, Bigge respected him as a magistrate. Accordingly, this chapter looks at the various sides of his public life in the decade ending in 1820, not forgetting that energetic and constructive men invariably attract criticism.

In spite of displaying humanity and good sense, William became the target of complaints from his fellow settlers for favouring himself in the allocation of skilled convicts. He also incurred a considerable number of complaints by convicts themselves, originating from his time at Bathurst. These never resulted in action being taken against him. Nonetheless, Bigge was highly critical of the way he had employed convicts on the other side of the mountains, which the Commissioner claimed, 'excited much surprise in the colony'. As mentioned earlier, there is little evidence that it did.[4] Bigge's investigation into the state of the colony was the most exhaustive survey of all aspects of life in New South Wales carried out up to that time and he made that survey immediately after William's term of office at Bathurst ended. He also took an unusually large amount of evidence from William, most of which is examined in Chapter 9.

Administration of the law was a central feature of William's activity, both at Bathurst and on the Hawkesbury. Bigge particularly asked him about punishment.[5] His replies, and the details of cases he heard, shed light on much more than William's own attitudes. They illustrate the daily aspects of life in what was, after all, a penal colony. In England corporal punishment was a harsh fact of daily life for many children, criminals and men in the military forces. Despite the horrors of the lash, Bigge appears not to have thought its use controversial. William's own earlier reluctance to order flogging had slowly moderated. As a magistrate he was not empowered to deal with the worst crimes, but those he and his fellows on the Windsor bench did deal increasingly strongly with such as fell within their jurisdiction. The later sentencing possibly reflected a more severe regime of punishment in the colony, following Bigge's visit, which had an impact long before his reports were presented to parliament in 1822 and 1823.

Three sentences given at Windsor between 1811 and 1825 contrast with the six lashes William ordered for the mutineers on the *Minerva* in 1799, although it is impossible to know how far, as senior magistrate, William prevailed over differing opinions on the bench. At the commonsense end of the scale he twice sent a man to another master, with no punishment, after unreasonable complaints by the original intemperate employer .[6] Other of his sentences were proportionate to the offence and vividly illustrative of daily life on the Hawkesbury.

Thus on 10 June 1820 William and John Brabyn heard a case brought by William Bowman (the employer) against James Turner 'Convict servant', revealing behaviour by Bowman which was unnecessarily harsh. It is probable that this master employed very few convicts. Turner was accused of 'neglecting his work and that he does the same in an improper manner and also for being insolent when reprimanded. That Complainant pushed him [i.e., Turner] out of the garden and directed him to Windsor, which he refused and abused Complainant greatly.' Turner responded by saying that had lived with his master five years and a half, 'in the whole of which time his Master has never expressed any dissatisfaction of his conduct'. The circumstances were that he had been told to wheel some dung in a barrow, but the ground being soft he took the dung out with a shovel when the sides (of the barrow) came out. His master kicked him for the delay and 'brought him to the gaol with his hands bound behind him with a silk handkerchief'. Mr Loder, the gaoler, stated that 'untieing his arm it was so stagnated he could not use his arm to bring it forward'. William and Brabyn dismissed the complaint and gave the man to another master. A similar case was heard later that month with a similar result.

The bench was a little tougher on 30 October 1822 when Patrick Smith 'was submitted for amelioration of sentence', after having been convicted 'of the most insubordinate conduct' towards his master (Roger Connor). William asked the Colonial Secretary that 'the indulgence intended to have been bestowed on him this year now be suspended'.[7] To lose a ticket of leave was a penalty, but not a harsh one. On 6 April 1825 William declined to pass a sentence when a Mr Baldwin said that an assigned convict, Fletcher, had robbed him and been convicted 'four years since' and 'he has also neglected his work, although he has not brought these charges before the Bench'. Reporting this, William explained to Goulburn, the Colonial Secretary, that: 'The Bench have ordered Fletcher to work for another person until your instructions are received on regard to him'.[8] He was benign when the employer had been unreasonable.[9]

William, or the bench he chaired, inevitably did order floggings. On 14 July 1817, sitting with the other magistrates Cartwright and Mileham, they sentenced William Jones to 50 lashes and to be sent to Newcastle for three years to hard labour for stealing a bullock, which always had been a serious offence, both here and in England. Jones also forfeited all his personal property against claims and had the 'overplus paid into the hands of the Treasurer of the Police Fund at the Hawkesbury'.[10] George Lawford, a free man, was tried for 'a very aggravated felony and ... sentenced by a Bench of Magistrates on 18 October 1820 to three years hard labour at Newcastle'.[11] Newcastle, north up the coast from Sydney, was a penal colony within the penal colony, where men mined coal. Bigge thought that convicts being sent to the Coal River 'is felt, and sometimes dreaded by them as a punishment; and that it succeeds in breaking dangerous and bad connections, but that it does not operate in reforming them'.[12] Given William's belief in rehabilitation, the sentences sound uncharacteristic of him, though the crimes had been serious.

In general the administration of the law ranged alongside religion and education as part of the paternalism which characterized New South Wales society.[13] As far as religion was concerned William not only helped what was then the established church (of England), he supported the Catholic church as well and indeed the Presbyterians. On 24 May 1822 he wrote to Governor Brisbane to support the Reverend M. Therry who had 'applied to me as Senior Magistrate' for a piece of ground belonging the Crown at Windsor 'for the purpose of erecting a Chappel for the performance of Roman Catholic worship' and that 'the late Governor [Macquarie] had been pleased to express his approbation of the same'. He enclosed a sketch. It was built.

Four years later, in June 1826, he even-handedly supported a memorial to the Governor from 27 free settlers from the Scottish borders at Portland Head, who had mostly come out in 1802. They had established a church in 1809, but been without a minister for 17 years. One had now arrived, for whom they had built a house. They asked for him to be granted a salary, in addition to the small stipend which they could raise themselves. William certified that he had known the original settlers for upwards of 20 years (a mild misstatement given that 20 years before he had been on his way to trial in England) and that their 'conduct was worthy the consideration of His Excellency the Governor'.[14]

Paternalism infused most things that the magistrates did. For example, the Cawdor bench, at the Macarthurs' Camden estates, was more lenient than most. 'Yet,' its historian observes, 'its hand could fall with great brutality'. People felt 'the machinery of justice was a lofty elaborate thing. It was a system of paternalism, in which the magistrates tempered their sternness … with just as much personal discretion as each case … seemed to require'.[15] That early on William overstepped the mark is shown by his being reproved on 14 February 1811, along with other JPs, in that 'he conceived that he could … convict and sentence persons for the illegal distillation [of liquor]' when such prosecutions could only be carried through at Sydney.[16]

There is every indication that the views and judgments of William, and his colleagues on the Windsor bench, were paternalistic in many contexts. Unfortunately for our knowledge of his personal views, a printed questionnaire sent out by Macquarie to all magistrates and chaplains in February 1820 so infuriated Commissioner Bigge that he demanded the suppression of the answers. This was on the grounds that they were pre-empting his enquiry. The 13 questions did indeed, in Secretary Campbell's words, cover 'the Comparative State of the Colony'. They were very similar to those posed in opinion polls today and included some which were transparently hopeful of vindicating Macquarie's social policies over the previous ten years, such as whether attendance at church had been more regular or less so and whether the 'lower Classes' were 'more circumspect in their Conduct'. What would have been revealing were the questions on corporal punishment and on the attitudes and behaviour of the free-born offspring of convicts.[17]

The majority of magistrates are recorded as having replied. William's answers would by no means necessarily have been the same as those he later gave to Bigge in person. Thus when Bigge interviewed him about punishment for neglect of work, he answered that it would be '100 lashes & to the coal mines [Newcastle] for terms not exceeding three years'.[18] Asked if he approved of that, he replied: 'If Newcastle was so situated as that the convict could not escape, I should think it an excellent place of punishment', adding 'I think that the Punishment has salutary effects upon those who return'.[19] The fear of pain was always a part of the penal system. However, William had long shared Macquarie's beliefs and may have deliberately been saying what Bigge wanted to hear. In a later memorandum he recorded that 'Severe punishment only hardens them [i.e., convicts]'.[20] This was a view later shared, for example, by the chaplain at Norfolk Island, the Reverend Thomas Atkins, who believed that the lash 'merely brutalized and hardened the prisoner'.[21]

William's punishments for assigned females were lenient. In June 1819 one of his own servants, Ann Keogh, most unusually, came up before him on the bench, accused of being drunk and of stealing articles belonging to Rebecca Cox, immediately after her drowning. Keogh was sentenced to six months at the Female Factory.[22] The Female Factory at Parramatta was not exactly a prison, but more like a workhouse to which women who had offended, were refractory or were pregnant were consigned. It was too crowded for all the women to live in and many were boarded out in the town, sometimes turning to prostitution. William also sent one Anne Walker there, on 29 April 1820, for absconding from her husband after meeting one James Anderson in a public house and going to live with him. The background to this was that the woman was a convict, but allowed to live with her husband. Anderson, being a free man, was only fined.[23]

The intricate domestic situations with which a magistrate had to deal are further shown by a case heard on 7 September 1824, when the bench listened to a statement from Thomas Wright, relating to his wife Anne Wright, alias Ann Hubbard. Thomas had 'the honor to inform you that the

The Female Factory at Parramatta – magistrates sent recalcitrant women convicts there (National Library of Australia, ref NK/12 47)

said women is resident in this district, having a certificate of her freedom, but is now under Bail to appear at the Quarter Sessions to a answer to a charge of Felony'. He added that 'the child [she] has with her has been adopted by her and does not belong to her husband, but to one Mr Dillon, a man with a large family'.[24] Today the story would be sensational tabloid material. Such domestic situations were further complicated if one partner in a marriage was a free person, like Anderson, while the other was a convict. In this situation the convict was permitted to live with the free person, who effectively acted as a guarantor.

Being superintendent of the government labourers in the District of the Hawkesbury involved deciding on the assignment of convicts to private masters sent to the district from Sydney, normally in batches. The register of the Colonial Secretary's letters shows how frequent this became, as more and more convict transports arrived. Peace in Europe brought unemployment, a surge in crime in Britain and sent an increasing – in fact unmanageable – number of convicts to New South Wales. Commissioner Bigge commented that 'in perusing the list of persons to whom mechanics have been so assigned, I find them to consist either of the magistrates or of the officers of the government'.[25] He might well have enlarged on this. The settler complaints certainly did.

This had not been Macquarie's intention. At the start of his vice-regal rule there had been a serious shortage of convicts available for assignment. On 24 December 1810, after the transport *Indian* docked, the Governor's secretary, John Campbell, wrote to the magistrates saying that it was 'totally impossible for His Excellency the Governor ... to meet the third part of the demand [for assigned convicts]'. On 18 June 1813 he wrote to Samuel Marsden and Cox, as magistrates, ordering that the distribution of stockmen was to be made 'by ballot and none but industrious and deserving Persons or such as have fair claims to such indulgence shall be admissible to the benefit of the Ballott'.[26] Ballots were frequently invoked, being drawn at Windsor for the entire Hawkesbury district, where William evidently considered himself to be an 'industrious and deserving person', although less conspicuously so in the early days than later on, when more prisoners arrived.

The Cox family, father and sons, had already received assigned convicts as part of their land grants, starting in 1804. William himself never received large numbers at any one time, acquiring men and some women in dribs and drabs, particularly after the ending of the Napoleonic Wars. Thus on 5 February 1816 William received two from the *Ocean* and on 18 October that year the Governor directed that three named men be sent to him. On 21 March 1817 he received three of a total of 25 sent from the *Sir William Bensley*. Whether by coincidence or not, this was three days before he was despatched by Macquarie to explore the Lachlan River from Bathurst. When the number of convicts arriving quadrupled in 1817 and 1818, and Macquarie was hard put to find employment for them, it was more understandable that William got the men he wanted – who were of course primarily 'mechanics'. On 28 September 1819 Cox again headed the list for Windsor with three men assigned to him.[27] By 1819 the number of convicts he employed 'free of expense to the Crown' was 86; by 1821 it totalled 104.[28] In 1822 the convict indents at the Records Office in the Rocks show he was employing 128.

An analysis has been made of those convict indents of 1822. A sample of one third (actually 48) of the 128 employed was taken. It is not always easy to reconcile names on a later muster with arrival records and with declared job skills. Only 38 could be so identified. Of these, two belonged to government clearing parties working on William's estate and three were free men or women. Of the 33 remaining, only 13 were servants or labourers, while 20 had skills useful to the estate, including farm men, stable boys, a carter, seamen and a waterman, plus a gamekeeper. Even if an indoor servant and two seamen are excluded, the total of skilled men was still above 50 percent. The wheelwright at Clarendon was a free man, who chose to work for William. So did at least three others, who were free by servitude, plus three ticket of leave men. This route towards emancipation had closely engaged William, ever since the building of the mountain road.

Macquarie defended Cox to Bigge, saying that those 'who have been useful servants to the government ... have surely a prior claim to men who had not been employed in public service'. As recounted earlier, Bigge himself was critical of the rewards given to some men who worked on the mountain road, in at least one case unfairly, and followed this by paying William a very backhanded compliment when he commented on the giving of tickets of leave:

> It is to this influence that is attributed the success that Mr Cox has met with in his improvement of the convicts that were placed under him. Men who had been rejected by others ... have willingly entered into the services of Mr Cox, and worked for him industriously, under his

A ticket of leave – the vital pass that enabled a convict to work on his own account promises to obtain tickets of leave, or emancipations for them.[29]

This was indeed a part of the secret of William's success in dealing with convict employees, though hardly the whole of it: his personality did the rest.

William continued to seek special favours long after Macquarie had left, such as when he asked the new Colonial Secretary, Alexander McLeay, to find him a teacher for his children. On 30 July 1827 he asked for a Robert Turner, belonging to the town gang at Windsor, to be transferred to him for a period 'as I stand very much in need of a man of his description … he is either a brickmaker or has been accustomed to work in a brickyard'.[30] This demand was in spite of the skill being in short supply. Bigge had noted six years before that there were only 17 brickmakers in the entire colony. He commented further that:

> Cox got men transferred from working on the roads and obtained services from them gratuitously, which other persons could with difficulty obtain, and must have paid for. Evidence … is very pointed upon this subject and has not been denied by Mr Cox.[31]

Not surprisingly, William's skilled workforce aroused envy. John Blaxland was asked by Bigge: 'Do you know any other persons who have succeeded in obtaining mechanics?' He replied: 'I have heard that Mr Cox of Clarendon, Mr Fitzgerald … at Windsor, Mr Meehan, Mr Wentworth'. Blaxland complained that of four he received himself from the *Three Bees* two were ruptured, one lame and the other incapacitated by old age.[32] Samuel Marsden told Bigge that convicts came already assigned to individuals, including 'To Mr Cox, several', in spite of having benefited himself. [33] A. G. L. Shaw comments that 'Only about two dozen "superior settlers" could employ mechanics full time … Marsden had ten, Macarthur was "reasonably satisfied" and so were Cox and D'Arcy Wentworth, though Jamison, Bayly, Blaxland, Howe and Dr Townsend had been aggrieved'.[34] D'Arcy Wentworth was similarly accused of misusing his position as a magistrate. Neither side fooled Commissioner Bigge.

At the same time, William was being kept extremely busy at Bathurst, having become a fully accredited expert on expeditions. A short summary of the Colonial Secretary's correspondence gives an idea of what he was involved in, both at Bathurst and on the Cumberland Plain. In 1816 he constructed a new 'Western Road' from Parramatta to Emu Ford, improving access to the mountain road, where he erected new buildings at Springwood. He dealt with an outbreak of hostilities between Aborigines and settlers. He supplied bricks for the new church at Windsor, one of the colony's most substantial and architecturally notable buildings. On the other side of the mountains he was administering and provisioning government road workers at Bathurst, an activity which continued in 1817.

In March 1817 William was sent by Macquarie to explore the Lachlan River, as already mentioned, and thereafter was responsible over a period of a year for equipping the surveyor John Oxley's expeditions. It was all very well ordering Mr Cox on 14 June 1817 to have articles such as '8 gallons of spirits, 40 lbs sugar, 4 lbs tea, 6 cotton shirts … conveyed to the Depot on the river Lachlan' for Oxley's 'Journey of Discovery'.[35] But William had very limited resources and the demands must have seemed incessant. On 29 October 1817 the Colonial Secretary gave more instructions to the Commissary to send stores for 'the intended expedition to trace the course of the Macquarie river in the country west of the Blue Mountains'. These were for 10 persons, the stores to be sent to Parramatta to be delivered to Mr Cox at Clarendon, 'he having undertaken to forward them to Bathurst for the Party'.[36] Oxley was awarded £200 for this exploration.

The next year the surveyor was asked to try again, with an expedition which began on 4 June 1818. Macquarie reported to Bathurst that 'If Mr Oxley and his former Companions can be again induced to embark in it [following the course of the Macquarie River] I feel it will afford the best hopes of a satisfactory result'. The Governor thought the river might lead to a great inland sea. This inevitably involved William in organizing the equipment and supplies. The deputy commissary general, Mr D. Allan, was told to send rations for 15 persons for 24 weeks – for example, 2000 pounds of flour, 90 pounds of tea and equipment including a tent, 4 frying pans, 15 suits of slop clothing and 15 pairs of blankets. These were to be 'packed up and sent off as soon as possible … to be forwarded from thence [Parramatta] by Mr Cox'. On 15 April Allan was told to send more articles 'being immediately required' for Mr Oxley's expedition. Responsibility for the completion of such constantly repeated, very detailed, orders rested with William at a time when Bathurst was only a tiny settlement offering very few facilities. This time Oxley took 12 men, two boats and 18 horses. The horses were important, which explains William's problems over horses generally, described below. At the same time, in 1817 William himself was preparing to explore the Macquarie River further. Even for a man of William's organizational ability, this must have been a strain. Obviously he had assistance from supervisors, notably Lewis, who was now on the government payroll. All these demands on his time must have been exhausting and that he carried them out puts the subsequent convicts' complaints against him in perspective as petty and often malign.

Such constant activity continued until his commission as commandant was revoked by Macquarie on 23 August 1819. The complaints only surfaced more than a year later, on 1 December 1820, when William was summoned peremptorily by Bigge to answer questions about the execution of the Bathurst road, about buildings at Bathurst, the employment of government men and the conveyance of stores to Bathurst 'by you and one Richard Lewis', also the receipt of government stock from the public herds. Lewis had been a superintendent in building the Blue Mountains road and in 1815 had been appointed by the Governor 'to be a Superintendent in the new discovered country to the westward of the Blue Mountains, under the orders of William Cox Esq, with a salary of fifty pounds sterling per annum and the usual indulgences'.[37] Bigge seems to be unaware that Lewis held an official post. He was not always as well informed as his assistants might have kept him. Lastly he cited 'the promises made by you to several convicts of obtaining tickets of leave … in consideration of certain services performed'.[38]

The origin of these accusations was a short letter to Bigge, dated

2 August 1820, from Charles Frazer, the Colonial Botanist, who had visited Bathurst when William was superintendent in 1818.[39] He accused Cox of having misused his position as commandant at Bathurst, telling Bigge that, when superintending the Bathurst road, Cox had procured an extravagant number of pardons and had defrauded the government by misappropriating government material and labour.[40] In fact William, even if he had used government facilities himself, had usually been fairly meticulous in accounting for what he had done. Thus in a three page letter to Macquarie on July 1818 on the state of the settlement, he reported in his neat carefully spaced writing, on the arrival at Latt 31.49.40 Long 147.52.13 of Oxley's party. 'I immediately made preparations for leaving Bathurst, having previously had inventories taken, horses tools etc.' He gave details of horses, cash receipts books and rations, also enclosing 'for Your Excellency's perusal' a list of 16 convicts with 'their claims for remission of sentence' and went on to explain the state of crops and the need 'to repair the [mountain] road from the 16th mile to the 21st'.[41]

This sort of evidence of William's stewardship is absent from a book on the evidence to the Bigge reports by John Ritchie, in a chapter headed 'Roguery' and featuring 'Conduct of William Cox'. His collection of convicts' complaints is editorially heavily weighted against William, despite the author saying in an introduction: 'Paternal, yet politically radical, Cox earned the reputation of being a humane employer and magistrate'. Ritchie then recites the allegations.[42] Quite apart from its having taken Frazer two years to draw attention to the complaints, all his accusations were hearsay and six out of eight do not stand up to examination, although two were potentially serious. Thus William Price's evidence states, 'I have never received any payment from Mr Cox since I got my Ticket of Leave, but I was in debt to him'. Evidently William had advanced him money, hardly a condemnation. Patrick Hanigaddy had wanted William to sign a petition to the Governor for land, but William had refused saying he had too many petitions. Elijah Cheetham was contesting methods of payment by another man accused by Frazer, named Fitzgerald, which were totally irrelevant.

The most bizarre accusation was the complaint of Richard Kippas. He was a life prisoner who worked for William, who he said 'allows me £40 Per Annum. He pays me in Property and in money. I now work at Wheelwright's business and received my emancipation six months ago.' The pay was almost triple the official rate of £14 a year, but Kippas said he was annoyed that William had not given him a pass, which he had given to several others.[43] Earlier he had most unusually not been punished after an escape attempt and went to work for William at Bathurst. In other words, he had of his own free will continued to work for William after achieving emancipation. The complaint by John Emblett, William's groom, was similarly farcical. He had been recommended for liberty by William, but granted first a ticket and then emancipation by the Governor, not by Cox.

Thomas Smith's complaint was one about which Ritchie does not appear to have checked the relevant government orders, which illustrate how the system worked at Bathurst. Smith had worked for William in 1816 and in 1817 with bullock carts and told Bigge, 'I don't know whether they belonged to him or to the Government'. But on 3 February 1816 Mr Rowland Hassall, the commissary superintendent at Bathurst, had been instructed that 'William Cox Esq having undertaken to find conveyance for the Provisions and stores required on the part of Government at Bathurst', he should provide William with 'ten strong young bullocks [as working oxen] for such conveyance of stores and provisions' in part payment.[44] Again, on 25 October 1817 and in February 1818 the Colonial Secretary's records show William being issued with oxen in 'part payment for the carriage of government stores and provisions to Bathurst'.[45] Smith's real grudge was against Macquarie. He said that William had given him a pass and that 'on presenting it to the Governor he [Macquarie] tore it, saying it was of no use and that he would not have people going about the country with a pass'.[46] This sounds unlikely, even though Macquarie could be both imperious and impetuous. Overall, it is understandable that William complained so bitterly to Bigge about labouring 'amidst a den of thieves and a nest of hornets'.

The only serious accusations came from Blake and Byrne, of which Macquarie testified he had received no complaint, as explained below. Both men nourished a grievance against William because he had accused them of poisoning government horses – of which they had been acquitted, the horses being considered to have 'died of poor condition'.[47] This was in the context of providing horses for Oxley's expeditions. William had been under pressure for many weeks in 1818 over provisioning Oxley's expedition into the mountains and horses were in short supply, although the two horses were not intended for the surveyor. William told Bigge that 'they were bought for Govt to work a two horse cart at Bathurst'. He remained 'convinced in my own mind that these two men [Blake and Burne] were the cause of the death of the two horses'.[48]

Blake also told Bigge that a stockyard of two acres had been erected by William, who had sold it and a brick hut to the government, the hut having been built by a government employee named Brown. This was presumably the one at Crooked Corner. William was alleged to have used the stockyard for his own sheep. He also had a house, sheepyards and stockyards built by government men. Then again, Cox and Lewis had used government horses and bullocks to draw a cart to bring provisions from Springwood to Bathurst 'to save their own'. In reality they were paid for the hire of the cart with cattle from the government herds and William had been ordered to build the stockyards, for which he was paid £49 17s 6d. [49]

In total Bigge gave William the evidence of 33 people to read. His reactions to some of it were intense. He pointed to the Bathurst Book of Expenditure, which tended 'to refute the Ill grounded complaints that are made by a Sett of designing and malicious men, thereby to injure me because as a magistrate I have been obliged to keep a strict watch over their Conduct and punish it when required'. He considered that 'as a free man James Blackman [the Lawsons' supervisor] stands pre-eminent in the mis-statements ... instigator of the others'. When William wrote again to Bigge on 20 January 1821 he was unusually vehement, reminding the Commissioner of his many years service as magistrate and the efforts he had made for the government.[50] He followed this up with a vigorous rebuttal of various convicts' accusations that he abused his office when superintendent of Bathurst, saying, as quoted in the Foreword: 'There is not a magistrate in the Colony who has given as much of his time to the business of the Crown & the public these ten years past as myself'.[51]

The evidence does suggest that William had been maligned. The use of the bullocks and carts had been repeatedly authorized by Macquarie. He had not sold a stockyard to government: he had been paid to build it at Crooked Corner, although it is probable that he also used it for himself. [52] But the real crux lay in William's accusations over the horses. Both Blake and Byrne revealed personal grievances against him. Blake's included that: 'Mr Cox promised me an emancipation in the year 1816, if I would go to his stockyard & mind his sheep'. He had received emancipation, but not from William, as had John Emblett. Byrne had been sent to mark out 56 miles of road from the Lachlan River to the Limestone Rock but 'Mr Cox never paid me for the work'. He told Bigge about a black horse named Scratch that 'had been employed by Mr Cox in drawing his Caravan was employed in taking down wool from Bathurst. He had a Government mark upon him.' But Scratch had been acquired legitimately for the Blue Mountains road in 1814. In his 30 January letter William said, 'The old horse Scratch was the one allowed me for my caravan'.

Byrne continued about a team of government bullocks bringing up provisions for Oxley's expedition and taking down a load for Lewis.[53] But on 3 February 1816, one of the occasions mentioned by Byrne, the commissary superintendent, Hassall, who seems to have been assisted by his son, had been told that William should receive bullocks in part payment for the conveyance of stores.[54] On 5 October 1816 the Deputy Commissary (the son), had written to the storekeeper at Bathurst, Thomas Gorman, instructing him to issue to 'Wm Cox Esqr' or his order, 'fourteen cows and five oxen, being the balance due to him for carriage of provisions and stores from Parramatta to Bathurst'. Furthermore, Gorman had been told: 'you will be careful to see the above cattle branded with Mr Cox's brand before they are delivered'.[55]

Macquarie, when questioned by Bigge about 'Mr Cox's conduct at Bathurst', defended William. He emphasized over the stockyard question that: 'he could not credit the Charge as now made. If any Cattle were drawn improperly by Mr Cox, it must be attributed to the neglect of the then Superintendent of the Government stock.' Protecting himself, he added, 'The Governor does not however feel himself called upon to explain imputations against Mr Cox or any other person'.[56] However, it had been at Macquarie's direction that William had been paid in cattle and oxen.[57]

William spiritedly denied any wrongdoing on his part, whilst claiming that the storekeeper Gorman had been a rogue. Bigge picked up on this, criticizing him for recommending Gorman, when 'Thomas Gorman, who acted as storekeeper to the Bathurst road party, and afterwards at Bathurst appears in the language of Mr Cox ... to have been "a consummate villain"'. William had earlier described Gorman as 'not equal to the task' and had asked Macquarie for a replacement, unsuccessfully. He now protested that he did not appreciate what Gorman had been doing: 'I perfectly understand the mode of common accounts, but am unacquainted with Commissariat Terms or Accounts'.[58] Bigge then devoted a whole page of his parliamentary report to criticism of the temptations created by 'the system upon which Mr Cox had been suffered to conduct the government works, and the issues of provisions at Bathurst': in other words, which Macquarie had forced on him.[59] Part of the Commissioner's private instructions from Lord Bathurst had been to investigate the alleged extravagance of Macquarie's public works. This fitted the hidden agenda.[60]

Referring to Byrne and Blake, the only convict complainants he appears to have taken seriously, Bigge wrote: 'It must be observed, that Mr Cox had sent these men to be tried before a criminal court on a charge of poisoning the horses ... a charge of which they were acquitted, but of which Mr Cox still thinks they were guilty'. Both were acting as superintendents of farms and 'were much trusted and commended by their employers'. But Bigge did refer to the 'difficulty of obtaining concurrent testimony respecting the character of convicts'.[61] A logical conclusion is that William had lost his temper with Byrne and Blake over the horses dying. Bigge failed to understand that they were not for Oxley's expedition, but there was a shortage due to Oxley's needs. The other accusations were not pursued. It is likely that, over the matter of the stockyards, William had been mixing private and government business, as he often did. No official action was ever taken against him as a result of the complaints.

Overall, when surveying William's contribution to the governance of the colony in those years 1816 to 1819, when he was the administrator at Bathurst – the only period in his life in which he served as a representative of the Governor – he unquestionably gave a very great deal more to the colony than he took. But, as elsewhere throughout his life, he did have what can most politely be called an eighteenth-century attitude to the perquisites of office. Nor did he cease acquiring land.

The 1819 list of grants from 1812 to 1821 shows that William obtained two grants of 820 and 200 acres at Bringelly (Mulgoa) on 8 October 1816 and a further 760 acres there on 18 January 1817. His sons George got 600 acres there on 8 October 1816 and Henry 400 on 18 January 1818, while William Jnr was allotted 800 acres at Melville and Henry 200 at Minto.[62] These were all in the County of Cumberland, south of the road from Parramatta to Emu Plains. Whether the Bringelly plots were adjacent is not clear, but it must be highly likely that they were and they underline the 'family business' concept which William pursued. Macquarie was generous to the Cox family, and to others, no doubt partly because it furthered his idea of allocating all the land on the Cumberland Plain before making grants beyond the mountains. He also granted land to James Cox at Fort Dalrymple in Van Diemen's Land, to which James had been permitted to move with one convict servant in 1819, where he eventually formed his own Clarendon estate. Whatever disadvantages representing the Governor at Bathurst had involved, they did not halt the Cox family enterprise.

9 Toughly Interviewed by Commissioner Bigge

If the acquisition of land was the essential building block in the establishment of pastoral estates in New South Wales, and of family enterprises such as William Cox and his sons created, the assignment of convict workers to their owners came a close second. When John Thomas Bigge was sent out in 1819 to investigate the state of the colony he had been instructed by Lord Bathurst that transportation to the colony was:

> intended as a severe Punishment ... and as such must be rendered an Object of real Terror to all classes of the community ... If ... by ill-considered Compassion for Convicts ... their situation in New South Wales be divested of all Salutary Terror, Transportation cannot operate ... as a proper punishment.[1]

This applied as much to convicts assigned to private masters as to those employed on government work.

William Cox, though a disciplinarian, was far from lacking in human compassion towards convicts. His replies to Bigge's questions were therefore both illuminating and potentially fraught with difficulty for him. They also reveal a good deal about William's own character and attitudes, as well as providing an unusually clear exposition of what he thought about convicts and their management, with Clarendon as the backdrop. He appreciated that Bigge's report might be crucial to the future of the colony, as had made been clear to the public by Macquarie's announcements when the Commissioner arrived.

It has been remarked that Bigge and his assistants were 'as assiduous as ants in gathering and storing a vast quantity of detail for carriage back to Whitehall.'[2] There has also been much academic dispute over how far Bigge's conclusions – which were to have a decisive effect on the colony as a whole and which greatly enhanced the fortunes of the pastoralists – were in fact based on the evidence he had taken and how far they derived from the private instructions he was given before he left England. The allegations made against William, which are in the collected evidence but were not published in the main reports, as well as comments in the main report itself, were discussed in the previous chapter.

From the start in 1788 the colony had been almost entirely dependent on convict labour, as the pastoralists themselves came to be. Without labour an estate could not be run or developed. An understanding of convict assignment and its role in both the landed gentry's growing dominance overall, and in the running of William's estates in particular, is therefore essential in forming an impression of the colony at that time. For the convicts, life on a farm estate, such as Clarendon, was far preferable to working on a purely pastoral one, where the shepherd's life was lonely and miserable, although at the time of Bigge's visit estates beyond the mountains were few.

It will be worth taking a look at the character of the Commissioner himself. John Thomas Bigge was a former Chief Justice of Trinidad, who socially had more in common with the Macarthurs than with Macquarie, whose regime he was investigating as a result of discontent with the Governor's actions, voiced both in the colony and in London. Bigge had been commissioned to conduct a comprehensive enquiry into the state of the colony and to report back to the Secretary of State, Lord Bathurst.[3] He delivered his conclusions in three reports, the first in June 1822, the second later that year, and the third in 1823. The first was on *The State of the Colony of New South Wales*.[4] This dealt almost entirely with the transportation and servitude of convicts. The second was on *The Judicial Establishments of New South Wales and of Van Diemen's Land*, for which William was not specifically interviewed, in spite of his being a magistrate. The third report was on the *State of Agriculture and Trade in the Colony of New South Wales*.[5] This criticized William for giving indulgences to convicts, whilst being highly complimentary about his and other farmers' agricultural methods.

Bigge's directive from the Prince Regent had been 'to enquire into the Laws, Regulations and Usages of the Settlement … and into every other Thing in any way connected with the Administration of the Civil Government'.[6] However, Bathurst had given his own private instructions to the Commissioner three weeks earlier. The Secretary of State first asked for alterations that would render the colony 'available to the purpose of its original Institution' (as a penal colony) and then wanted Bigge to investigate the alleged extravagance of Governor Macquarie's public works.[7] This heavily loaded subtext also referred to:

> the difference of opinion which has prevailed in the Colony. I allude to the Propriety of admitting into Society Persons, who came to the Settlement as Convicts. The opinion entertained by the Governor, and sanctioned by the Prince Regent, has certainly been, with some exceptions, in favour of their reception … upon terms of Perfect Equality with the Free Settlers.

No matter what the Prince had approved, Bathurst was aware of the hostility which Macquarie's ideas had aroused, both in the colony and in parliament.[8] Many of Bigge's questions derived from this instruction.

Bigge travelled widely and took evidence from a considerable variety of people, supplemented by numerous letters. His main report concluded that 'the expediency of promoting … the growth of fine wool and creating a valuable export … appears to be the principal if not the only source of productive industry within the colony'.[9] The Commissioner, therefore, recommended employing convicts in a pastoral economy as the solution to future development. This was to be the key to the pastoralists achieving pre-eminence in the colony.

Assignment had originated under Governor Phillip as a means of improving agricultural productivity. It soon became essential for reducing the costs of the penal colony by taking prisoners 'off the store', that is to say fed and housed by employers, not the government. As the historian George Rudé has commented, 'once the convicts arrived in the colony they were cast for an economic role and if they became reformed in the process, so much the better.'[10] The obvious role was in food production. Officers of the New South Wales Corps were assigned up to 10 convicts per 100 acres to work their land in the 1790s. Initially the assigned convicts were fed, clothed and, if necessary, housed by the government. But in 1797 Governor Hunter was instructed by the Duke of Portland that this was to be done by the employer.[11] In 1805 the Secretary of State began specifying that new free settlers, such as the Blaxland brothers, should be assigned 10 convicts for each 1000 acres of their land grants.[12] After 1815 assignment became even more fixedly the cornerstone of the colonial system, where private masters 'should carry the cost and supervise the labour of convicts at every moment possible'.[13]

The convict population increased rapidly during Macquarie's tenure as governor. In 1814 the total number of convicts to arrive was 819, of whom 72 mechanics (skilled men) out of 194 were assigned to private employers. In 1819, 2376 arrived, but only 92 out of 477 mechanics were able to be assigned.[14] These figures are significant in terms of Macquarie's problems in dealing with the vastly increased number of arrivals after 1815. However, assignment was not the slavery condemned by Sir William Molesworth in his highly partisan parliamentary report of 1838, which reflected how the system had become politically controversial at home.[15] It was abandoned in 1840.

For those convicts who went along with the system and did not cause trouble (or managed not to be provoked into it by intemperate masters, as some of William's court judgments showed they could), the system provided a way of learning practical skills and securing a far better future than a convicted felon in Britain could hope for. But convicts could be recalcitrant and an employer who did not allow extra rewards and indulgences to a skilled man would have been unlikely to have got much work out of him. As was seen during the building of the Blue Mountains road, William Cox did have a keen understanding of the convict mentality and an appreciation of the value of giving convicts incentives to work well, which was one of Macquarie's reasons for giving him the job.

The way in which Governor Macquarie, and likewise William, viewed criminals had progressed beyond the classicist crime-is-in-the-blood school of the late eighteenth century and towards the idea of rehabilitation, anticipating aspects of the positivist approach of the 1820s. One commentator considers that 'In Macquarie's personality ... were mixed a broad sense of justice and a humanity far ahead of Georgian concepts'.[16] This attitude was very different to the terms of Bigge's agenda. After Macquarie's departure the belief in rehabilitation faltered and the aims of punishment reverted to the classical view of the eighteenth century. This had been expressed by Lord Portland when he told Governor Hunter back in 1798 that 'crimes of a more heinous nature ... can only be repressed by a sense of the certainty of the punishment that awaits them'.[17] There was less concern with understanding the nature of the 'criminal' and more with developing rational and systematic means of delivering justice, which Bigge had been told to consider.[18]

So the Commissioner's enquiries into how the assignment system operated under Macquarie, and how it could lead to tickets of leave, or even pardons, was highly charged politically. The ticket of leave was explained to the Molesworth Committee by a later Chief Justice, Sir Francis Forbes, as giving the holder 'the right ... to work for his own benefit', thus freeing him from assignment, but he could not leave the colony. Tickets were 'as a reward for good conduct and also formerly as a remuneration for extra work, skill or ingenuity'. That was before Governor Brisbane established a scale under which a ticket was allowed after four years of a seven-year sentence, after six on a 14-year one and after eight on a life sentence.[19] The tickets were close to essential for providing a pool of free labour. A convict had also been allowed a ticket if living with a free spouse. By 1837, when

Forbes gave his evidence, that privilege had been abolished.

William had been a major contractor on public works in the 'Macquarie towns' on the Hawkesbury. Immediately after constructing the Castlereagh Glebe House, he had built the Blue Mountains road and had been highly praised by the Governor, who had written, *inter alia*, 'I cannot therefore too highly Appreciate the Merits and Services of Mr Cox on this occasion'.[20] Bigge must have read this correspondence between Bathurst and Macquarie before he came out and such praise was unlikely to have impressed him. In the end he devoted more than a whole page of his main report to sniping criticism of the way the road building was conducted and its rewards for the convicts employed.[21] Perhaps sensing that Bigge might be hostile to the rewards he gave convicts, William's answers to the Commissioner's questions were often guarded and on occasion he plainly said what he guessed Bigge wanted to hear. Having made a statement, he frequently modified it when checking the transcripts and was not always consistent.

The first interview was on the subject of agriculture on 25 November 1819, the transcript of which William signed on 14 February 1820, but he was not interviewed on convicts until 14 December 1820, shortly before Bigge's departure.[22] The records of his evidence were corrected by him personally, in his own hand. The interview on agriculture, which covers 49 pages, largely about assignment, suggests that Bigge expected to attach importance to what William had to say. He sought the views of only 25 individuals on agriculture and his talks with other landowners were much shorter.[23] John Ritchie, in a biography of Macquarie, suggests that Bigge 'took precautions to ensure that their replies favoured his vision of a pastoral economy which would remove prisoners from government work in the towns'.[24]

In his agricultural interview William told Bigge, in a way that underlined the primitive nature of farming of the early days, that when he first came to the colony in 1800, 'Tillage was conducted entirely by hand hoes', as was explained in Chapter 8. Nor were harrows used, 'the seeds being covered in by the hoe'.[25] George Caley, the botanist, wrote in 1803: 'Nothing further is done than break up the ground with a hoe and throw in the wheat which is again chopped over with a hoe or harrowed ... the stumps that yet remain in the ground are against it'.[26] However, it has been considered that the labour intensive method of hand hoeing and hand-setting or sowing seed 'was intrinsic to improved husbandry on the light soils of the Port Jackson hinterland'.[27]

When the surveyor general, John Oxley, was interviewed by Bigge in 1819 – he was one of the handful of landowners praised by the Commissioner – he was asked whether he thought the removal of stumps and trees 'contributes to the augmentation of the produce?' 'I certainly do,' Oxley replied, 'at least one eighth is gained by grubbing the trees.' He went on to explain: 'It is a practice newly introduced and only freemen work at it ... the price generally given is about 40s an acre'. Convicts would not perform enough to even pay for their rations, unless 'they are overpaid as free men'.[28] Although John Macarthur had brought out the first iron plough in the 1790s, landowners were too well aware of the labour costs involved.

When the Commissioner asked by what means productivity could be improved, William gave specific examples, in addition to grubbing out the stumps, which had now begun. 'A farmer can by raising artificial food such as rape, clover, turnips & English grapes, maintain a flock of sheep & the manure from them will enable him to raise his crops of wheat.' Using sheep manure was exactly what was done in Dorset. William's enthusiasm was, probably unknowingly, despite his growing agricultural expertise, echoing the agricultural revolution of 'Turnip Townshend' 90 years earlier. Viscount Townshend had introduced the cultivation of turnips on a large scale and a four field-field crop rotation system at his estate in Norfolk in the 1730s. William had similar ideas.

Wheat crop yields had declined from 20 to 25 bushels per acre on the Hawkesbury. Asked by Bigge if 'it will soon be necessary to adopt a better system of husbandry', William was emphatic that it would. 'Most certainly,' he replied, '& if they [the fields] were appropriated to the growth of maize according to a new system lately & successfully adopted of ploughing for maize and clearing it likewise with the plough I think the crops of the Hawkesbury district could still be very productive.'[29] The fertility of the Hawkesbury soil was becoming exhausted.

The Hawkesbury river in 2010, seen from the road bridge (Author's photo)

Bigge asked: 'Were the convicts of that day [William's first years] better fitted for the purposes of agriculture?' The development of agriculture had always been part of the intention of the assignment system. At this, the general tenor of William's evidence became a grievance – one frequently expressed by other settlers – that recent convict arrivals were less useful: 'The convicts which arrived here in the early part of my time, were generally able bodied men, & who had been accustomed to country labor and capable of performing the duties required of them'. Many of the able-bodied had been Irish. By 1820, William lamented, one fourth of those arriving were aged under 21 and 'not fit to send into the field for labour, being incapable of performing a day's work.'[30] By then there were indeed very few country labourers being sent out.[31] At the same time the constructive potential of the young convicts was being overwhelmed by their numbers.

The termination of the Napoleonic War had made matters radically worse for Macquarie, loading convicts on to him without consultation in numbers for which he could not find employment. The end had brought economic depression to England. Men were no longer being recruited to the armed forces, while some out-of-work ex-servicemen turned to crime. There were unemployed half-pay officers, some of whom later arrived as squatters. Even Jane Austen, in her novel *Persuasion*, written in 1815 and 1816, introduces naval officers looking for places to live.[32] Men and women convicted of 'serious' crimes, which could include petty theft, posed an immediate problem and were transported.

In 1817 Bathurst admitted that 'The Number of Convicts transported has increased beyond all calculation', but still complained at the cost of lodging them. The situation had soon worsened.[33] In 1818 Macquarie drew Bathurst's attention to five ships having arrived in one month and five days, bringing 1064 more convicts in that 'Short time' alone.[34] Meanwhile, the disastrous floods of 1817 had not only damaged farmland, they had reduced the demand for farm labour, with convicts who had been assigned being returned to government by employers. The Governor had attempted to tackle the 1818 influx by shipping some 440 of them straight on to Van Diemen's Land. Bigge simply disregarded the difficulties which would have undermined his case.

Macquarie employed the majority of arriving convicts, and those already in New South Wales, on public works. This classic solution benefited William as a contractor and also meant he had no problem obtaining men for Clarendon. T. G. Parsons argues that Bigge 'consistently ignored' evidence that landowners were adequately supplied with agricultural labour, notably Jamison, Bayly and John Macarthur, 'whose 47 convicts included 45 percent of mechanics and agriculturally skilled men'.[35] William told Bigge: 'Myself and my sons employ about 100 men' and described the many trades carried out on his own estate.[36] By 1823 he was employing 123 himself.[37]

Bigge might have been concerned with the treatment of assigned convicts by their masters and, by implication, what kind of men those employers were. In fact, he devoted very few questions to the subject. What did emerge was to William's credit, also illustrating the disparities between different employers' attitudes. He told Bigge: 'Our ploughmen and labourers are paid by the year from at not less than £10 and many as high as £15. When we employ them by task & they are good working men they are capable of earning considerably more. Some mechanics are given from £15 to £25.'[38] At this time the official wage had recently been raised by Macquarie from £10 to £11 and for women to £7. It was intended to cover necessary domestic expenses (wages were abolished by Brisbane in 1823). Task work was paid for on completion of a specific job, after which the convict was 'on his own time' and both could, and often did, get up to no good. Macquarie would have liked to abolish it.[39]

Overall, William estimated his workers cost him at least £25 12s a year each, some of this in rations. John Blaxland stated that each of his convicts set him back a very similar amount, £24, charging the rations at £14, while free shepherds earned between £15 and £25, with rations added.[40] By contrast, Gregory Blaxland, thought: 'The ration is fair, but the wages are too high. £4 in necessaries would be sufficient.'[41] A sterling coinage, as opposed to local notes and coins, known as 'currency', was firmly established in 1818, when the Bank of New South Wales was founded. William told Bigge that 'they now receive their wages in money or in cloathing [sic] and other articles of necessity at a sterling price.'[42] This was much better for the convicts. William was also opposed to clothing being given in lieu of wages and in a significant letter to Bigge emphasized the need to give assigned men some extra small comforts. He wrote:

> It is laid down in law that 'the Master shall not give his servants any money or useless thing unless they have a proper stock of clothing' … what is he to do for Tobacco, Soap, thread to mend his clothing and little comforts that they want when unwell … or now and then getting a day's recreation? … he would be like a slave without any stimulus for exertion.[43]

Providing a stimulus to convicts to work well was important, not that Cox was alone in realizing it. With the currency stabilized, labourer convicts in the colony could be better off materially than they would have been as countryside workers in England, except for their lack of freedom and the threat of the lash. By the time of the mid-1820s in England William Cobbett recorded that farm workers would be earning only seven pence a day, six days a week, without board or food.[44] Convicts were fed, clothed and provided with some sort of medical care.

This was certainly true of William's community at Clarendon, where his first manager, the Irish exile Joseph Holt, referring to his early days at Brush Farm, recorded that 'His good treatment of the convicts in his service had the happiest effect upon many of those who were so lucky as to get into his service'.[45] As quoted earlier, William's idea of a desirable relationship between master and servant was encapsulated when, in the later interview on convicts, he told Bigge that 'where the man is capable of performing the task with ease to himself, he pleases his Master who makes his life more comfortable'.[46] He also made the point that there was more control over convicts if they were with a private employer, although not if they were with an emancipist smallholder, when he considered that master and servant would get up to mischief together.

William saw female convicts as either wives or domestic servants, as most of them were. But not, as so many others did, as inevitably being drawn into prostitution. Macquarie had soon after his arrival unequivocally condemned all cohabitation unsanctified by marriage ties in an official proclamation.[47] William, less puritanically, saw women as a stabilizing influence in society, although his frequent references to the desirability of marriage validate the contribution which he felt women made to family life. This reflected what they could become. From the moment of their arrival females were treated differently to men and were sent to employers almost immediately. Numerically they were far fewer. Charles Bateson estimates that from 1810 to 1819 the number of women transported was 1934 as against 11,650 men.[48] But they possessed many skills which the colony could increasingly utilize. Deborah Oxley summarizes a wide range of prior occupations, with 40 skills predominating, including nursemaids and laundrywomen, while 22.22 percent were housemaids. There were milliners, bootmakers and even five schoolmistresses.[49] Female skills needed no adapting to the environment and convict domestics played a vital role in the households of William and other landowners, although he and they sometimes suffered from their thefts.

Strangely, William thought female servants should not be paid at all, because they were living with the family, as he told Bigge in a letter of May 1820. Generally speaking, domestic servants were 'provisioned well', although they slept 'outside the house in a detached kitchen or outbuilding' for fear of theft.[50] This does not seem to have been the case at Clarendon, although the kitchens were separate, while Elizabeth Farm had 'A Kitchen with Servants' Apartments'.[51] William's female servants really did live in, much as they slept in the attics or basements at English country houses, which William Jnr's did in the basement at Hobartville, but in England they were paid.

The second role of convict females was as women available to men. Nothing that William told Bigge suggests that he thought women were merely providers of sexual services. Joy Damousi suggests that convict women were 'assigned only one function – they were there primarily as objects of sexual gratification'.[52] True, some employers did take convict servants to their beds. D'Arcy Wentworth lived with and finally married a convict woman, which hardly fits Damousi's description, but it did cast doubt on his being a true gentleman. Between 1826 and 1831 Darling gave inducements to women who found husbands, so that husband and wife could be assigned to the same master. In 1831 William Jnr encouraged two employees, Agnes Wicks and Samuel Leicester, to marry so that the man could get a ticket of leave.[53]

Bigge devoted more attention to the Female Factory than to any other aspect of the women's lives, on account of its cost. It was William's belief that women ought to be in domestic service and that the factory had given them 'an aversion to service in the respectable families in the country'.[54] His main concern was whether the factory produced potential domestics, a narrow-minded approach, which characterized his views on female convicts.

The Commissioner also asked William if 'the encouragement held out to Prisoners to marry by giving them the privilege of tickets of leave is attended with good effects'. Convicts were allowed a ticket of leave if married to a free person. William expressed doubt about this change to 'comparative freedom' through a convict marrying and settling down. In practice, in 1818 he had helped a life prisoner, named William Price, to establish himself at Bathurst and to start a new life when he got married.[55] He did not share the strong views of the chaplain at the Hawkesbury, the Reverend Robert Cartwright, who was robust in attacking the exemptions attendant upon marriage, telling Bigge that such indulgences would be 'making an holy Institution subservient to the vilest purposes, which is frequently done in this colony'.[56] Subsequently, marriage was increasingly seen by the authorities as a reward for good behaviour, rather than as a right.

There were various ways in which a convict could attain freedom. Convicts could become free by completing their term of servitude, or relatively free through indulgences, emancipation and, for a few, full pardons. These could be recommended to the governor annually. The men employed on the Blue Mountains road had been rewarded with pardons for their work, Macquarie telling Lord Bathurst, 'They being a considerable time in this Country and of Decent Conduct'.[57] This was the focal point. If men worked and behaved well, in William's view also, they merited encouragement and the starting point toward emancipation was the ticket. Yet when Bigge asked him whether issuing them led to good conduct among the convicts, he replied guardedly: 'I think that tickets of leave are preferable to emancipations. In the first instance the holder is always amenable to the magistrates as a convict in case of misconduct ... an emancipated man is out of the reach of the jurisdiction of the magistrates for offences committed by him.'[58]

This was a considerable admission. On 9 November 1819, two weeks before William's interview on agriculture, Macquarie had admonished all the magistrates over the issuance of memorials (for indulgences) 'on behalf of any person whatever', no doubt at Bigge's insistence.[59] Not that this stopped William doing so. In May 1820 he tried to obtain a relaxation of sentence for a John Stubbs who had been sent to Newcastle. Campbell, the Colonial Secretary, responded that unless the man's conduct had been 'steady and correct' he should be retained there, 'as in the late case of another person who had been recommended by Mr Cox'.[60] However, Macquarie himself performed a *volte face* by later strongly defending William's recommendations, which he said 'must necessarily rest with those who have the superintendence of men confided to them'. He went on to tell Bigge: 'I feel that too much stress has been laid on the rumours to his [Cox's] prejudice, and perhaps they have had even too much influence on my own conduct towards him latterly'.[61]

Pardons had become another explosive subject. In his report the Commissioner said: 'In consequence of the suspensions on the annual distribution of pardons ... Mr Cox and the magistrates of Windsor have thought themselves justified in giving passes to these men [who had laboured on the normal roads] to work as it is termed "upon their own hands" ... such a pass having been given more frequently than by any other person, was vulgarly termed "Captain Cox's liberty"'. Bigge seems to have been criticizing both tickets given for government work and private employment.[62] He concluded that 'Mr Cox, a gentleman much distinguished for experience and sagacity, has observed a want of authority over their convict servants'.[63] This begs the question of whether William was considered a 'soft touch' by the convicts. The complaints laid against him at Bathurst, summarized in Chapter 8, suggest so.

Macquarie saw emancipation as the route to bringing convicts back into society. As a magistrate, William did not object to emancipists being appointed to the bench, and had long collaborated with Simeon Lord. This was another major source of disagreement in the colony between the Governor and the exclusives. Macquarie: 'saw the necessity ... of extending to them [ex-convicts] the same consideration ... had they never been under the sentence of the Law'.[64] William's neighbour and fellow magistrate, Archibald Bell, also a former New South Wales Corps officer, saw convicts as 'once having been tainted, unfit for associating with afterwards', except for those sent out for 'political errors'. For prisoners to become emancipated was one thing, but for them to be raised to an official position, like the magistracy, was unacceptable. He had refused to sit alongside the emancipist JP Andrew Thompson, who Macquarie so admired, and believed that 'the feelings and sentiments of the respectable persons in this Colony are uniform on that subject'.[65] Bell's position was less extreme than Marsden's, less liberal than William's.

Back in London Bathurst decreed that 'No emancipist was to be appointed to civil office or the magistracy until he had proved himself qualified by his conduct and character'. By 1817 he had been 'compelled to conclude that most of the emancipists elevated to positions of trust were unfit for such preferment' and urged restraint on Macquarie.[66] This was to be the official line, and the attitude of the majority of the settlers, for the next two decades.

Almost equally controversial was the Governor's policy of allotting ex-convicts small land grants as the foundation both for their rehabilitation and the development of agriculture, even though its origins went back to Grose's time. To then give them convict servants was even more so. Interviewing William about convicts in December 1820 Bigge probed him over it. Had the 'practice [of assignment] been changed since the arrival of Govr Macquarie?' William replied that it had changed about 1811 and 'it is now customary to assign convicts to those who hold as small a quantity as five or ten acres of land, provided the District Constable reports to the magistrate they are enabled to maintain them'. This frequently meant assigning them to ex-convicts. William said Macquarie had 'informed me for my guidance that it was his wish that this should be our general mode of distributing them'.[67]

Ritchie describes what had resulted: 'Only two fifths of the ex-convicts to whom Macquarie had granted land throughout his administration continued to occupy their farms in 1821 … they lived in rudimentary hovels and exhausted their soil by overcropping; they worked in paddocks beside their convict assignees in shared defeatism.'[68] William was all too familiar with this miserable situation on the Hawkesbury, which Bigge himself observed in the aftermath of the 1819 flood. He did not approve. Back in 1811 he had 'been careful to prevent Prisoner settlers being set down for servants' as a magistrate and rejected many without 'the Means of Maintaining themselves.'[69] He now told Bigge, 'If a convict is badly inclined he has a greater opportunity of doing wrong than if placed with a respectable settler', adding that 'many instances have occurred where they both have combined to commit the same crime.'[70]

Giving evidence on agriculture in 1819, William had said that 'an emancipated convict had much better remain as a labourer'. A 'great majority have sold their lands and are reduced to poverty.'[71] Possibly he was recalling the numerous failures after the March 1819 floods (or those of 1817). But Bigge had reminded him that some emancipated convicts were thriving and successful people. 'Certainly,' he later contradicted himself by admitting during the interview on convicts, '& I would point out many who now have large families and considerable stock, who began with nothing more than the land they got.'[72] In the end Bigge concluded that: 'an emancipated convict, without capital or means of cultivation' could not so manage 30 acres 'as to derive subsistence or profit from it.'[73]

The convicts' true character, on which the future of the colony would depend, was ever controversial. 'Let a foreigner, a stranger,' William later wrote to Bigge, 'be told that it is the convict, the refuse of our country, that have performed nearly all the labour that has been done here in the short space of thirty years and I think he would be astonished.'[74] That they were indeed not the refuse of Britain is shown by Stephen Nicholas and Peter R. Shergold's researches. They write: 'All three of our separate measures of the convict workers' human capital – their occupations, literacy and height –

point to the same conclusion: the convict settlers sent to New South Wales were ordinary members of the British and Irish working classes'.[75] In the early decades of the colony the inherent wickedness of criminals had been a commonly held belief. But it has been calculated that in the period 1810–19 those transported were overwhelmingly aged between 15 and 29, which meant they had the youth and energy, once free, to develop the colony.[76] Would they, and their children, enjoy the rights of British citizens?

Transported felons had common law rights in the penal colony which they would not have enjoyed as prisoners in England, such as the right to petition, bear witness, own property and marry. Trial by jury could have been considered implicit in this. But at the time of Bigge's visit all trials were conducted initially by magistrates, then if necessary by the Supreme Court in Sydney. Both trial by jury, and more particularly having ex-convicts serving as jurors, would have been steps too far for both the authorities and many settlers, even though several ex-convicts were magistrates. Bigge asked William if the idea of ex-convicts acting as jurors had been discussed. As he probably knew, William had been at a meeting on 12 February 1819, resulting in a petition to the home government asking for 'that great and valued inheritance of our ancestors, trial by jury', with 1260 signatories. This was refused by Bathurst the following year.[77] The petition had been 'a fresh and historic conjunction of nearly all exclusive and emancipist interests'.[78] It was of keen concern to Bigge.

William told him: 'It was considered at the meeting that persons whose sentences were expired would be legally capable of acting as jurors and that no further objections could or ought to exist to their so acting'. But there had been disagreement over whether those privileges ought to be allowed to convicts pardoned by the governor or only those given freedom by the higher authority of the King. 'Are such persons morally competent to Discharge the office of Jurors?' Bigge asked. William retreated, suggesting that some ex-convicts would be unfit 'as they are too much tainted with effects of crime'. He then prevaricated, saying 'but I do not think the time has arrived yet for introducing the Trial by Jury upon any Plan'.[79]

Here William was reflecting a serious division in the colony between those who saw the convicts as future citizens, and those like Archibald Bell and Marsden who could not countenance their being given public responsibilities. In any case, there might by then have been enough free citizens to sidestep that possibility. Gregory Blaxland, when interviewed, thought there were enough 'persons who had not been transported' to form a jury.[80] William's own response was half-hearted. Bigge eventually found 'among all ranks' a desire to see jury trial introduced '[but] the time was not ripe for its introduction in the penal colonies.'[81] When trial by jury was introduced, many years later, no emancipists were selected.

A second 'right' which William told Bigge about was imaginary. It was the convicts' 'right' to own the land of the colony they had laboured to create. William explained: 'They give a Decided Preference to those who have been convicts … they think that the Free People have no right to the possession of lands in this colony'. Did 'convicts look on a grant of lands as their right?' Bigge asked. William replied cautiously: 'latterly they have been inclined to hold that opinion.'[82] He was evasive, even though others had made similar observations (which he was unlikely to have known). This careful conversation presaged a crucial later change in the colony, when the offspring of the emancipists asserted their rights as native-born citizens in the 1840s. The naval surgeon Peter Cunningham noticed, on a visit in 1826, that 'currency lads', children of convicts, did not like working for settlers as 'they naturally look upon that vocation as degrading.'[83]

Thanks to a shortage of skilled men among the predominantly young convicts arriving, there was resentment against William for favouring himself, as a magistrate, in the allocation of 'mechanics'. Chapter 7 includes discussion of Commissioner Bigge's investigation of such allegations. Surprisingly, however, Bigge's interviews with William Cox, Archibald Bell and the Blaxland brothers did not touch on how the assignment system helped the government or the welfare of the colony. Atkinson is critical of the landowners' behaviour at that time when he writes: 'Until the mid-1820s employers in both New South Wales and Van Diemen's Land thought of the assignment system as an employment exchange … To a progressive mind many employers seemed to do too little for the improvement of the country. They also failed to understand that they were agents of the state in the management of their men and women.'[84] Bigge did not appear interested in how the private interests of landowners could be reconciled with and support the needs of government. Yet from its inception the assignment system had been intended to do exactly that, both to boost food production and save government expense by taking prisoners 'off the store'. However, Bigge had his agenda, and 'once he developed an approach, his investigation was directed to reinforcing his opinion'.[85] However he did end up shedding an unprecedented light on how the colony was run.

Two pictures emerge from the evidence just reviewed; one general to the colony, the other individual to William Cox. The effect of the report in terms of the economy was an encouragement of pastoral enterprise, which attracted new free settlers. But Macquarie had believed in development 'by means of small land settlement … linked with the redemption of the wicked.'[86] That ideal of rehabilitation was abandoned. Recognition of the part emancipists could play in developing the colony was set back a generation. The rights which convicts should have had, as British citizens, were not recognized. Bigge's brief had been to reduce public expenditure. As the jurist J. J. Spigelman points out: 'He focussed on the idea by which increased severity of the convict experience could … also reduce public expenditure in the colony. This could be achieved by ensuring that a greater proportion of convicts were assigned to private employers, especially pastoralists.' Bigge was a bureaucrat and, even though he identified sheep farming as the future of the colony's economy, a wider vision for the future was not on his agenda.[87]

William himself emerges as liberal and humane, understanding convicts' feelings about the country their labour was creating. If he was evasive in giving evidence to Bigge, it was not without reason. In public life he is revealed as continuing the eighteenth century's blurred distinctions between public and private property. That he exploited his official position, as did others, cannot be in doubt. But the complaints levelled against him were, if seen in proportion, minor compared to his achievements. His assigned servants were well treated, clothed and housed. He gave them incentives and assisted them towards tickets of leave and emancipation. Such liberal instincts would lead, in the 1820s, to his assuming a benevolent public role in the colony.

10   A Wife Drowned and a New Marriage

Rebecca Cox was drowned in a flood on the Hawkesbury River on 19 March 1819, the rising waters being so dangerous that her body was only able to be recovered by boat. Although this sad event ought to have burnt itself into the ancestral memory of her descendants, the *Memoirs* merely say: 'In 1819 Mrs William Cox died, leaving five sons. In 1821 William Cox married again.'[1] This follows a relatively lengthy discourse headed 'Over the Ranges' about the family's pastoral expansion beyond the mountains, which does, however, put his activities into perspective. It explains how he and William Lawson found the grazing land around Mudgee, being guided towards it by a 'blackfellow named Aaron', who had been terrified of the natives there. Lawson was appointed to succeed William as 'magistrate and commandant of the County of Westmoreland' on 23 August 1819, as recounted already.[2]

The two ex-officers, and their sons, both collaborated and competed in opening up that country over the ensuing decades. The historical arguments as to why development was slow beyond the mountains have centred on Macquarie's desire to the see land on the Cumberland Plain fully allocated first and his fear of convicts escaping. When the Governor made his semi-ceremonial journey along the Blue Mountains road in May 1815, he wrote in his journal about William's 'incredible labour and perseverance' in constructing it and referred to 'the New Discovered Country' beyond.[3] However, he proved restrained in allowing settlement there. His reluctance to allow expansion is shown by William's 2000 acre reward for building the road having still not been officially laid out when Bigge visited Bathurst in 1819.

The significant expansion westwards only took place between 1825 and 1830. As noted in Chapter 7, Chris Cunningham suggests that this was really due to lack of interest.[4] On the other hand, few men were needed to shepherd large flocks and stock had been allowed to be pastured temporarily beyond the mountains in 1816, after a drought.

Contrary to Cunningham's theory, when William Lawson acquired 30,000 acres near Bathurst in March 1819, he did so *before* taking over his duties. In terms of the pastoralists' territorial ambitions his letters are revealing. On 29 March 1819, he wrote to his agent in England, saying he had accepted the Bathurst appointment because: 'my sheep and stock are more of them over the mountains … I have increased my Estates and property to three thousand acres'. He had already been rewarded for the 1813 expedition with a land grant. Now he told his agent that he also had land well outside the official limits.[5]

Nor was Cox far behind in this expansion. Bigge noted that 'The more opulent settlers have begun to fence their estates with strong railings' and that

This gentleman [Cox at Bathurst] has erected farm buildings, and made inclosures [*sic*], in which he is making experiments with the artificial grasses [clover, lucerne, sainfoin]. It is here that he has considerable flocks of sheep, amounting to 5,000, and herds of cattle, which from the late accessions of other occupants, have been obliged to resort to new and more distant tracts. Twenty four flocks, of which ten belonged to Mr Cox, were distributed over the Bathurst Plains and adjoining valleys in the month of November 1819, and the whole number of sheep then amounted to 11,000.[6]

This was in spite of the land still not having been made over to William officially. The *Memoirs* name other families in that area that time. Hassall was on the McConnell plains, Lawson himself on the Macquarie Plains, while 'On the right bank of the river were the brothers West, Mackenzie, Cox [the Hereford Estate], Hawkins, Piper and the Rankin brothers, Kite, Lee and Smith. Some of them had small farms.'[7] In fact several, like John Piper, had a fair amount of land. What they were not were pioneers like Cox and Lawson. They simply aspired to be country gentlemen. This undermines the historians' claims that few people were interested in the land beyond the mountains, although they were relatively few.

Commissioner Bigge's account makes it transparently clear that it was the settlers who were pioneering development beyond the mountains, not the government. As the historian Geoffrey Blainey remarks: 'Successive governors faced the dilemma: should they foster the wool industry or should they prevent the sheep and their shepherds [from] … endangering the prison? In the end the sheep were victorious.'[8] Thus to a substantial extent it was the settlers, like William and his sons, who drove settlement policy in the colony.

In practice, the pastoralists were pursuing the only realistic economic development possible at that time, as was soon to be encouraged by Bigge's report on agriculture.[9] Pastoralism, it must be explained, was quite separate from the continuing allocation of smallholdings to ex-convicts, which had been official policy since the arrival of the First Fleet. It was also distinct from Governor Darling's small grants in the late 1820s to the native-born and to the ex-officer migrants who arrived after 1815 and were often regarded as squatters. If William came relatively late to the ranks of the pastoralists – and it could be argued that, due to his liberal actions, he never was a true Pure Merino – he had first to rehabilitate himself and secure an alternative income. The New Discovered Country was to be where he achieved his family's most lasting farming success.

Up to 1810 and the arrival of Governor Macquarie, land policy had been largely driven by acquisitive officers and officials. Six of the future landed gentry pastoralists had started off as New South Wales Corps officers: John Brabyn, Anthony Fenn Kemp, William Lawson, John Macarthur, John Piper and William Cox himself. Others included D'Arcy Wentworth, the medical officer, and Samuel Marsden, the chaplain. In the mid-1800s a new driver of land allocation had emerged: the patronage of the Secretaries of State for individuals. This continued for more than a decade, with grants proportional to the settler's 'means of cultivation'. In 1818 it was decided that prospective migrants, if they possessed £500 capital, could apply. John Ritchie records that 56 men did so in 1818, in 1819 applicants numbered 133, and in 1820 the number was 237, most saying that they 'wished to farm sheep'. As explained earlier, Lord Liverpool restrained the move. But it had helped to increase 'demands that New South Wales should be treated less as a gaol and more as a colony'.[10]

For most of his time Macquarie's energies had been concentrated on putting Sydney in order and laying out the five towns of Castlereagh, Pitt Town, Richmond, Wilberforce and Windsor. In doing the latter he was invariably accompanied by William, who became a leading contractor, building the Glebe House at Castlereagh and repairing the court house at Windsor (which he later completely rebuilt, also constructing the rectory there for Marsden). During this decade William's own holdings on the plain were supplemented in a chequerboard of *ad hoc* acquisitions. Several appear not have been too scrupulous, as was noted in the case of James Watson.[11] It is clear that William put pressure on him, as he did on a constable, to sell him a town plot.

The momentum of pastoralist expansion was only temporarily checked by Viscount Goderich, the Secretary of State, in 1831. Appreciating that the government had effectively lost control, he ordained that land should only be sold, not granted or leased. Until then, as John Darwin observes, 'local free settlers … forced the abandonment of London's attempts to restrain inland expansion'.[12]

From 1812 until 1827 the Secretary of State was that thoughtful politician, Earl Bathurst. He was dedicated to the goal of improvement and interested in the contribution the colonies could make to the mother country. This gave a measure of direction to the patronage, despite Bathurst combining his colonial responsibilities with being Minister at War, which kept him busy. New South Wales was far from being the most significant among many colonial possessions. The wars with France preoccupied the government from the mid-1790s until the defeat of Napoleon in 1815. Thereafter a severe depression, and unemployment, brought a rise in crime, during 'a period of dramatic economic and social change'.[13] The government was more interested in the colony as a repository for criminals than in its development, so Bathurst may have been something of a lone voice in the government on that score, even though it was he who commissioned Bigge's report to ascertain what was actually going on and wished the sanction of transportation for crime to be more effective.

In terms of the expansion of settlement, the most important event of the second decade of the new century had been the 1813 expedition across the Blue Mountains, although Blaxland, Lawson and Wentworth were motivated not so much by ambition for land as by problems on the Cumberland Plain. These included drought and caterpillars (army worm) eating the grass.[14] The three men were warmly praised by Macquarie for their 'enterprising exertions'. He granted them 1000 acres each on the other side in February 1814.[15] This was followed by the completion of the Blue Mountains road in January 1815, which was William Cox's great achievement and for which he had been rewarded.

A further factor hindering western settlement, quoted by W. C. Wentworth in 1819, was said to be the cost to users of the road, in terms of labour and time. It took ten days to bring carts or livestock from Bathurst to Sydney. Wentworth called the road 'excessively steep and dangerous', whilst admitting 'yet carts and waggons go up and down it continually'.[16] In 1831 Bathurst settlers were still complaining about the cost of bringing their produce and stock to market and asking for a rent reduction in consequence.[17] The crossing of the mountains and the building of the road did help to drive policy, but not fully until after Macquarie's departure, as statistics show. There were only around 120,000 sheep in the entire colony in 1820.[18] By 1830 there would be 504,775, mostly west of the mountains, and in the next five years wool exports would more than quadruple.[19] Bigge had recommended 'The growth of fine wool … [as] the principal, if not the only, source of productive industry'.[20] Sheep needed pasture and the graziers eventually obtained it.

Bigge recorded that in 1821 William held 4000 acres beyond the mountains, with 5200 sheep, while William Jnr had 1270 acres, George and Henry between them 4500 and young Edward 300.[21] Given Macquarie's restraints, they were doing pretty well. Nothing that William told Bigge about agriculture mentioned the plight of the Aborigines.

By 1821 some half a million acres in the colony were owned by free settlers. True, most of the arable land was farmed by some 2000 ex-convicts. But of those half million acres, only 32,273 were under arable cultivation. The hugely greater part was 'used for running sheep, cattle, horses, goats and swine'.[22] This matched Bigge's concept. He named William as one of 'the principal proprietors of sheep and cattle', along with Palmer Jnr, Throsby, Macarthur, Wentworth, Jamison and Marsden.[23] Placing convicts with such farmers, who resided on their own estates (which not all owners did), was the model for the colonial landed gentry, whose westward impetus greatly increased under Governor Brisbane, utilizing the mountain road.

After William was succeeded at Bathurst by William Lawson the two agreed upon a joint venture in an area known to the Aborigines as 'Munna' along the Cudgegong River, which they called Mudgee. Lawson also took up 6000 acres on the Cudgegong. George Cox kept a journal of his energetic first inspection of the country around Munna. He rode out on 30 November 1821, accompanied by Richard Lewis, his father's long-term supervisor, a settler named William Lee and four others 'including one Native man and five horses'. They left Hereford at 6.30 am, with George noting the character and potential of the country and drawing maps. They covered between 22 and 27 miles a day, reaching a place named Mudgee at 2 pm on Sunday 2 December. In that time they had covered 137 miles (220 km) and established two cattle runs.[24] Rolls comments: 'These men were instinctive bushmen. The maps they made might be wild, but they never lost themselves.'[25]

In January 1822, George and Henry Cox mustered 500 head of cattle, some belonging to William Lawson and some to their own father, and set out for the nearer part of Munna. Here they built huts and stockyards and the same again 20 miles further on at Guntawang, leaving in charge the convict stock overseer, Theophilus Chamberlain. Over time Lawson's sons, Nelson and William, and George and Henry Cox, acquired adjoining runs, over which they occasionally quarrelled and where they were attacked by Aborigines.[26] Mudgee soon attracted more settlers. Rowland Hassall, Richard Fitzgerald and James Badgery were among the first.[27] In 1820 Bigge had noticed that William had 'from the late accessions of other occupants, been obliged to resort to new and more distant tracts'.[28] Indeed William attempted to became a squatter far beyond Mudgee. This implies mounting settler pressures on land and the succeeding phases in the westward expansion, under Governors Brisbane and Darling, support this reading.

The first phase, under Brisbane, was of very short-term leases. There was much correspondence, for example on 'the circumstance of considerable Tracts of land coming into the possession of persons, who do not possess capital sufficient to cultivate and improve them'. Others held on to uncleared land in the hope of selling later at a profit.[29] The price to be charged was constantly debated. The leases produced a quick response from both Cox and Lawson. On 5 January 1822, Frederick Goulburn, the Colonial Secretary, who had taken over from Campbell,[30] wrote to William conveying Sir Thomas Brisbane's 'sanction for your occupation of all the land extending two geographical miles in every direction from the spot where the 32-30 parallel of South latitude cuts the Cudgegong River for the use of your flocks and herds as a grazing run'. The lease could be revoked with six months notice.[31] There was no mention of rent. A radius of two miles comprises a considerable extent of land, but this was now normal in the area. William Lawson was allotted a similar six monthly lease, adjacent to that given 'on the 5th January last to William Cox'.[32] When the six month leases were asserted to give inadequate tenure, Brisbane issued annual tickets permitting longer occupation.

By Brisbane's time, expansion west of the mountains was becoming something of a Cox family business, as it was for the Lawsons and a few others. Lawson, originally a New South Wales Corps officer, had been the surveyor on the 1813 crossing of the Blue Mountains, as a reward for which he was given his first 1000 acres west of the mountains. After retiring from being superintendent at Bathurst, he settled at his mansion at Prospect Hill, near Springwood, on the Cumberland Plain side of the mountains, and called it Veterans Hall. Eventually, his estates totalled at least 195,500 acres.[33] The Lawson sons managed their father's interests beyond the mountains, as did William Cox's. It had been on Lawson pére's advice that George Cox took up land around Mudgee. The 1822 Muster shows that William Cox's holding had risen to 6955 acres, of which 3500 were cleared, with 5525 sheep. His sons' holdings had not greatly increased.[34] But the family enterprise was central to William's thinking. Although he had a hierarchical view of society, his actions as related throughout this biography demonstrate that he had quickly appreciated that, in practical terms, the confining English tradition of entail, which placed an estate in the hands of trustees, and primogeniture, which passed it to the eldest son, had no reality in the colony. In New South Wales it appeared that land was unlimited and pastoralists were creating dynasties within a generation, which was impossible in England.

Brisbane's tickets were superseded by Bathurst's concept that purchases and leases should be allowed in equal measure, while he also wanted the allocation of Crown lands to contribute more financially through sales. He was now, in 1824, following up his emissary, Bigge's, proposals regarding the alienation of land and a pastoral economy, whilst under considerable domestic financial pressure. At home, in England, between 1820 and 1822, the collapse in the price of wheat and inflation had forced tax reductions and 'exacerbated the ongoing fiscal crisis'.[35] But although Bathurst wanted to help the colony pay its way, his orders became a confusing factor. They were passed on in a long letter from John Oxley, the surveyor general, to Major Ovens, the Colonial Secretary, in May 1825.

There were to be two 'Distinct Classes' of settlers, 'the first class obtaining their Lands by purchase, the second by Grant ... under certain limitations'.[36] One historian comments: 'In giving priority to sales [as opposed to grants] Earl Bathurst sought to increase the prospect of land being employed productively'.[37] Among the limitations were that no land could be alienated as a grant until it had been on the market for six months and not purchased. The second class of settler was to be apportioned land in proportion to the 'Extent of Capital' intended to be spent on bringing the land into cultivation. But Oxley himself commented that there were no 'important or essential' differences between the new provisions and the previous rules.[38] Matters were further complicated through an earlier provision regarding convicts. Brisbane had adopted a suggestion made by Oxley that emigrants should take one convict off the store for every 100 acres granted them. But from 1827 to 1833 the demand for assignees exceeded supply by about 200 percent.[39] Brisbane may have created this situation deliberately by reducing the number available for assignment.[40]

The way in which Bathurst's ideas complicated matters is also shown by the lengthy correspondence with Darling, Brisbane's successor, over several years. Thus on 22 July 1826 the Governor reported the Executive Council's fear that land having to be on the market for six months would cause 'the total ruin of Persons who Came to the Colony as Settlers in the full and well grounded expectation of obtaining Grants of Land immediately after their arrival'.[41] In September 1826 he was expressing the 'expediency of deviating from the Instructions ... in the case of Settlers ... wishing to purchase'.[42] Darling also raised the question of whether land should be allocated in 'the immediate neighbourhood of the established Counties' or only anywhere 'within the range of the Settled Districts'.[43] William Cox tried to exploit the former idea, as will be seen.

Further expansion followed when the Nineteen Counties were defined within the 'prescribed area'.[44] Holdings were to be in blocks of 1920 acres. But there was a lack of surveyors and the Secretary of State sent instructions allowing land to be allocated before it had been surveyed and valued. On

16 October 1828 Darling allowed unoccupied land adjacent to leases to be taken over, although half the applications were rejected, because the lands were not adjacent. The underlying story of the official letters is one of continual settler pressure on the boundaries of permitted settlement shown on the map on page 136.

William Cox asked, on 5 June 1825 if, as an official surveyor was at the Cudgegong River, he could purchase for his son Edward 'two thousand acres at Dabee on this river and higher up than the stations furnished out by his brothers George and Henry'.[45] Dabee was near Rylstone. This relied on the requirement for settlers to prove That they possessed at least £500 of capital as well as paying their own passages. William wrote to HE Sir Thomas Brisbane:

> I have the honour to state to Your Excellency that my son Edward Cox, who is arrived from England as a Free Settler, has applied to me as a reference as to his means of bringing a farm into a proper state of cultivation. In answer to which I beg to inform Your Excellency that independent of his own income [? may have meant capital], which is worth upwards of a thousand pounds sterling that I intend adding the same sum in stock to that amount, making in the whole upwards of two thousand pounds sterling.[46]

Edward was still only 20 years old and had been sent to Rawdon in Yorkshire at 16 for five years to learn sheep farming. In calling him a free settler William was realigning the truth, as he had when William and James had arrived as boys. Edward had been born in the colony at Windsor in May 1805 and was not a 'free settler'. Although he did acquire the estate, which he named Rawdon, his true home was at Mulgoa, where at that time he was living in the unostentatious Cottage which William had constructed in 1811 for his sons. He later built the elegant mansion called Fernhill.

The next year an attempt by William to stretch the limits of occupation for his family failed, revealing a gap between the old tickets of occupation and the new leases and sales. On 9 December 1826 he wrote to Alexander

McLeay, the new Colonial Secretary saying that:

> the whole of the Tickets of Occupation, occupied by Myself and
> sons, in the Districts of Mudgee and [illegible] & to the N. East of
> Bathurst, having been taken up [with] Grants or Purchases by different
> individuals, I find it necessary to send my young cattle to a place called
> by the Natives 'Binnea', it lay about N. N. East from Mudgee & is
> supposed to be distant from thence about 50 to 60 miles.[47]

The surveyor, Oxley, quickly pointed out that Binnea was 'considerably
to the northward of the limits within which settlers are permitted to
settle' and 'if the distance from Mudgee be accurately stated the situation
requested by Mr Cox is on the SW side of Liverpool Plains'.[48] It is worth
commenting that although William had laboured hard and long in 1817
and 1818 to equip Oxley's expeditions, there is no hint that he attempted
to call in favours in return.

Oxley was writing only a few weeks after the problem of unauthorized
occupation of Crown lands had caused Darling to create the new 'limits
of location' on 5 September. Settlers were only allowed 'depasturing
licences' within these limits. But the pressures from them when they
saw sparsely wooded open grazing land ahead of them forced a policy
change only three years later, although no settler was permitted to
receive more than 2560 acres. William Cox, William Jnr and William
Lawson were among those who applied for 2560 acre grants. The end
result was that eventually Earl Bathurst ceased to insist that purchasers
should have priority.[49] The 1826 regulations had been promulgated
'until His Majesty's pleasure shall be known'; those of 1829 were issued
'for the present'. This had the stamp of yielding to pressure, not of
permanence. Despite Bathurst's intentions, by 1831 Darling had only
allotted 496,270 acres out of 1,700,000 acres of officially alienated
land.[50] The good intentions had been almost completely subverted by
their own complexities, from which the Coxes benefited.

The grants brought conflict between neighbouring settlers as the result of land having been inadequately surveyed, if surveyed at all. Lawson had leased land adjoining Cox's on the Tulbragar, 35 kilometres west of Mudgee. In March 1830 William's overseer, Michael Lahy, found a notice signed by Nelson Lawson. It read: 'Within one month of the date of this you are to remove the heifer herd of Mr Cox in your charge now despasturing at Cox's Point as the land is rented to me'. The herd was eight miles from Nelson Lawson's stockyards and William promptly asked the Colonial Secretary if he was allowed to come near another person's grant 'when there were large quantities of land in various directions adjoining Lawson's land'.[51] The dispute then seems to have died.

In 1831 the new Secretary of State, Viscount Goderich, concluded that the way in which land was legally transferred (in distinction to the squatter occupations) was unsatisfactory. 'The scheme of deriving a Revenue from quit rents,' he wrote to the Governor, 'seems to me also to be condemned both by reason and experience ... the great bulk of the land, on which they are due, continues unimproved' and 'large tracts of land' were 'being appropriated by persons unable to improve and cultivate them.' Accordingly he ordered that: 'in future, no land shall be disposed of otherwise than by sale'. There would be a minimum price, but the highest bidder would 'in all cases be entitled to the preference'. The revenue would help finance 'the emigration [to the colony] of the unemployed British labourers, which would be of real and essential service'.[52]

This followed the ideas of a most unusual man, a former junior consular officer called Gibbon Wakefield. During three years of imprisonment for abducting a 15-year-old heiress, Wakefield had begun asking his fellow prisoners about their offences and devised a system for colonization. In his *Letter from Sydney* of 1829 he had argued that there was a chaotic granting of free land and that: 'if settlement were concentrated, waste lands of the Crown could be readily sold and the proceeds applied to the emigration of labourers ... ensuring a balanced, fruitful clinical society'.[53]

This sponsored emigration for unemployed English farm labourers was begun in the early 1830s. At the time of Goderich's order Governor Bourke had not been persuaded. His biographer, Hazel King, writes: 'The great territorial expansion of settlement in New South Wales during Bourke's governorship had been carried out on the initiative of the colonists themselves ... The Governor was able to convince the home government ... that it was wiser to make a virtue of necessity and try to guide and control a movement which it could not prevent.'[54] William Cox, with his sons, was one of those displaying that initiative, despite his advancing years and the serious illness he had been stricken by in 1828.

As might have been expected, Goderich's orders were not received well by the Pure Merinos, who would now only be able to expand by buying and were going to be expected to pay the immigrant labourers, instead of enjoying cheap convict labour. In response to Goderich, a committee, uniting the exclusives, the emancipists and the relatively recent colonial bourgeoisie, petitioned the Governor about the level of quit rents. Its 52 signatories of both generations included William Cox, his sons William and James, the Macarthurs, John Blaxland and the Lawsons. 'The value of land,' the petitioners claimed, 'must depend upon the demand, and the quantity to be disposed of ... The Interior ... discovers exhaustless tracts of land ... suitable only for grazing.' The more territory there was the less its value would be. That, and the reduced price of stock, would ruin farmers if the quit rents were not reduced.[55] Darling received the petition in April 1831, but did not forward it to Goderich until September.[56] By then 'the grumbles, groans and apprehensions of the landowners had swollen into a roar of anxiety.'[57] If the reforms put a brake on expansion, they certainly did not halt it. William Cox continued buying land until his death in 1837. In the longer term the land sales did provide revenue for assisting immigrants.

Although Francis Forbes, the Chief Justice, had supported the protest it was to no avail.[58] A government notice of 16 September 1831 decreed that 'persons desirous of completing the purchase at five shillings per acre, of the whole, or any portion ... not less than one square mile [640 acres], shall pay in portions'. Characteristically, William lost little time in applying. He asked, under an old warrant from Governor Brisbane of 3 May 1825, to purchase 4000 acres, of which he intended to retain 2560, or four square miles.[59] Land was being assessed in square miles, or the equivalent acreage. Next, on 16 April 1833, William was granted 640 acres (one square mile) of the government reserve at Mudgee 'bounded south by the Cudgegong river, east by Mr George Cox's 4,000 acres'.[60] William Jnr made similar approaches. Notwithstanding Goderich, the late 1830s were, in Atkinson's words, 'a time of great economic expansion … the Macarthurs themselves had never been richer; they were leaders among the landed gentlemen'. The Coxes also prospered, unaware of the disasters to follow in the 1840s.[61]

Nor did the Goderich reforms stop the parallel pressures from the much loathed (by the exclusives) squatters. The exclusives had their capital tied up in their land, whereas the squatters had theirs in cattle and sheep, having taken the land for nothing. The initial squatter image was first applied to poorer farmers who made use of vacant land, both within and beyond the limits of location. But the use of the term broadened from its original pejorative sense. By the time when the great age of pastoral occupation began, around 1835, the term 'squatter' covered a wide range of people, from predatory ex-convicts robbing their neighbours to such respectable immigrants as the younger sons of the gentry, officers of the army and navy, clergymen, lawyers and doctors, even a few women, who all considered themselves to be, or aspired to be, gentry.

The situation was complicated by many exclusives having themselves been partial squatters. In 1834 Chief Justice Forbes himself, who had stock depastured on the Liverpool Plains, beyond the limits of location, told Bourke plainly: 'I am a squatter in the District'. Not many exclusives would have been so honest.[62] In 1836 Bourke sought to legalize squatting beyond the limits of location.[63] Competing territorially with squatters for land, and for political ascendancy with emancipists, the Pure Merinos were slowly eclipsed, although not until after Bourke's day. 'It was the next Governor, Sir George Gipps, who was to see the immigrants and the native-born absolutely in the ascendant, although the transition was becoming evident even in 1835.'[64]

Obviously either obtaining land from government, or squatting on it, was not the only way of expanding an estate. Making direct purchases from individuals was less problematic. As always, William Cox seized opportunities. In the 1820s his old friend John Piper had been earning more as the Naval Officer at Sydney than the Governor did and had accumulated extensive properties, including 2000 acres 'at Bathurst'.[65] He got into financial trouble in 1827, through deficiencies in his collection of customs duties and his chairmanship of the Bank of New South Wales. On 29 June 1827, having become one of Piper's trustees, William wrote suggesting paying off £500 of his debts in exchange for land, saying he was glad 'the lands were all sold ... Vaucluse not selling would have thrown us out.' This meant Piper was spared having to sell his elegant Henrietta Villa at Point Piper.[66]

On 11 October 1832 William wrote from his Hereford farm at Bathurst about an exchange of land 'from the other side of the water', presumably to acquire it. He was in touch again on 24 March 1835. These friendly letters always began 'My dear Piper' and concluded with family news.[67] As well as helping to save Piper, the purchases resulted in an enlargement of the Cox estates west of the mountains. As mentioned earlier, by no means all the settlers around Bathurst were pioneers. Piper, like Mackenzie of Dockairne and others, had simply aspired to be country gentlemen.[68] There was even a Bathurst Hunt, whose riders wore green coats and chased dingoes.

The frequent changes in the way land was allocated in the first three decades of the nineteenth century meant that there was no standard pattern by which estates were accumulated. There was no inherited land, apart from Jamison's original 500 acres. John Macarthur's vision had been of 'an extensive wool exporting country controlled by men of real capital, with "estates of at least 10,000 acres each"'.[69] But few early settlers possessed substantial capital, in the way the Blaxlands had done. Most collected land piece by piece, like William Cox, who was more typical of his generation, with his 29 different plots as well as various houses and urban plots.[70] But this was misleading. He had worked collectively with his sons in a family enterprise from as early as 1804. The family's Mudgee holdings alone eventually came to 100,000 acres. Quite a number of pastoralists were bankrupted by the 1840s depression, including John Blaxland's estate (he had died by then). Yet the landed gentry did not collapse. The Coxes themselves suffered, but survived, having a great measure of determination in their genes.

Early on during this turbulent time, just as Bigge was leaving the colony, William, bereft of his first wife for two years, remarried. His new bride was Anna Blatchford. She was 32 years younger than him and they were married by Samuel Marsden a mere month after she arrived in Sydney. A copy of the marriage certificate provided by the (now) Cathedral Church of St John Parramatta shows that the wedding on 23 January 1821 was by special licence.[71] Given that William was a contemporary with whom he had both collaborated and quarrelled for many years, Marsden might have mentioned the occasion in his correspondence (now in the Mitchell Library), but he was evidently too preoccupied with

St John's Cathedral, Parramatta, location of William's second marriage. Mrs Macquarie designed the towers, copying Reculver church in Kent (Author's photo)

missionary work in New Zealand. The witnesses are given as George Cox and Mary Ellen Lenouf, the latter an incorrect transcribing of Leroux, the family with whom Anna had arrived from Hobart aboard the *Queen Charlotte* on 18 December 1820. On the way out there from Sydney the brig had set a record run of 48 hours. Returning, she sailed from Port

Dalrymple with a cargo of 20 tons of salted meat, 60 bushels of wheat and four passengers. They were Captain Watkins of the 48th Regiment, Lieutenant Leroux of the same, Mrs Leroux and 'Miss Blackford' (a frequent misspelling of her surname).[72]

Anna was the daughter of Joseph Blachford, a London merchant, and Susan Pike, and was born at Brading in the Isle of Wight in 1796. Her gravestone in New Zealand has inexplicably been altered to suggest that she died at the age of 80 and so would have been born in 1789. Although Mowle's *Genealogical History of the Pioneering Families of Australia* gives this date, the Isle of Wight records show that her parents were only married at Newport on 22 April 1793 and contemporaries commented on how young she was. She died on 26 August 1869. It is said in the same Cox family document that she was both the niece of George Wilson Leroux, and that she was Mrs Leroux's sister, but Mowle has her being the niece. It is more likely that she was the sister. She had travelled out with them three years earlier, when he was posted to Hobart as part of the 48th Regiment, taking over duties in the colony. Van Diemen's Land was then administered as an integral part of New South Wales. They had reached Port Jackson on 30 August 1817 and the *Hobart Gazette* reported their arrival at Hobart on 27 September.

Leroux himself became District Coroner at Launceston. In 1820 he was also the Naval Officer (in charge of customs duties) for which he received a barrack allowance.[73] He was bound to have been in contact with James Cox for two reasons. James was a magistrate at Port Dalyrymple in 1820 and was also a merchant supplying meat to the army garrison. It is a reasonable presumption that James provided an introduction to his father when Leroux was posted to the mainland.

The 48th Regiment continued to form the colonial garrison until 1824. Leroux must have been provided with accommodation, where Anna would have stayed. The family memoir quotes a letter from Robert Murray to D'Arcy Wentworth, saying:

Old Mr Cox has got a licence to be married to Lt Leroux's wife's sister of the 48th Regiment. They landed from the Derwent a fortnight ago. He saw her three times, approved and they consented She is not yet twenty.[74]

Anna was a lot older than that, but the rapidity of the engagement is unquestionable. There is an often quoted account of her elaborate sarsanet wedding dress, with a lace pelerine, in a letter to Elizabeth Piper dated 21 December 1829, but it unquestionably refers to the 1828 wedding of her sister, who had followed her out and married Francis Beddek, the Windsor solicitor.[75] Governor Darling's despatch of 22 December 1828 shows that he had granted Anna's sister and another lady, a Miss Wylde, 'a Reserve of two Square Miles of Land each on their Marriage, subject to His Majesty's confirmation … Miss Blachford is sister to Mrs Cox, the wife of the second Magistrate in point of seniority in the Territory, and is married to a very respectable professional Gentleman of the name of Beddek, who arrived here last year … the measure will, in this Community, be attended with many beneficial consequences.'[76] Beddek was Windsor's first solicitor. It was commented wryly that the area needed one, the locals being so disputatious. He became entwined with the Cox family, living for a time in The Cottage at Mulgoa and eventually drafting William's will. It seems from the 'Reminiscences' of Edward's wife, Jane Maria, that their mother also came to join the Coxes. If Leroux's wife was indeed another sister, she must have written very encouraging letters home about colonial life. Anna herself, because of her youth, quickly made an impression on the way of life at Clarendon. The number of servants was increased, William built a new and elegant dining room as an addition to the house, and – as the *Sydney Gazette* recorded – they began to give parties and dances in a way that William never had before.

11   Dispossessing the Aborigines

Inescapably, William Cox and other landowners became involved in conflicts with the Aborigines, when as settlers they moved into territory which was traditionally occupied by the 'natives' and on the natural fruits of which they depended for their living. This had a second dimension for settlers who, like Cox, were magistrates responsible for the security of their districts and had to deal with attacks by Aborigines – and who often could have done more to prevent settler outrages against them. The fighting was brutal, and reprisals by Aborigines were savage and indiscriminate.

The potential for conflict had been recognized at the start by Governor Phillip, who strove to understand the Aborigines. He had been ordered to establish contact with them and, in the words of the *Australian Dictionary of Biography*, 'proposed to treat the Aboriginals kindly and to establish harmonious relations with them' in accordance with his orders and, undoubtedly, with his nature.[1] He placed two native men, Colebe and Bennelong – the latter to feature prominently in early accounts of the colony – in his personal care. Any among the very few settlers who interfered with the Aborigines' traditional pursuits were liable to heavy punishment.

However, the Governor was eventually forced to take punitive action against the natives after he was himself speared in the arm at a meeting with some at Manly Cove. It is unclear whether he realized that the spear used against him was not a fearsome killing spear, studded with sharp stones, which could not be withdrawn without inflicting great and fatal damage, but was of a lighter kind that gave a warning wound. It says much for his character that the attack did not cause him to abandon his policy. But even the small area of 3400 acres (1392 ha) which Phillip alienated for white settlement was sufficient to cause conflict. In consequence he ordered plots to be set out side by side, rather than with ten acre spaces between them as planned, since the Aborigines could hide therein. This illustrates that, even with the best of white intentions, conflict became inevitable as settlement expanded. Archibald Bell much later told Commissioner Bigge that the natives 'are naturally mild, inoffensive and indolent, but pertubaceous in seeking revenge which is indiscriminately visited upon the first white man they meet with.'[2] William was to experience the results of this at first hand in 1816.

Thus from the beginning a central question regarding the acquisition of land in the colony was how the government and the settlers saw semi-nomadically occupied territory. The legal concept of *terra nullius* – land belonging to no one – had not yet been formulated. The historical commentator Inga Clendinnen points out that: 'During those first years … only a handful of First Fleet observers began to grasp the great fact of the Australians' [Aborigines'] intimate dependence on what the British continued to think of as a "wild", indeed empty, land.'[3] It has been argued that 'there was no legal doctrine maintaining that uninhabited land could be regarded as ownerless' and that 'early legal interpretation was supported by government policy which recognized indigenous title to the land.'[4]

There is little in the recorded attitudes of a succession of governors to support that claim. Their aim was to see the colony's lands developed. King did tell Bligh that he considered the Aborigines to be 'the real Proprietors of the Soil' and tried to protect their 'persons and property.'[5] Macquarie wrote to Bathurst in October 1814: 'Those Natives who dwell Near Sydney or other principal Settlements, live in a State of perfect Peace, Friendliness and Sociality with the Settlers … it seems only to require the fostering Hand of Time … to bring these poor Un-enlightened people into an important Degree of Civilisation.'[6] Before he left he told the Secretary of State that New South Wales had 'been converted from a barren Wilderness of Woods into a thriving British colony'. Lord Bathurst's land regulations of 1825 contained 'no mention of the Aboriginal people ... it continued to be assumed that they had no prior claim on the land'.[7]

This was William Cox's basic attitude. Although he did express sympathy on occasion for the Aborigines' predicament in becoming dependent on settlers for food, as the result of having been dispossessed, none of his recorded remarks support the idea that they had any right to the land. Nor was it understood then, which is fully recognized today, that in Richard Broome's words: 'Aboriginals viewed land symbolically as the land created by great ancestors ... labour [thus] reflected the deepest meanings of life and one's place in it'.[8] Their labour, as William saw it when employing them at Mulgoa, did however deserve fair pay and treatment, not the exploitation to which they were often subject when given work.

There had been incidents on the Hawkesbury long before William's time, including settlers gratuitously killing Aborigines. The new farms at what was than known as Mulgrave Place in the 1790s had increasingly restricted the access of the indigenous Darug people to waterways and traditional sources of food. These included wild yams, honey, tree grubs, fish, eels, birds such as quail, and of course kangaroos. Governor Hunter had refused to punish the few taken captive, recognizing them as victims, but King was the first governor to meet Darug elders to discuss grievances caused by settlement. Although they asked King to be able to use the ungranted areas around the rivers, this proved impossible in practice due to settlement pressures and the Aborigines responded by seizing settlers' corn and provisions and killing the settlers themselves in most brutal ways. It was left to the farmer to decide when he could reasonably shoot at Aboriginal raiding parties to protect his own and his family's lives.[9] Grace Karskens comments that 'the Hawkesbury was in a state of war for years, from 1799 to 1805, while violence broke out again on the Nepean to the south in 1814–16'.[10]

On the Hawkesbury there was a particularly savage outbreak in late May 1816. The bodies of three white men were discovered, 'badly disfigured', and probably killed by Aborigines.[11] William received instructions from the Governor dated 1 July and 6 July and as a result made military dispositions to deal with the problem. He informed Macquarie on 11 July of his preliminary dispositions:

> went to Capt Forrests's farm to get a place for Sgt Broadfoot's party to sleep in case they came that evening ... Finding no shelter they went to the left bank of the Grose and have now a position a little below Mr Bell's in an empty house that commands the ridge leading to the roads north and west, as well as the Grose.

William's writing was as neat and controlled as ever. He folded his letter three times so as to fit into an 'envelope' made of one piece of paper about six inches wide and four inches deep, marked 'H M Service'. Macquarie recorded down the side "Recd 12 July 16. Answered 13 ditto.' The original is in the Mitchell Library. The text continues explaining an incident that was typical:

> I have now the honour of reporting to Your Excellency that I formed a party on Saturday last to go in quest of the Hoschen [sic] Natives and sent two Constables and two friendly natives as guides [names given] and on Monday morning they were joined by Mr Luttrell and seven other men making 12 ... On Tuesday they proceeded towards Singleton's mile and in the evening information was brought to Mr Bell's that the Natives had been to Joseph Hobson's farm and murdered him. I received this information at one o'clock on Tuesday morning and after directing [the] Sgt and his men to get the track of the Natives, I went the same route with the Sergeant, but they lost track of them and I deemed it prudent to drop the pursuit.

On the Wednesday morning the coroner's inquest on the body was held. William attended and 'explained Your Excellency's determination as to the four Natives ... and gave directions who to give the alarm to in case they saw or heard of any Natives. I also settled my plan with the Sergeant.' Macquarie replied on Friday 19 July, in haste judging from the handwriting, accepting William's advice.[12] It appears that the natives were not caught.

William explained after the inquest that 'Hobson was a very hard working, quiet man and always on the best of terms with the Natives. His death wound was on the head and he was also stripped quite naked. He had removed his family after the murder of the 2 stockmen.' He further told Macquarie that 'The Natives here appear so determined on mischief that very prompt measures are necessary or the Settlers and Stockmen will be murdered in future'. The stockmen are likely to have been convicts. The Bell mentioned was presumably Archibald Bell, who from 1812 to 1818 commanded a detachment of the 73rd Regiment at Windsor and had a property named Belmont at Richmond. It seems odd that he was not involved directly in the operation, although this was evidently a job for the magistrate (Bell was appointed as one in 1820, with a salary and a house). Very probably he had the murder of Hobson in mind when he told Bigge that the natives took revenge on the first white man they encountered.

During 1816 a number of orders were sent out by the Colonial Secretary regarding 'Aboriginal activities', notably on 9 May when a proclamation was circulated to all JPs about 'Aboriginal hostility' and on 26 July 'respecting the sanguinary Disposition and Outrages still manifested by the black Natives of the Colony'. On 19 October the need for protection against the natives was certified and on 2 November a circular was sent concerning the cessation of hostilities and the treatment of natives, which was also sent to the Aborigines themselves.[13] This marked the end of that series of conflicts. The precise cause of the 1816 conflict was not identified, although there had been a brutal and unnecessary attack on an Aboriginal boy by settlers. But provocation was seen completely differently by settlers and Aborigines, as Bell explained.

These events may well have conditioned William's attitudes at Bathurst in 1824, detailed below. This author's reading of events, taken amongst other sources from records of meetings, is that when conflict became inevitable on a larger scale around Bathurst in the next decade, William's view was again pragmatic: effectively a version of stick and carrot, of attack followed by negotiation. Indeed the 1816 incidents took place when he was already dividing his time between the Hawkesbury and Bathurst, where he was the commandant. What took place at Bathurst has become extremely controversial to historians, even if it was not at the time.

The Aborigines' predicament was sometimes recognized by settlers. Thus William was one of 15 men, headed by Sir John Jamison and including the lieutenant governor and the judges, who petitioned Macquarie on 24 August 1819 about the formation of a 'Society for promoting Christian knowledge amongst the Aborigines'. It is not clear if this was related to the Benevolent Society of New South Wales, of which Macquarie was patron in 1818.[14] In their petition the residents said that their long experience in the 'Interior' made them aware of the 'important necessity' of doing something to raise the Natives from their 'degraded and very wretched state ... not only on principles of justice but of humanity to the Natives, who have been deprived of great parts of their means of subsistence by our clearing the lands of its timber, by which they were [provided with?] the greater part of their animals' food'.[15] The petitioners referred to the Native Institution of 1814, founded by Macquarie, which had educated Aboriginal children, although William was not involved in this. The institution only educated a half dozen boys and half a dozen girls, who one by one deserted it, so that it failed. The land question does not seem to have been pursued by the society, possibly because of the speed with which events developed.

By the early 1820s matters had become far from happy west of the mountains. Aborigines were often killed or taken hostage without any effective trial resulting, although Saxe Bannister, the attorney general in 1824, recorded that Macquarie had once caused a white man to be executed for murdering a native.[16] The simple truth was that the Bathurst plains were not expansive and fertile enough to accommodate two hugely different cultures without hostility. Inevitably, William's sons became involved in attempts to recover stock stolen from their increasing landholdings. On 7

February 1822 William reported from Clarendon to Governor Brisbane that 'my son Mr Henry Cox is this instant returned from Bathurst ... with information that the Natives have driven away the persons who was [sic] in charge of the stock at the river "Cudgegong"'. They had let the cattle out of the yards and got possession of the sheep.[17] There had been no killings.

On this occasion George Cox had asked the sergeant at Bathurst to allow four soldiers to return with him and deal with the problem, but the sergeant had refused. 'My son [George] was therefore driven to the necessity of arming 5 or 6 persons ... and set off with them.' William's letter continued and he asked the Governor for soldiers 'to protect our people and property'.[18] The soldiers do not appear to have been sent, while George's action would have been spontaneous. To have obtained orders from his father would have taken ten days, Clarendon being five days ride on horseback. But that he did sometimes receive orders from his father was shown by William's evidence to Bigge in November 1819, when he told the Commissioner that soon after Lawson's appointment as superintendent: 'I wrote to my son Mr George Cox directing him to withdraw our Flocks from a place called Swallow Creek ... to be shorn.'[19] The transmission of orders from father to son, if completely normal at the time, has since become an element in the 1824 historians' controversy.

In 1823 William wrote to Goulburn, the Colonial Secretary, saying that he had received a letter from George who 'had been to visit our distant cattle stations at Mudgee and I have the pleasure to say the natives had continued friendly with our people'. He had conversations with about 25 of them on 'the late disturbances' and urged them to go Bathurst to talk further, which they agreed to do. William concluded this letter by hoping 'that no more deaths will occur in retaliation, it being of so much importance to the public'.[20] This episode can be construed as showing William approving of violence to recover stolen cattle, but also wanting conciliation to be effective. This reading of it is confirmed by meetings that took place after the situation had deteriorated in 1824 and seems to be more characteristic of the older generation of settlers than the younger.

After the conflict at Bathurst worsened William Cox chaired a meeting of stockholders, including Samuel Marsden and William Lawson, at Sydney on 3 June 1824. They sent a memorial to Brisbane 'representing the late Calamitous events at Bathurst and praying for assistance'. Their memorial was signed by William Cox and said:

> Your Memorialists having learnt with feelings of horror and consternation the late disastrous accounts from Bathurst and in which no fewer than seven individuals, the servants of your Memorialists have been barbarously murdered and the other Shepherds and stockmen compelled … to desert their charges and leave the entire property of your Memorialists unprotected.

They asked for 'prompt and effective assistance'.[21]

A month later, on 16 July, at a meeting of magistrates called by the Governor and attended by William, Lawson and seven others, similar views were expressed, but if anything more strongly. They considered that since the previous November 'the black natives in the Districts about Bathurst, from some unhappy cause, not as yet ascertainable, have been incited by some of the chiefs or others to assail at different periods the huts in occupation by the stockmen of the numerous stock proprietors … to kill sheep and cattle'. These 'Native attacks' were 'acting upon a determined spirit, rather of general plunder than personal revenge' and 'measures of strong, sufficient and <u>immediate</u> resistance' were needed. 'A large military force' should bring the natives 'to a state of due subjection', although the magistrates also envisaged that 'Upon the happy restoration of a harmless spirit, the Chiefs of each Tribe have given to them some personal Badge of distinct and be victualled at the Public Expense' and be occasionally given supplies such as blankets.[22]

This approach, advanced by senior magistrates, explains both the highly charged atmosphere at Bathurst during the 'Black War' and much that happened during it, with a younger generation of impatient settlers on the spot, where talk of 'massacres' became widespread. Furthermore, William's stock overseer at Bathurst was the 34-year-old life sentence convict Theophilus Chamberlain, who was noted for his brutality to Aborigines.[23] The stock overseers in pastoral areas enjoyed considerable independence, even though they were usually convicts, and their freedom of action was boosted by their having horses.[24] From the sequence of events it is evident that Chamberlain exercised his own discretion to a very considerable extent and that he was mounted. William, whilst legally responsible for this employee, was not in a position to control him from Clarendon, although George was.

The commandant at Bathurst was now a Major Morisset, who had succeeded Lawson in 1823.[25] He reported on 25 June to the Colonial Secretary that Chamberlain, following up the spearing of cattle, had encountered a party of natives who would have killed him had he not been mounted.[26] Morisset responded by sending a detachment under a sergeant to arrest 'a mob of black natives', but the soldiers failed to find them.[27] In July he asked for mounted troops to pursue Aborigines, which was refused. When Bathurst eventually heard of it he was so angered at the idea of using cavalry against natives that Morisset was relieved of his command in 1825.[28] The events which followed included what amounted to a massacre by Chamberlain in August.

The circumstances were that the overseer and his men had pursued the thieves of cattle belonging to Cox and Lawson. The whites had been set upon, whereupon they dismounted, tied their horses together, opened fire and then charged the Aborigines with the bayonet, killing three at the first skirmish and sixteen at the end.[29] It seems extraordinary that they were allowed to have bayonets, as if they were soldiers. John Connor records that about a week before Morisset's expedition of September 1824 passed through Mudgee:

> a man named Chamberlane ... and two stockmen killed sixteen Wiradjuri, probably all men ... for a small group like the 'Mudgee tribe', it was a high percentage casualty rate for a single action ... followed in swift succession by the total disruption to food gathering caused

by Morisset's parties [it] would have convinced the Wiradjuri that negotiating peace was the only option to ensure their survival.[30]

This they began to do in October. The delay was because 'they were clans … if a major issue had to be discussed runners would be sent out to other clans for a national conference'.[31]

Articles in the *Sydney Gazette* show that there was much general talk about 'extermination' of the Aborigines during 1824. In October it was reported that the district was 'engaged in an exterminating war'.[32] Earlier, on 24 June a young Lawson son wrote to his brother Nelson, who was in England, saying of the Aborigines: 'We have now commenced hostilities against them, in consequence of their killing a great number of shepherds and stockmen, but afraid we shall never exterminate them'.[33] An accusation was made by a missionary against William Cox that he had advocated the same. The accusation has been frequently repeated and discussed academically, although the alleged incident does not seem to have aroused indignation at the time, if it took place at all. For the purposes of this biography, it is necessary to relate the full events, so far as they are known, although they are commonplace to historians of the period.

In June 1824 the missionary L. E. Threlkeld, as quoted by the author Niel Gunson, stated: 'A gentleman (Mr Cox) of large property recommended at a Publick meeting … that the best measure towards the blacks would be to "Shoot them all and manure the ground with them"'. That the 'Mr Cox' was of large property implies that he was William, while Gunson identifies him positively in his edition of Threlkeld's *Reminiscences*.[34] No date was specified for this remark.[35] Furthermore, the missionary was not there himself; although the attorney-general, Saxe Bannister, was.[36] Yet there is no mention of the incident in Bannister's own account of the colony.[37] Leaving aside Threlkeld's long delay in reporting the alleged speech, the missionary was given to exaggeration. Marsden later felt obliged to write him in 1826, referring to correspondence with the London Missionary Society, saying 'I cannot but observe that your language is very strong; and I should apprehend, would give unnecessary pain to the Society'.[38] Both the episode and the attribution must be treated with caution, especially since no first name was given by Threlkeld for the 'Mr Cox'.

Despite its vagueness, Threlkeld's accusation is taken up by Jan Kociumbas in her *Oxford History of Australia*, with a series of often inaccurate references. She writes:

> In spite of the views of land takers like Meares, Lawson, Wentworth or Cox, who either overtly or implicitly advocated the slaughtering of Aboriginal families, not all those devoted to the new concept of the colonies as a place where people were replaced by sheep believed that this should imply a policy of extermination.[39]

The names she quotes are of the younger generation and in a footnote she adds: 'For killings on behalf of George Cox of Clarendon see *Sydney Gazette* of 30 September 1824, for Cox's advocacy of total extermination, N. Gunson'. In fact, the 30 September issue of the *Gazette* reads 'Mr Chamberlane came into Bathurst, to report the above circumstances [his killings] to Mr George Cox, who took him to the Commandant', *not* that George ordered killings.[40] Nor did George Cox live at Clarendon.[41] Equally, in attacking William Lawson, Kociumbas quotes the letter of 14 June.[42] But Lawson's son wrote it. Kociumbas has failed to distinguish between the two different generations.

The earlier 1822 incident does show that George Cox did not hesitate to send armed men after Aboriginal stock thieves. However, pursuit of stock thieves was a different matter to advocating wholesale slaughter, let alone carrying it out. George, although then young and aware of his on-the-spot authority, was later referred to in the *Sydney Morning Herald* as having 'consideration for the wants and infirmities of others', while his later letters reveal a modest and understanding character.[43] This does not, of course, mean that he did not make the remark, which was in keeping with the general feeling. But nor does it mean that he personally killed Aborigines, as the stock overseer did. This is not to pretend that the Coxes, or others, were saints, although they did remove the overseer in 1825. As regards

Lawson Snr, Eric Rolls cites an instance, on 22 December 1823, when he brought to trial a white man who had shot a native and says: 'William Lawson got along with the Aborigines better than most men ... when he retired as commandant ... the Aborigines still turned to him for advice'.[44]

The records of senior officials' meetings quoted earlier make it clear that the authorities pursued a policy of strong action combined with conciliation. What actually followed was Brisbane's belated declaration of martial law on 3 November, which legitimized killings.[45] But Wiradjuri attacks had ceased during October, as recorded above, and in November their leaders came to Bathurst to ask for peace. Brisbane revoked martial law on 11 December 1824. He was recalled the following year, partly because of Bathurst's displeasure at his handling of that situation.

Was William Cox in the area at that time at all? He chaired the meetings in Sydney on 3 June and 16 July, when his recorded remarks fell far short of recommending 'manuring the ground' with bodies. He usually avoided public controversy. He was well known for his absences from Bathurst and it could take five or six days on horseback to get there from Sydney. On 6 November 1818 it had taken him from a Monday until a Saturday.[46] Finally, in November 1824, Brisbane submitted his name to the Secretary of State as a potential member of the new Colonial Council. Would he have done so if William had been so uncharacteristically rash in public?[47]

It is true that William was now 60 and was inclined to be irascible and that his herds had suffered repeatedly at the hands of the Aborigines. But his letter of 7 December 1823 to Goulburn had emphasized that he encouraged remaining friendly with 'the natives', although this would have been consistent with the 'violence and conciliation' approach. He also employed Aborigines himself. Even Gunson concedes self-contradictorily that: 'Apart from his callous attitude to the Aboriginals, he was regarded as a man of unimpeachable integrity'.[48]

It seems more likely that, if the offending remark was made at all, George Cox made it, although Kociumbas' *Gazette* quotation about his giving orders is simply wrong. A reasonable conclusion is that, as the conflict between Aborigines and settlers came to a head, the younger ones, at least, believed that the native inhabitants had to be driven out before they murdered more settlers (not to mention the convicts they killed). The authorities colluded in this, or encouraged it. The view of an older settler, Archibald Bell, had been expressed in his evidence to Bigge in 1820, quoted earlier. He had also explained that when cheated by a white settler over payment for work, 'this caused retaliation ... [Aborigines were] tenacious in seeking revenge'.[49] Even if it was the result of provocation, their reprisals were seen by settlers as increasingly intolerable. After the 'Black War' at Bathurst, more emphasis began to be laid on the prevention of conflict, without a great deal of effect. Vengeance against Aborigines who took cattle continued and they suffered all sorts of outrage from squatter woolgrowers in later years.[50] Furthermore the concept of an exterminating war continued, although it has been argued that the words 'exterminate' and 'extirpate' had become familiar in colonial conversation, with reference to indigenous people, during the 1820s and 1830s ... originally meaning nothing more than 'banish' or 'excommunicate'.

The *Sydney Gazette* of 21 May 1827 reported the trial of Lieutenant Nathaniel Lowe of the 40th Regiment 'for the wilful murder of one Jackey Jackey: an Aboriginal native'.[51] Lowe had ordered him to be shot. Lowe was defended by Dr Wardell (W. C. Wentworth was the junior counsel, who 'followed on the same side'). Jackey had killed a white man and it was argued that he 'could not be amenable to the English law because he could not comprehend the form'. He had 'merely done that which was recognized to be lawful, according to the notions of the tribe'. Wardell went on to say that 'even if the natives committed no offence, but possessed that propensity to eat human flesh, they would justly be proscribed, that an exterminating war carried on against them would be justifiable'. Lieutenant Lowe was found not guilty.

The Aborigines did not suffer outrage from William. He had earlier employed a few as guides when building the Blue Mountains road and in 1826 he had a number as farm workers at Mulgoa, despite earlier bloody attacks on that farm. At Mulgoa conflict had become inevitable over the usage of the Nepean River, especially during times of drought. In 1811 Robert Luttrell, the violent son of the surgeon Edward Luttrell, was killed during a fight with the Mulgowie tribe. In 1826 Peter Cunningham, the naval surgeon, met 'a gentleman at Mulgoa … who had … thirty acres of wheat reaped by a party of them … in fourteen days, as well [done] as by whites … they were fed and paid a regular price', whereas others disliked working for whites as they were being cheated by small convict settlers.[52] Karskens identifies this gentleman as William, who was happy with them.[53]

This was a much more positive approach than that of, for example, Archibald Bell. When asked by Bigge if they had 'shewn themselves capable of performing any European labour', Bell replied, 'I have seen some few reap and one or two hold the plough for amusement'.[54] With William it was the familiar story of his understanding how to motivate men, in this case by treating them fairly. The Aborigines around Mulgoa, some of whom settled on his farm, became known as the Mulgowie, but by the 1840s they were, if not actually extinct, no longer identifiable as a tribe. Later on, Broome writes, 'Aboriginal people provided farm labour on many properties in New South Wales'.[55]

12 The Exclusives Lose Their Dominance

William Cox's activities acquired a new and philanthropic dimension in the 1820s, as did those of many of his Pure Merino contemporaries. These activities, even if often tinged with self-interest, might have continued colony-wide to the great advantage of the landed gentry. But by the 1840s the gentry's influence had become so diminished by a variety of factors, not least their own intransigence and squabbling, that the benevolence only survived locally, much in the manner of that practised by English squires. This period proved to be one of the most disputatious of the colony's early history, when the oddness of local conditions turned most of the gentry, most squatters and native-born 'Australians' into political activists.

Bathurst and Bigge had between them outlined a future for the colony in which the pastoralists would be dominant, employing convict labour, even if nothing that the civil servant Bigge proposed could be described as visionary. But, in the historian Michael Roe's words: 'Time and space and growth all undercut the Bathurst–Bigge design, yet its upholders fought back, demanding attention. Their failure was nearly as significant and as interesting as any success in Australian history.'[1]

William's role during these years was not entirely typical of the gentry, because he was liberal minded and often – but not always – supported the emancipists' aspirations. His liberalities had their limitations, for example the possibility of having ex-convicts potentially sitting on criminal juries, which he could not accept. Yet his experiences, together with those of Jamison and a few others, do cast a useful light both on his own character and on that curious period of history, with its internecine political infighting, before the gold rush of the 1850s changed everything again. Nor did anything stop William continuing to expand his estates and build his family dynasty, right up until his death. This was as well as executing government construction contracts and sitting as a senior magistrate, not to mention raising a second family with his new wife, Anna Blachford.

Up to the 1820s, the public role of the landed gentry had been held back by Governor Macquarie. If William's great patron was 'the father of Australia', he was also capable of being an unyielding parent, especially where matters of the larger public interest were concerned. Local benevolent initiatives he fostered, colony-wide ones – except those promoted by the Church – he often prohibited. This was unrealistic, since long before he departed the leading landed settlers had become established as citizens of substance. As such they were natural leaders of the community. They had come to believe in their authority and rights, which Macquarie ought to have recognized. At the same time, so far as the overwhelming majority of them were concerned, the ownership of land was at the heart of everything. It certainly was for William and, to a slightly lesser extent, his sons.

The possession of land was not only associated, in the English gentry's mind, with birth, political power and stability, it was the reason why so many of the exclusives had come out to the wide spaces of the colony in the first place.[2] Land remained inextricably linked to progress and to the quarrel between the 'ancient nobility' and the new squatters, even though most gentry had engaged in squatting at some time or other themselves.[3] The established gentry's status was compromised by the squatter arrivals in two ways. The Pure Merinos had invested their money in acquiring land. The squatters simply took territory for nothing and invested only in stock, including some very small-scale farmers, often ex-convicts. Secondly, many among the larger scale squatters aspired to the same social standing as the gentry, which by origins and social standing they enjoyed at home, such as ex-officers. This complicated situation has already been explained.

The landed gentry's wealth and status had indeed been greatly bolstered by the Bathurst/Bigge pastoral concept. From a sociological point of view it had adverse effects, at least from William's liberal standpoint; the Bigge Report led immediately to the abandonment of Macquarie's constructive views on the rehabilitation of ex-convicts, to which he subscribed. It was true also, although apparently not appreciated by many settlers, that the ex-convict emancipist population was certain to assume a much wider significance, fuelled by the ex-convicts' belief that they had the right to the colony's land, as William and others had observed to Bigge in 1819. Two decades later, in 1837, James Macarthur published his classic book *New South Wales, its Present State and Future Prospects* in London. In this he deplored that ex-convicts thought 'the colony theirs by right, and that the emigrant settlers were interlopers upon the soil'.

Adding to this pressure, the emancipists' free-born children were becoming a growing influence and one which, if the authorities had thought about it at all, had been inevitable once women convicts were sent out with the First Fleet in 1788. In all, some 12,500 female convicts were transported. In the 1820s those born before 1810 were coming of age. By 1828 one quarter of the population of New South Wales had been born in the colony.[4] These young people were entitled to the rights of British subjects and they began to be joined in the 1830s by an ever increasing number of young free immigrant workers, encouraged to come out with assistance from the home government as part of Goderich's plans of 1831. In the whole of the 1820s such free immigrants had totalled 6500, but between 1831 and 1840 over 40,000 arrived.[5]

To further this inflow Governor Bourke gave a bounty to settlers who employed their own agents to bring in mechanics or agricultural labourers; single men from 18 to 25 years old, unmarried females between 15 and 30, and couples under 30. This was on top of government-assisted schemes. Both offered real attractions for the immigrants, but little for the great landowners. Although, in practice, the wages paid were not as high as those proposed in 1831, workers' pay was still high compared to the cost of employing assigned convicts. In 1833 immigrant female domestic servants received £8 to £16 a year, men more, and they also had to be housed and fed.[6] Thirteen years later, in 1846, convicts whose sentences had expired were being sent as labourers to Port Phillip and paid £20 a year, hardly a crippling increase.[7]

Although there was heated dispute locally about the character of the female immigrants, for both sexes the colony was a welcome change from the deeply impoverished state of rural southern England. Far from improving, this had became more intense since the 1790s. In November 1825 William Cobbett recorded that 'the honest labourer' is fed worse than a prisoner and existed 'on 7d a day for six days of the week and nothing on Sunday'.[8] In Hampshire, Wiltshire and Dorset there were rural riots in 1830, while the first would-be trade unionists, the Tolpuddle Martyrs, were transported from Dorset to the colony in 1834. Thus immigration brought an influx of men and women who were already politicized from their bitter experiences in the home country. 'Pastoralism encouraged militancy among the working class … many urban workers yearned to become yeomen and most free workers hated the thought of employment on outback sheep stations.'[9] However, they usually seem to have put that old resentment aside when given new opportunities.

Under Bourke's scheme the Macarthurs successfully 'brought out forty one families between April 1837 and March 1839, together with a small number of single men … This was only possible because the late 1830s were a time of great economic expansion [in the colony]'.[10] The Coxes do not appear to have done anything similar with whole families, although William's sons imported craftsmen to build their elegant mansions at Mulgoa, where building progress was only checked by adverse economic circumstances in the 1840s.

In the 1820s and in the 1830s, more and more 'gentlemen' squatters arrived, also encouraged by the home government. Bourke's Crown Lands Occupation Bill of 1836 systemized and extended the granting of temporary licences to be issued to persons of good repute on 'runs' beyond the official limits of occupation, effectively legalizing the squatting.[11] A decade later, in 1845, Gideon Scott Lang defined squatting: 'The first principle of squatting is that the squatter shall have full power to settle without restriction wherever he can find unoccupied pasture, and to take possession of as much land as his stock can occupy'.[12] Donald Carisbrooke writes: 'Many of the immigrants with capital who came to Australia in 1838 did not intend to make it their permanent home, but to return to Britain with their fortunes made'.[13]

Some doctors and lawyers might have planned to return. But the ex-army and navy officers put out to grass by the recession which followed the Napoleonic War, and their half-pay brethren, were different. They had been allowed to commute their half pay into land purchases in the colony, especially in the Hunter River valley, and came to have considerable influence. Most considered themselves to be gentry, although Jane Austen, in her novels of that period, considered naval officers (who were unquestionably socially superior to those from the army) to be on the borderline. To read Austen's *Persuasion*, for example, is to understand how intensely small distinctions were felt. A knight was considerably inferior to a baronet and an admiral was barely on calling terms with either. Her characters include naval captains of 30 who had been promoted due to others being killed in action, who were no longer employed. Men like these became squatters in New South Wales, where the English social distinctions were copied.

Some newcomers really were of the English gentry, or better. The Wyndhams, cousins of the Earl of Egremont, England's largest landowner, and of a Secretary of State, were genuine aristocrats who built Dalwood in the Hunter.[14] George Wyndham became a custodian of British ways in the Hunter. Governor Gipps called him a 'gentleman greatly respected and of high repute for talents and education in the Colony' when asking him to stand for the Legislative Council in March 1839 (which he declined on the ground of his private affairs requiring his undivided attention).[15] Nonetheless, or perhaps because of it, Wyndham was seen by emancipists as a symbol of squatter arrogance. On that same occasion William Cox Jnr was approached by Gipps and also declined for similar reasons. This demonstrates one way in which the 'the ancient nobility', in Mudie's pejorative phrase, were being asked to share their pre-eminence with relative newcomers.

An important point about these arriving families was that they were almost a generation younger than the original exclusives, whose natural political enemies they became, whilst – as happens with immigrants almost anywhere – they in turn became resentful of those who followed, because the more numerous the squatters the more competition there was for land and labour. In so far as the original landed gentry were concerned, squatting was only acceptable if it was brought within the framework of ownership and attachment to the soil. They were particularly hostile to the small squatters, who ran a few sheep or cattle and were accused of stealing sheep and sheltering bushrangers. These men were usually on unclaimed land within the county boundaries. The main squatter territory, the area around the Hunter River, was quite different to either the Cumberland Plain or the land west of the mountains, having terrain suitable for both grazing and agriculture.[16] It spawned a different society, obviously different to the small opportunist squatters and also to the genuine gentry. They included the viciously reactionary 'Major' James Mudie (a former officer of the Marines who had been a lieutenant, never a major).

William Cox did eventually extend his interests to the Hunter too, although conflict between the old colonists and the new immigrants reached its worst proportions there, in an extreme reflection of the colony overall, where the free immigrants were generally disliked by both the native-born and their fathers, the emancipists.[17] In the 1830s Chief Justice Forbes told Governor Bourke that 'as he saw it there were two political groups in the colony – the immigrants and emancipists'.[18] This was a simplification. Within the political stewpot there were also the increasing subsidiary groupings already mentioned; the emancipists' native-born offspring; the squatters, the would-be gentleman immigrants and the increasing number of immigrant workers. They all contributed to the pressures on the exclusives.

Looking at it from their angle, the historian John Ward asks, referring to the Macarthurs, how the squatters could have a credible commitment to the colony, as against the 'ancient nobility' who 'had been granted land or bought it, who by skilful breeding had improved the quality of the fleeces and who by immense expenditures had built up permanent homesteads and establishments'. Freehold ownership of land, according to the Macarthurs, gave independent gentlemen their title to political and social authority.[19] By the end of the 1820s, before the squatters began to arrive in any number, the Macarthurs' Camden Park incorporated over 60,000 acres. By then John had died and the family's authority was being exercised by his thoughtful son, James, and his nephew, Hannibal, while William Cox's authority was increasingly being wielded in conjunction with his sons in a family enterprise which would be of much greater eventual extent than the Macarthurs'.

It was against this increasingly agitated background that the landed gentry attempted to exercise 'political and social authority' from the 1820s onwards, once Macquarie had left. They were largely held together by the concept of respectability underpinning their position and they tried to shape society not only by participating in politics, but also through their role as economic men.[20] As has been observed, Macquarie had kept a close eye on any activities rivalling his own and limited what the established landed gentry could do. He had increased the muscle of the Sydney Benevolent Society and given his approbation 'in the most flattering terms' to a petition for trial by jury, the 'valued inheritance of our ancestors', as well as supporting the lifting of restrictions on the burthen of trading ships, explained below. But he stopped the formation of an agricultural society, which could have helped the farming community as a whole. Archibald Bell's replies to Bigge's questioning on 27 November 1819 show that it had been a genuinely disinterested idea, although with one qualification:

[Bigge] 'Was any attempt made to form an agricultural society?'

[Bell] 'Several attempts have been made & proposals offered ... by the Gentlemen of the Colony, but the application was negatived'.

'Can you recollect the names of the persons who joined in the application?'

'Mr Cox, Mr Marsden, the two Messrs Blaxland, Sir John Jamison and I think the Judge Advocate, there were others who names I forget & I think it took place about two years ago ... this was submitted to the consideration of the Governor with a request that he would become the Patron.'[21]

Bell also explained that there had been objections to the possibility of emancipists being allowed to join the society, which qualification the Governor disliked:

I heard that he [Macquarie] objected to it as persons who had been convicts were not likely to be admitted ... the mode of admission was to have been by ballot & although no specific article was framed to exclude this description of persons, we [supported] the principle of their exclusion.[22]

Nor until after Macquarie had left were the more intellectual Philosophical Society of Australia and the Sydney Institution able to come to life, and leaders like Sir John Jamison become free to launch new initiatives. Jamison himself, for many years an associate of William's, was to prove an energetic liberal and supporter of the emancipists, becoming a contentious figure as a result.[23] Liberals like Jamison and Governor Bourke supported ex-convicts' aspirations out of intellectual conviction, while William appears to have done so out of sympathy and understanding for their situation. It was also no coincidence that this energetic discussion of possible improvements came about after Bigge's long visit in 1819–21. The Commissioner had been very concerned with improvements, which his report reflected.

The landed gentry's inclination towards disinterested benevolent work had been evident long before Macquarie left and Bigge took his report to parliament. As might be expected, the magistrates appealed for help for the Hawkesbury community after floods, as they had done under Bligh. Thus in June 1817 William headed an appeal to the Governor about the 'great distress occasioned by the recent inundations', to which Macquarie responded on 17 June, giving relief.[24] William also led the Hawkesbury Benevolent Society, jointly with magistrates Brabyn, Cartwright and Mileham. On 20 May 1819 Macquarie acknowledged a letter from them about a general meeting and replied:

> For the interests of the Poor of the Districts of the Hawkesbury ... I shall be happy to give the said Committee in trust for the support of the Benevolent Institution, one thousand acres of land in any part of the Colony where Crown lands remain still unappropriated.

The gift evidently paid results over the years. It was noted at Windsor on 3 December 1827 that:

> Members of the Select Committee [of the Society] having perused and made ourselves fully acquainted with the Method adopted by William Cox, Brabyn and Bell Esqrs ... the measures resolved upon are most conducive to the interests of the Society.[25]

Income came from the sales of cattle bred from a donated herd. Since the stockholders were careful to cull their own herds of the worst animals when making donations, the society was reckoned to have 'owned the roughest mob of Colonial cattle'.[26]

Similarly, on 3 May 1823 several JPs, including William, wrote to Governor Brisbane about relief for aged persons 'who have been discharged from the benefit of His Majesty's stores [and] ... are in the utmost distress, nearly the whole of them being incapable of labor and subsisting on the precarious bounty of their neighbours'. The oldest was 90 and the 20 included two soldiers' widows of 60. Brisbane's secretary, Goulburn, agreed to put them 'on the stores'.[27] William also made more directly personal efforts to help those in distress. On 2 February 1823 he asked Brisbane to be 'graciously pleased to grant [a 78-year-old] a ration from His Majesty's stores'. This was an ex-convict 'oppressed with infirmities and [who] can no longer labour to procure a subsistence', having been employed 'as a labourer on my farm for the last fifteen years and conducted himself with the strictest honesty'. Brisbane replied: 'Most strongly recommended to be admitted to the Benevolent Fund', although William might have been expected to help a long-serving employee himself.[28]

Overall, with government assistance, he and the other magistrates were often successful in combating the great poverty there had long been among smallholders on the Hawkesbury and, unlike Jamison, he was not in conflict with Brisbane. He resigned from the presidency of the Benevolent Society in January 1824. William Jnr, who lived at Richmond after he left the army, was elected treasurer in 1827. This was a small sign of the next generation of Coxes giving some thought to the society they lived in. As will be seen in the next chapter, they were more inclined towards simply living like gentlemen, whilst accepting the kind of local obligations that their parallel squires in England performed.

Such charitable activities were ones which Macquarie would have had little reason to impede. In the larger, colony-wide, sphere, resistance to his restrictions mounted. In January 1819 the Governor yielded to the extent of giving permission for a meeting of gentlemen, clergy, merchants, settlers and other free subjects to draw up a petition to the King, mainly on the subject of trade. The petition was formulated at a meeting on 12 February 1819 of 'Gentlemen, Clergy, Settlers, Merchants, Landholders and other respectable inhabitants of New South Wales', as the *Sydney Gazette* phrased it, and presided over by Sir John Jamison. William Cox was a signatory. The petitioners also requested a repeal of the weight limit of 350 tons burthen on ships trading between the colony and the Cape of Good Hope, over which the East India Company exercised a monopoly and which prevented small colonial-owned ships from operating. The petition was presented to the Governor with 1260 signatures and he forwarded it to London.[29] The committee had included the emancipists Simeon Lord and William Redfern, thus uniting exclusives and traders, presaging alliances which William would later form in opposition to many of his own class. The following year Bathurst permitted the shipping measures, but not civil government. Changing the shipping measures would have suited the home government's purposes, since in 1813 it had removed the East India Company's monopoly of trade with India and was increasingly trying to regulate the way in which the company ran the subcontinent.

The petition had also raised the extremely contentious subject of trial by jury, the institution of which it solicited from the home government. At the meeting of 12 February 1819 the petitioners had asserted that there was now a great number of free, respectable inhabitants competent to act as jurymen, although the politically charged question of whether they should include ex-convicts was not touched on. The petition was sent off by Macquarie on 22 March.[30] It can be seen as a landmark event in leading citizens making positive, if polite and respectful, efforts to change colonial policy. William would have been unlikely to have taken part if it had been at all extreme in its presentation.

Thanks to Macquarie's restraints, the colonial landed gentry was only able to reach a form of responsible social maturity in the decade of the 1820s, in the middle of which of which the aggressive young W. C. Wentworth returned from England and began championing the emancipists through his *Australian* newspaper. The freedom of the press then became a major issue with Governors Brisbane and Darling, and not to the exclusives' advantage either, even though James Macarthur had convinced both Darling and Whitehall of the importance of having an upper class of landed settlers and that government should be carried on according to the wishes of the dominant landowners.[31]

Conservatives usually sided with the governors, until Bourke, an Irish Whig, took the emancipists' side. There was increasing agitation, promoted by Wentworth, for the controversial jury trials and an elected legislature.

William had long before taken a cautious position on both in his evidence to Bigge. Now he sometimes sided with the emancipists. Bourke, perhaps reflecting this measured involvement, described him as 'one of the many free emigrants of great wealth … who advocate liberal principles'. Others he named included Jamison, John and Gregory Blaxland, William Lawson, James Macarthur and, rather surprisingly, in view of the evidence to Bigge, Archibald Bell.[32] Bourke himself was described by the Reverend James Dunmore Lang as 'capable of the most comprehensive views in matters of state-policy and civil government'.[33]

Long before Bourke arrived, when Macquarie's immediate successor Brisbane was governor, a potentially most significant initiative – in terms of the landed gentry's status – was launched, with which William was strongly involved. This was the delayed creation of an agricultural society. Stimulating improvement in the colony's farming methods might have been the vehicle for the exclusives' greatest contribution to the colony's development, since this was where their expertise lay. The enterprise it aimed to encourage was vital to the economic life of the colony, yet the way in which it gradually collapsed was symptomatic of the exclusives' own decline.

Bell had told Bigge in 1819 that the objects originally proposed were 'For the purpose of communicating our own experiments & information … in our practice of farming & to have an exhibition of live stock for the purpose of further general improvement'.[34] That was the potential for good. There was no apparent direct profit for the promoters, although as farmers they would be the first to benefit from any improvements. The bad outcome lay in the conflicts which rapidly enveloped the society, demonstrating how even the gentry's most well-meaning initiatives could end up undermining their own standing.

The Hobart Agricultural Society had been inaugurated on 8 December 1821 and the Sydney one came into existence on 6 July 1822, with Jamison as president and William as one of four vice presidents, along with Mr Justice Field, the Judge of the Supreme Court, and Samuel Marsden. The

Judge shared many of the exclusives' views.[35] A large committee, all but five of them JPs, included John Piper, John Blaxland, Archibald Bell, William Lawson and George Cox. It was very much a committee of exclusives, paying the substantial annual subscription of five guineas and immediately pledging to form a subscription fund to import 'a more important breed of cattle, Horses, Sheep etc'.[36] The Governor's patronage was hoped for, just as Macquarie's had once been. This time there was no official objection to emancipists not being involved – most would have been excluded by the five guinea subscription anyway.

The society's first dinner was held a week after its formation and the first show was held at Parramatta in 1823. The two brother societies 'went beyond discussion of farm science and holding of shows to become quasi-political organizations'.[37] Unfortunately, Jamison had issued a political statement in the Sydney society's name, reflecting one of the Hobart society's objectives, which was the protection of stock against felonies (i.e., bushrangers): hardly a disinterested purpose. William and others strongly objected to this at a special meeting on 20 August 1822.[38] They did not wish to set themselves up as arbiters of the community, which would not have been acceptable to the Governor. This resulted in Jamison's immediate resignation, although according to one bowdlerizing history of the society, he resigned because he was going to visit England, from whence he did not return until 1825.[39]

It was not until 1826 that Jamison did deliver a presidential address.[40] He was again president in 1827, by which time it had been renamed as the Agricultural and Horticultural Society. In that year he attempted to stand down, but was firmly re-elected by Cox and Marsden, so evidently the quarrel had been resolved. One factor must have been the pre-eminence which Jamison's title and wealth gave him. The other vice presidents were now Hannibal Macarthur and John Blaxland.[41]

After his own return from England, in February 1824, Samuel Marsden addressed the Society on 15 July and attempted to brush aside the early political embarrassment. He complimented Field, 'under whose direction our Society made rapid advances towards the accomplishment of our immediate objects of pursuit'. This would, Marsden hoped, excuse the delays that 'had arisen out of the difficulties thus unfortunately encountered in the infancy of our Establishment'. It was now 'acquiring the strength to ensure our prosperity as a public body. We hope by the nomination of a President to see the Society placed again in active operation' and for 'steady perseverance in maintaining the Rules laid down for our governance'.[42]

Since the Society's articles specifically abjured political activity, which was where Jamison had offended, Marsden's remarks might have been thought apposite. But Brisbane responded in fury, apparently because of the plaudit for Field, vividly illustrating the in-fighting which bedevilled public life in the 1820s and 1830s and which obstructed the efforts of the exclusives to play a leading role. The Governor claimed to Bathurst that 'the manner this Address was got up proved that a party purpose was the sole object of the few members concerned'. He forbade its publication, which as governor he had the power to do.[43] He appears to have completely disregarded the fact that 'over a thousand pounds was sent to England in 1822 in order to acquire more livestock, with another hundred pounds for fresh seed and agricultural textbooks ... raised by the infant Agricultural Society'.[44]

Brisbane next accused 'Mr Field, late Judge of the Supreme Court' of being behind attacks on him in letters to the (London) *Morning Chronicle*.[45] On 9 February 1825 he wrote to Bathurst transmitting 'some hasty replies to many of the foulest, most unjust, ill timed and most unprovoked attacks on my character ... in the Morning Chronicle of last August.' There seems to be no proof that Field, by then back in England, did have anything to do with the letters, although he and the society were referred to in one of them, which attacked Brisbane's 'littleness of mind' in suppressing Marsden's address. Other letters in this long-distance dispute included a highly pertinent attack on the government being 'occupied in the most ridiculous cabals and private intrigues', while Brisbane was particularly stung by the accusation that he spent 'the greater part of his time in the Observatory or shooting parrots' (he had built an observatory at Parramatta).[46]

Thus in the colony Brisbane had contrived to offend both sides: the emancipists, whose influence he had undermined, and the landowners, who resented the rising economic power of the new settlers and denounced him to London.[47] When he was removed by Earl Bathurst, after badly mishandling the imposition of martial law at Bathurst in 1824, his valedictory despatch was critical of various members of the landed gentry. He reported that he would have had 'difficulty in restoring' Marsden to the magistracy 'independently of his clerical office'. He had himself recommended Jamison for a possible legislative council, but 'his character is so fallen in the Country that he is no longer respected nor in fact associated with by the better class of Colonists'.[48] Jamison had been one of the principals in accusing the Governor of having 'improperly sent convict women to the penal settlement at Emu Plains for impure purposes'. His Regentville estate was nearby, on the other side of the Nepean River. The 260 or so convict workers lived in a variety of small cottages, which no doubt did contribute to promiscuity, while William's road to the mountain ran across the Emu plains at an inconvenient angle in terms of isolating the settlement. But Jamison's accusation seems to have been unjustified in terms of Brisbane's intentions.[49]

Under these intense and partisan pressures, the Agricultural Society lost its sense of direction and its activity lapsed in 1836, although it was reconstituted in 1857. It is now the Royal Australian Agricultural Society of New South Wales, bringing 'expertise to rural, business and professional pursuits'.[50] In the 1840s local agricultural shows continued, however. In February 1847 George Cox won a prize for his Mulgoa wine at the Richmond Show, even when he was suffering financially in his main activity of stock rearing from the collapse of cattle and sheep prices.[51] So the impetus for improvement was still there. But the larger issue for the Pure Merinos was that the pursuit of public interest goals, which had begun as the objective of some of their leaders, had been so discouraged during Brisbane's intemperate governorate.

Throughout the 1820s the policy arguments became stormier. On 16 January 1827 Jamison, William Cox, Gregory Blaxland, John Blaxland, Archibald Bell, W. C. Wentworth and others wrote to Sheriff Mackaness requesting 'that you will be pleased to convene a further meeting of the free inhabitants of the colony for the purpose of petitioning the King and both Houses of Parliament for trial by jury and a House of Assembly'. This Mackaness did and a deputation to the Governor told Darling that Gregory Blaxland 'intends to proceed to England, and is charged with the petition to the two Houses of Parliament'. The petitioners felt it was within the competency of the colony to furnish the 100 members they proposed for the assembly, thus avoiding involving emancipists.[52] A part of the objective was to control the powers of the Governor.

This démarche infuriated Darling, who promptly removed Mackaness from office as being 'a Common Associate' of Wentworth and Wardell (who had jointly founded the *Australian* newspaper at the end of 1824).[53] In his valedictory despatch, after receiving notice of his recall in July 1831, he later asked Goderich to make allowance for the 'Persons I have had to deal with, Men I may say habitual Drunkards filling the most important Offices, Speculators, Bankrupts and Radicals … If it is your Lordship's will that I should be the Sacrifice, I must submit'.[54] Those words speak for themselves of Darling's extreme attitudes and self-pity. Nor did the removal from their posts of two fractious governors in succession (Brisbane and Darling) help the transition of New South Wales towards being a free colony, inevitable though that was, with emancipists and their offspring becoming a growing proportion of the population, as more convicts completed their terms of servitude and had more children.

As to the jury trial question, Francis Forbes, the Chief Justice, wrote in November 1827 that 'it is now generally conceded that the colony is quite advanced to a state to fit it for this mode of trial, but … there must be a great number of details to arrange'. He then approached the delicate question of whether 'persons who had been transported to this colony' should be admitted as jurors, presuming that property would be the test of eligibility and that it would be set 'sufficiently high' to ensure respectability.[55] On 18 April 1828 the petition, taken to London by Blaxland, was presented to the House of Commons. But MPs decided in July that the time was not ripe for either jury trials or an elected assembly. Those discussions continued until 1842, when an Act of Parliament did provide for a partially elected council. Two of William's sons, William Jnr and George, were among those put forward in 1835.

Earlier, in 1827, Darling had felt that 'the Colony was by no means prepared for such an Institution as a Legislative Assembly ... which would be forcing it beyond its strength and powers'.[56] In fact popular agitation for one was limited almost entirely to Sydney, except that a large number of landowners were involved in the leadership of the campaign, including Jamison, John Blaxland and William. In fact they were principally concerned with the uncontrolled spending of public money.[57] But if they were active in asking Darling for financial reform, when in 1829 W. C. Wentworth attempted to have the Governor impeached over the death of a soldier named Joseph Sudds, who had been put in leg irons and an iron collar after committing a theft, Jamison, Blaxland, Cox and many others dissented. After all, Cox himself owed his career as magistrate and contractor to the authority of a governor.

Again, when Wentworth's *Australian* virulently attacked Darling, the same Pure Merinos were among 115 landowners and merchants who sent an address to him on 4 July 1829 regretting that he had been 'grossly vituperated by licentious public writers'. They somewhat slavishly asserted that 'We are convinced that every act of Your Excellency's administration has emanated from the purest motive'. The great majority of the signatories were identified as being 'L.D.' – landed proprietors – plus such merchants as Robert Campbell, now a considerable landowner as well. Their sons outnumbered them. The Blaxlands were represented by George, the Bells by John, plus Thomas Jamison, Charles Marsden, John Lawson, three Cox sons and many others.[58] William Cox was then 65 years old, John Blaxland 60, Jamison only 53, William Lawson 55, Simeon Lord 58 and John Piper

56. Even including their sons, the exclusives were still only a small group, even if now allied politically with such successful emancipists as Lord. When the Governor was challenged seriously, the sons also supported the legitimate authority.

Generally speaking, William appears to have trimmed his support between the authorities, his own class and the emancipist challengers. It might appear that a few exclusives lining up alongside emancipists, like Lord, would have potentially damaged them, but there is no evidence for that. More damaging was the active and growing presence of the 'gentry' of the Hunter Valley, whose settlers' motivations were directed to their own immediate enrichment.

If public life increasingly involved the next generation, that involvement was most prominent on the emancipists' side in the shape of Wentworth, the outspoken and populist lawyer son of William's contemporary, D'Arcy. The young Wentworth did not intend to make matters any easier for the exclusives and a brief conspectus of the life of this unusual man will explain his motivations. The furore with Brisbane had coincided with his return to the colony in July 1824, after studying law at Peterhouse College, Cambridge, where he had coined the famous phrase prophesying Australia becoming 'A new Britannia in another world'. This was in a poem written for the Chancellor's Medal at the Cambridge Commencement, called 'Australia', although it only came second.[59]

Shortly after his return Wentworth founded the *Australian*, jointly with a fellow barrister, Robert Wardell, who had run a newspaper in London.[60] In January 1825, soon after it started publication, Brisbane told Bathurst that they had published the newspaper 'shortly after the promulgation of the new Charter of Justice for the Colony' and 'These gentlemen never solicited my permission to publish their Paper', but as 'the opinion of the Law Officers was that there was no power to prevent it without going to Council, I considered it most expedient to try the experiment of the latitude of the full freedom of the Press'. He added that 'I shall beg to decline for the present my opinion in regard to its effects'.[61] One effect was to be unrelenting editorial attacks on the exclusives (which did not stop Wentworth acting as William's legal counsel).

Wentworth's mental outlook was greatly affected by his paternal origins. He was born illegitimate. His mother, Catherine Crowley, had been a convict sentenced to transportation in 1788, who had travelled out with his father. D'Arcy, once an officer in the Irish Volunteers, had trained as a doctor. He was going into exile after four trials at the Old Bailey for being a highwayman had ended in his discharge, and he agreed to go out as the assistant surgeon in the colony, in a kind of voluntary transportation. William Charles had been horrified when he discovered his father's unpalatable background. Nonetheless the Wentworths were related to Lord Fitzwilliam, who had helped William Charles to become a lawyer in London in 1817, when he described himself as thereby 'qualifying myself for the performance of those duties, that my Birth has imposed'.[62]

Wentworth had been mortally offended in 1819 when John Macarthur refused to allow him to marry his daughter, Elizabeth, after a quarrel over a loan. It was after this that he went to Cambridge University. The upshot was that, when he returned in 1824, whilst preoccupied with the greatness of his family and the glory of his country, he resolutely identified himself with the interests of the emancipists and their children. Effectively he went on fighting the battles of his youth throughout his life, despite rapidly becoming a highly successful lawyer and a major pastoralist himself.[63] When he retired it was to England, where, apparently coincidentally, he lived at the country estate of Merley, literally across the road from the Coxes' Fern Hill in Dorset.

Inevitably Wentworth campaigned stridently through his newspaper for jury trials and an elected assembly. Both involved the highly charged question of whether emancipists should be allowed to serve as jurors, and if so only in civil cases (for them to sit in criminal trials was unthinkable). These were two questions on which William Cox displayed a particular interest, although he usually tried to keep out of politics. Under Macquarie such public questions had been put on hold. Now, on the question of an elected Legislative Council the exclusives were in conflict both with the governors and with the governors' masters in Downing Street.

Jury trials and an elected assembly were seen as the birthright of Britons and were issues on which the exclusives might have provided leadership, had not so many been opposed to one or the other, or both. As time passed, the exclusives' role in public life was becoming increasingly contentious, not least in opposing emancipists potentially serving as jurors at all. Meanwhile the arguments over press censorship which had begun under Brisbane rumbled on under Darling. The landowners and their sons became more and more drawn into political positions, to the detriment of their more enlightened leaders' non-profit objectives. Indeed the exclusives' initiatives were increasingly being propelled by their sons, who became more overtly political in pursuing their class interests. William himself had been proposed by Brisbane for the first (unelected) legislative council in 1824, after the 'Black War' related in Chapter 11, possibly because he avoided taking contentious positions. But the nomination was rejected by the Secretary of State, who chose only officials.

In September 1828 a major personal event disrupted William's life. He fell ill with an irregular heartbeat. An article in the *Sydney Gazette* leaves no doubt about either the seriousness of the illness or how well he was regarded. 'A Correspondent' wrote that:

> Cox has for a few years past been frequently subject to the disease, described by the Hawkesbury people as 'a palpitation of the heart' ... by copious bleeding, cupping and the aid of cathartics, he is now considered to be out of danger ... The sensation on the public mind ... can more easily be accounted for by bringing to recollection, that very many of the inhabitants of the Hawkesbury enjoy sweet liberty under his auspices, hold land under his recommendation ... have reared families in his employ ... His humanity has been conspicuous.[64]

'Cupping' meant the use of leeches. The 'palpitations' must have been severe. Even allowing for a degree of journalistic excess, it is clear that

William exercised a paternal authority in the community. One example had been when in June 1820 he had helped the ex-convicts William Lawrence and Andrew Scott to obtain smallholdings (although, as has been seen in Chapter 5, he also pressured ex-convicts to sell him plots).[65]

Nor was the collapse surprising. In July 1827 William had felt so unwell that he had declined the chairmanship of the Quarter Sessions.[66] He had been combining his duties as a JP with a demanding range of activities, not least in continuing to acquire land, albeit in collaboration with his sons George and Henry. The 'Black War' of 1824 had involved him controversially as both a stockholder and a magistrate. He was very active in benevolent works and with the Agricultural Society. If Anna made running his household easier, she was many years his junior and William, now in his sixties, was not only fathering a new family, as a young woman Anna required a social life. He kept her happy by building extensions to the house and using it for parties. Among occasions which the *Sydney Gazette* reported in 1822 and 1823 were those marking the christening of a son, a race meeting at Richmond and a ball attended by 60 guests at Clarendon. At one party the guests sang the popular (among themselves) ditty, 'The Pure Merino'.[67]

Pressures on the exclusives continued to build under the more liberal, pro-emancipist rule of Governor Bourke in the 1830s, when the movement for an elected assembly took on a new vitality. In 1833 a public meeting was held to petition the King and the House of Commons for a house of assembly. Atkinson observes that: 'The names of Jamison, Wentworth, Robert Wardell, William Bland, Simeon Lord, Cox and Blaxland appear as usual' among the 68 signatories. A subsequent petition for an elected assembly attracted 6025 signatures and was an extraordinary 17 yards long.[68] Those just named were liberal minded landowners, including Lord. A surprising signatory was the hardline 'Major' James Mudie of Forbes Castle on the Hunter, but that was for the partisan reason of wanting a council as 'independent as possible of the Governor'.

Mudie's antagonism to Bourke stemmed from the Governor's Summary Punishment Act. This was intended to protect the convict 'from the tyranny of his master and the local [settler] magistrate'.[69] Mudie claimed that it undermined convict discipline. In his case it did not work, and culminated in the Castle Forbes revolt and the hanging of several of his servants. In fact he was expressing the views of many conservatives when he wrote that 'a convicted felon is unworthy both of future trust and of mingling with and participating in … the social enjoyments of his former associates and fellow subjects'.[70] Although at the time Bourke's Act was considered to threaten the colonial gentry, it was really an expression of the Governor's liberalism.

The petitioners were also confronting the squatters, who the gentry felt should bring their land within the official framework of land ownership, but to whom the government gave way. In 1837 Bourke appointed a retired officer of the 62nd Regiment, Edward Denny Day, a squatter, as a magistrate. Bourke reported to Lord Glenelg that Day had 'sold out to settle', married in the colony, and was so highly respected that other residents had asked the Governor to enable him to 'remain among them' (why he might not have been able to was unclear). 'This being out of my power,' Bourke wrote, 'I have named him Police Magistrate at Mussel Brook.' It had been the repeated desire of settlers to have such magistrates in remote parts of the colony.[71] This provides a good example of the dilemma facing the exclusives in objecting to respectable middle-class squatter arrivals. As Roe observes, the gentry, the nucleus of conservative power, were to be 'destroyed by the new [squatter] movement', although when the 1846 Land Act legalized their position the squatters' attitudes changed. They began to settle and raise families and became politically conservative.[72] This was what Day had done.

Further undermining the exclusives' authority, and preventing what could have been a gradual broadening of their narrow social base, was the seemingly everlasting quarrel about how to define a 'gentleman'. Even in the 1830s there was still bitter dispute over the extent to which a connection with trade was a disqualification. The Australian Club in Sydney, founded in 1838, had an upper membership limit of 300 and excluded anyone in trade, mimicking the snobbery in England. The unreality of the exclusives' attitude was underlined by there having long been in Sydney, as Roe observes, 'a handful of merchant princes having economic and social affiliations with the gentry'. Paramount among them was Robert Campbell, while another was the Australian Club's founder himself, S. A. Donaldson, and of course Lord.[73]

A recent commentator, J. J. Spigelman, refers to 'the social pretensions of an insecure upper class, desperately trying to mimic the social order and hierarchy of a distant aristocratic society' and says that for 'those who could not rely on the presumption of respectability conferred by ... "breeding", actual conduct alone revealed the character entitling one to gentry status'.[74] William Cox's conduct and leadership, not least towards the convict labourers on the mountain road, had fully earned him that status. Furthermore, he had the 'breeding' which so many did not. Where Spigelman exaggerates, in this author's view, is in suggesting that the English aristocracy was their inspiration, rather than the squirearchy. The true English aristocracy of the late eighteenth and early nineteenth centuries was almost absurdly grand. If it inspired settlers, it was of the next generation when William Cox Jnr, for example, had his coast of arms painted on his carriage.

The most lucid thinking of that second generation's thinking came from James Macarthur, John's fourth son. Ward suggests that: 'James Macarthur was our earliest systematic thinker on society. He wanted to build up in New South Wales a society and government based on a pastoral hierarchy with strong emphasis on the rule of law ... the family and property'. But by the time he took over his father's direction of family policy it was too late. 'Politically his attempts were in ruins by the end of the 1850s.'[75] The liberalism which Bourke had first supported, combined with popular politics, had eclipsed the pastoralists.

If William Cox's sons were giving thought to the society they lived in, as James Macarthur did, there is little sign left of it. William Jnr, the eldest, had been commissioned into the New South Wales Corps in 1808, survived its transition into the 102nd Regiment and been sent home with it. He fought in the Peninsula War at the siege of Badajoz and married the sister of a brother officer. He then returned to the colony to live as a gentleman, indeed somewhat as an aristocrat, developing an existing house at Richmond, called Hobartville, into an altogether grander mansion. His and his brothers' lives are explored briefly in the final chapter.

The Macarthurs – led by James Macarthur – reached a peak of prosperity during the economic expansion of the 1830s. At the same time, despite the much disliked Goderich reforms, which only allowed land to be sold, not granted, William Cox and his sons never ceased expanding their estates. In 1834 James Cox began building his own magnificent Clarendon in Tasmania. In 1835 William Jnr 'of the 12th Regiment of Foot' was using his commutation (of half pay) to buy land, just as the ex-officers immigrants did.[76] In 1836 William Snr bought 1100 acres in the Country of Roxburgh (near Bathurst) for £290. Even after he died, on 15 March 1837, his executors were dealing with an application for 2560 acres in the County of Ellis, Upper Hunter, originally made 'during the administration of Brisbane or Darling', for which he had paid £640.[77]

William died on 15 March 1837. A brief family notice was printed in the *Sydney Gazette* of 18 March, which read

DEATH. At his residence, Fairfield, Windsor, on Wednesday morning last, the 15th instant, after a long and severe illness, William Cox Esq, aged 72, deeply regretted by his numerous relatives and friends.

Surprisingly the paper does not appear to have published any obituary. By that time the sunshine of the Pure Merinos' day was already showing signs of fading. Whilst it has been easy for historians, from Samuel Bennett onwards, to explain their decline with the help of hindsight, the exclusives themselves do not appear to have realized that the pillars of their temple were cracking until it fell in the 1850s. If the gentry who survived the disastrous 1840s 'no longer played by 1851 the *undisputed* role that they had twenty years before' it was, to quote Dyster, due as much to 'diversification in society as to defeat in the field. In their home districts they were still the men given pride of place.'[78] Some of their descendants did fulfil the Victorian ideal of country squires, after which later generations simply became respected members of professions, such as the Coxes who pursued the law and medicine.

In William's time the gentry had continued to fight their corner, against both the squatters and what many of them saw as dangerous democratic and emancipist influences, disfiguring their own reputations. Bennett, writing in 1867, observed that the:

> early colonists indeed, to their honour be it spoken, in bestowing names upon their estates appear to have acted under the elevating ideas that they were not only the founders of families, but were helping to create 'a new Britannia in another world' … with whose glories they wished to identify themselves and their posterity.[79]

Bennett exactly identifies their aspirations. Some, like Jamison and Macarthur, named their estates after their aristocrat patrons. William drew on his Dorset and Wiltshire heritage. Bennett also refers to W. C. Wentworth pouring 'the vials of his wrath' on that class (the exclusives) and to 'the bitterness of the social and political quarrels which then raged in the colony'.[80]

However, it was as much economic catastrophes as political ones which made the 1840s so disastrous for the landed gentry, when the great prosperity of the 1830s gave way to the colony's first recession. The Bank of Australia failed in 1843 and the shareholders – who included members of the Cox family – had to pay up their shares of the default. The value of cattle and sheep collapsed and George Cox was forced into slaughtering his stock and boiling down the carcasses for tallow, which could be exported to England, as they had no other value. W. C. Wentworth had foretold this situation in his description of the colony as it was back in 1819. At that time, he wrote, 'Good milch cows may be bought for £5 to £10, fine young breeding ewes from £1 to £3 ... low as these prices may appear they are in great measure fictitious; since there is more stock of all kinds in the colony, than is necessary for its population'.[81]

Wentworth was proved right, if only three decades later. Although the Coxes survived, many pastoralists did not outlast the 1840s. In June 1848 John Blaxland's Luddenham

George Cox, William's fourth son, who established Burrundulla at Mudgee (Mitchell Library, State Library of NSW)

and Newington estates were in the hands of a trust company (he had died at Newington in 1845), their owner having 'ignored the transient, but more profitable benefits of squatting'.[82] The colony was almost littered with abandoned great houses, such as Aberglasslyn, overlooking the Hunter River near Maitland, whose builder, George Hobler, had been bankrupted in 1843, tried squatting and ultimately emigrated to South America. [83] Many settlers had 'their plans prostrated by the financial disasters ... Castles in the air had suddenly faded,' Bennett wrote.

However, in 1865 Bennett was still able to list 30 families who were 'the landed gentry of that part of the colony' within 30 miles of Campbelltown. The list included the Macarthurs, MacLeays, Wentworths, Jamisons and Coxes. He described the 'little clique of exclusives ... who regarded themselves as the only persons whose claims (to land, labour and social recognition) ... ought to be considered for a moment'.[84] Bennett was writing with a degree of ironical contempt, if also of recognition. Despite their pretensions, the 'ancient nobility' still captured some imaginations, not least their own.

Bennett also remarked that 'The fluctuating circumstances of colonial existence have always proved fatal sooner or later to the designs of those who have endeavoured to found a territorial aristocracy'.[85] It had done, even though the colonial landed gentry had evolved into a model significantly different to its home country inspiration, which is another aspect of the colonial experience that has seldom been discussed. By the mid-nineteenth century those of their descendants who survived the crash of the 1840s did become recognizable squires, accepted as leaders of their local communities, as the Coxes were. William had established a dynasty. His family had both arrived and survived.

13 The Cox Dynasty Established

William Cox died on 15 March 1837. It would be roughly a decade and a half before the dream of the exclusives also perished, both as the result of the social and political development described in the previous chapter and of the gold rush of 1851. Yet, because it is indeed an ill wind that blows nobody any good, the gold mining at Gulgong north of Mudgee enabled George Cox of Burrundulla to sell off building plots on the parts of the estate nearest the growing Mudgee township, where his descendants became archetypal squires, accepted as leaders of their local communities. Few of any family were national figures in the way that William's grandson, George Henry Cox, was or as ambitious as James Cox in Van Diemen's Land. An obvious exception to this dictum about the second generation was the thoughtful James Macarthur, who set out his vision of a landowning aristocracy in his *New South Wales, its Present State and Future Prospects* of 1837. By contrast the Coxes of that era were doers, not thinkers.

First, however, what of William Cox himself? How does he emerge? As a natural gentleman, as well as one by birth; as considerate of the ex-convicts who he recognized had created the colony by their labour; as someone genuinely concerned with improvement, both agricultural and in terms of citizen's rights. On the obverse side of this silver gilt coin, William remained more than a little unscrupulous to the very end. He was involved in a land acquisition dispute on the day he died, over which his executors were forced to admit he was in the wrong. He retained throughout his life an eighteenth-century view of entitlement to the spoils of office, even though that morality was changing around him. But *without* ambition, and *with* too much scruple, the pastoral economy of early New South Wales could not have been created, nor the colony developed.

No study of William's life and career would be complete without looking at what happened to his descendants and the dynasty he founded. The lives of William Cox Jnr, James, George, Henry and Edward further illustrate the continued rise and slower ultimate decline of the landed gentry. In acquiring land the first generation had been nakedly ambitious in the way that settlers on any new frontier have to be, although much less so than the settlers of the American West were. The second generation of Coxes were more socially ambitious and less obviously grasping, but they continued in their father's tradition of buying land, whenever the opportunity arose. It has also to be remembered that their lands were often heavily mortgaged, which helps to explain their continued antipathy to the squatters, whether gentlemen or not, who took land without paying for it. But mortgages did not stop William's sons continuing to expand their estates and build themselves suitably splendid houses.

George Cox's letters reveal that they took up the extraordinarily large area of 60,000 acres at Nombie on the Liverpool Plains in 1838,[1] while the State Records show land purchases by the sons both before and after their father's death. William Jnr completed the purchase of 4000 acres on the Upper Hunter on 12 June 1837 'permitted by Govr Brisbane's warrant dated 23 June 1825'(apparently the same warrant upon which his father had once relied) on 19 September 1831 and George purchased 958 acres at Mudgee for £239 17s on 10 December 1833,[2] while Edward applied for a further 1100 acres bounded by Thrall's Creek at Mulgoa on 31 August 1836, having paid £21 15s for 814 acres there on 30 May 1834. These were near to the grant that his mother had obtained for him in 1804, on which William Snr built The Cottage in 1811 for his sons' future use until they married.[3] Having been restored by the architectural historian James Broadbent, it is now the oldest inhabited house in Australia.

The sons displayed their social ambitions – far greater ones than their father ever had – through the houses they built for themselves. James

Broadbent remarks: 'second generation landowners, such as William Cox junior ... began to build or rebuild, confidently encouraged by the prosperous economy and uninhibited by their environment'.[4] William Jnr rebuilt Hobartville in Richmond in 1827. At Mulgoa, Henry built Glenmore in 1825. George added a second storey to his 1824 mansion Winbourne in 1842, the year before the Bank of Australia crashed. Edward was delayed by the 1840s depression and forced to compromise on a second storey at Fernhill, which he only completed in 1845. James began Clarendon in Tasmania in 1834.

The sons were thus somewhat different to the father, though not by a wide margin. If one believes in the effect of inherited genes, then the great fortitude of Rebecca, coupled with William's own determination, accounts for the sons of the first marriage turning out to be rather more enterprising than those of the second to Anna Blachford. Her son Alfred described her as 'remarkable for her commonsense, and her promptness in acting when ... called up to settle differences [in William's absence] among the men and women composing the little community in which she lived'.[5] Notwithstanding her household abilities, there is less to be said of her sons than might have been expected, although they were close to their half brothers. Edgar and Alfred both eventually went with their mother to New Zealand. Alfred moved in 1858, 20 years after Anna had married Dr Alexander Gamack, the surgeon at the Windsor Hospital, which she did in December 1837, the year that William died. They will be looked at first.

Edgar had inherited a considerable amount of land: the 1823 acre Hereford farm at Bathurst, where he bred racehorses, another 2000 acres, also in the County of Roxburgh, 2560 acres in the County of Wellington, 640 acres at Burrandong, another 640 which William originally bought from Bell and 100 acres also at Bathurst (presumably in the settlement). If Edgar died then these six properties were to go to Alfred, who inherited 1000 acres in Roxburgh directly.[6] Edgar married the old family friend, John Piper's daughter, Andrewina. Why he later abandoned this substantial pastoralist holding and followed his mother to New Zealand is not clear.

But something went badly wrong with the family subsequently, because their eldest son, Edgar William Piper Cox, died intestate at a great age in 1918, being described as an estate manager of Tomago, Hexham, New South Wales.[7]

Alfred too lived for a considerable time in the colony and in 1848 was involved with George Cox, the lawyer Beddek and with Gamack, in settling William's estate.[8] But in 1855, having been there several times, he decided to move to New Zealand, sold his New South Wales properties and obtained two grazing runs at Raukapuka, where he built a homestead in 1860 and was a magistrate. He died in 1911 at the age of 85. His 'Reminiscences', covering the years 1825, when he was a small boy at Clarendon, and up to 1911, give verbal portraits of his brothers and half-brothers, which no one else did. Overall, the second marriage produced no dynastic or leading pastoralist outcome, since Thomas also emigrated.

Thomas went to Cambridge, with money left for the purpose by his father, and after a short European tour to Germany and Switzerland did return to the colony in 1848, asking in advance for a horse to be bought for him. He and Alfred stayed briefly with George at Winbourne in June 1848.[9] Alfred commented of Tom: 'It seemed at one time there was a prospect of his remaining in the Colony and engaging in squatting pursuits, but the fancy was short-lived, he returned to England in less than a year with the view of reading for the Church'. He eventually became a country rector in Somerset. He had inherited a valuable house on O'Connell Street in Sydney, at the heart of what is now the Central Business District, and was no doubt helped financially by the house being rented to the government.[10] This property had been the subject of a brief official exchange, after it was built, when William got the better of Governor Brisbane over the latter hesitating to approve renting it for the new head of the Commissariat Department, called Boyes, before he arrived. William told the Governor that he now had 'an opportunity of letting the premises on a lease to a tenant I approve of. I am unwilling to let it stand over.' Brisbane capitulated and took the house.[11]

The sons of William's first marriage were more distinguished (Charles was killed by natives in Fiji on a voyage to China in 1813 at the age of 21) and truer to their father's ideas. One might have expected William Jnr to have continued the Cox tradition in public life. In fact he simply became a country gentleman at Richmond, largely declining major social responsibilities. He had been born on 13 November 1789 and had been left at the City Grammar School in Salisbury, together with James, when the rest of the family sailed for New South Wales.[12] As recorded earlier, the boys both came out to the colony in July 1804, when William was 14, and were given grants of land by Governor King jointly with their father.[13] He was described by his half-brother Alfred as being 'not strikingly like his father, either in appearance or character. He was of medium height, somewhat inclined to fleshiness ... more than any of his brothers he had the look of a well-conditioned Englishman, he was a well-set up man, having obviously been drilled in his youth'. No doubt he had been during his army service. At his death those living in the neighbourhood said 'they knew no-one ... coming nearer ... to their ideal of an English Country Gentleman'.[14]

William Jnr was commissioned into the New South Wales Corps on 10 March 1808 as an ensign and returned with it (as the 102nd Regiment) to England. He was said to have later transferred to the 46th Regiment, which had been posted to the colony, but that unit did not take part in the Peninsular War, where he served on the Staff Commissariat as a lieutenant. He took part in the memorably bloody siege Badajoz in 1812, under Wellington, when the British lost 4800 dead and wounded and Wellington wept when he fully realized the extent of the carnage. It is said of Badajoz that it made friendships of a kind that could not have been forged in any other way, although this has surely been true of most such bitter battles, from Agincourt to Arnhem.

One happy result was that William married the sister of an engineer officer, Captain Robert Sloper Piper, whom he had served alongside (and who ended up as a colonel). Confusingly, in Cox family terms, William's bride was called Elizabeth, but was unconnected to the family's close friend Major John Piper.[15] Their children carried the middle name Sloper. William's rank of lieutenant in the army dated from December 1812 and he transferred to the 46th Regiment in 1813. He went on to the Irish half-pay list on 11 June 1818, as belonging to the 12th Regiment of Foot, but only sold his commission as an unattached lieutenant on 5 June 1835.[16] These dates tie in with his return to the colony in 1814 to live as a gentleman of somewhat aristocratic pretensions.

Curiously, in spite of having been granted that land back in 1804, when his father had portrayed him as a newly arrived free settler, he was listed in April 1818 among 'persons permitted to become free settlers and who are to receive government cattle'.[17] As long after this as April 1835 he was 'allowed the commutation allowance on the purchase of land', as a half-pay lieutenant of the 12th Regiment of Foot from June 1818.[18] This was the same commutation of pay that ex-officer squatters benefited from, although William can hardly have needed the money. It was exactly the sort of thing that his father would have done.

Meanwhile in 1816 he had bought the estate of Hobartville at

Hobartville, William Jnr's house at Richmond (Author's photo)

Richmond, with its 'neat and commodious house', which he rebuilt in the 1820s to be a much more architecturally ambitious country house in a basic Palladian design with a Doric columned porch. The design by Francis Greenway is described by Broadbent as uninspired, but refined in design and detail.[19] The French windows of the drawing room look out over lawns to a lagoon, with the mountains beyond. The whole concept is of a true country gentleman's residence. Appropriately, today it is the home of a racing stud owner. Hobartville became known for the couples' parties and balls. A well-known watercolour of the reception hall in later years depicts a surge of young ladies ascending the grand staircase at a ball, although they are shown smaller than life size compared to the staircase to make it seem more impressive.

Alfred wrote of Elizabeth that the 'real secret of this remarkable [social] success was mainly due to the clever management and social instincts of his [William's] wife … who had few equals as a hostess in the Colony'. Her letters are indeed strikingly illustrative of the very different life that she led to that of her deceased mother-in-law, Rebecca, which was equally true of Edward's wife, Jane Maria, at their Mulgoa mansion, Fernhill. The first generation's wives left little correspondence and in instances when they did – most notably the letters of Elizabeth Macarthur – they reflected the practicalities of settlers' lives, not their frivolities. By contrast, on 26 September 1832 Elizabeth wrote to Mrs Piper saying, 'Captain Chetwode … gets plenty of his brother officers up from Parramatta to our Balls, which makes us look dashing'. Chetwode had been in the same regiment as her brother.

On 3 May 1835, she wrote to a relation: 'My dear Cousin, I hear you … are coming to the Ball and I need not say for as long as you like to make your stay at Hobartville'. She added that she had wanted to take her two girls to their grandfather (William Snr) 'but the measles being in the house, we may be prevented'.[20] William Jnr did not escape being hit by the financial disasters of the 1840s. George Cox commented in August 1846 that 'The Hobartville party was not near so large as last year … there were not forty altogether … did not break up until near two o'clock'. It sounds as though, financial depression or no depression, there was a major ball each year, not to mention other parties which Alfred mentioned and Anna would have enjoyed, since she was something of a party-giver herself.[21]

Later, on 3 October of 1835, Elizabeth wrote to tell John Piper, then at Alloway Bank near Bathurst: 'We had His Excellency, Sir John [Jamison] and Capt Wentworth here two days this week that I really began to think our house would never be empty. Mrs Blachford is still with us, but we look upon her as one of ourselves.' (This was Anna's mother who, after her other daughter married the solicitor Francis Beddek in Windsor, had evidently come to live there herself.)[22] These brief excerpts convey the flavour of a wealthy second generation enjoying itself, at the same time as the husbands acquired more land and fulfilled a modicum of community duties.

William's aristocratic inclinations were displayed in 1828, when Anna Cox (Blachford)'s sister was married at Windsor. He arrived with his wife in a carriage drawn by six plumed horses, adorned with his coat of arms, and which bore white favours as part of the 'gay turnout', as one lady witness described it to Mrs John Piper. It was an elegant wedding. 'Miss Blachford wore a clear muslin dress, beautifully worked at the bottom and lace let in, over a sarsenet slip, the hem of the skirt was satin and the body trimmed with pipings of white satin and lace and a lace pelerine, silk handkerchief, and watered ribbon band, a leghorn bonnet trimmed with satin ribbon and a handsome white veil.'[23] This description has been confused with Anna's wedding to William Snr, of 1821, but the original letter in the Mitchell Library makes it clear that it was not.

William did display his father's regard for helping assigned convicts if they deserved it. Agnes Wicks had come out on the *Princess Royal* in 1828 and been assigned to him in 1829 as a house servant. She stayed with him three years, being described by him as 'honest, sober and industrious', and fell in love with a carpenter he also employed, as described earlier. William helped the pair by promising to keep them in his employ until they got their tickets of leave.[24] The application to publish their marriage banns was made at Richmond on

16 May 1831.[25] William was less lucky in the same year with Ann Huldie, off the same ship, who stole things, tried to blame the theft on the nanny and wound up in gaol.[26] It is evident that William maintained a fair-sized establishment at Hobartville, in purely domestic terms greater than his father's at Clarendon. The basements in which the servants lived are quite extensive.[27]

Thus William Jnr basically followed the career of a landed gentleman, employing convict 'mechanics' and obtaining land grants. His half-brother Alfred considered that he had 'less energy and enterprise than the father'.[28] He did behave like a traditional squire in espousing some local benevolent causes, becoming treasurer of the Windsor Benevolent Society in 1828. He and his brother George were named among a long list of those proposed for the Legislative Council in December 1835, any 12 of whom were to be selected by Governor Bourke. The others included Sir John Jamison, W. C. Wentworth, John Blaxland, Hannibal Macarthur, James Macarthur and William Lawson, in an eclectic mix of two generations, with the exclusives prominent.[20] William was not chosen. In 1839, when Sir George Gipps was in near-desperation to find members, he was invited to stand, but by then had changed his mind and 'Declined on the ground that his domestic habits rendered him unfit for the duties of public life'. Gipps had described him as 'amongst our most respectable and wealthy Settlers'.[30]

However, in 1842 William did consent to be appointed as a magistrate of the territory, along with James Macarthur and three of the Blaxland sons.[31] In other words, he pursued much the same sort of life as a wealthy squire would have followed in England, though hardly that of an English aristocrat. In England the gulf between the squirearchy and the aristocracy was vast. Had he been an eldest son in England the family estates would have devolved upon him and been protected by entail. Here it had been unnecessary, emphasizing the way in which the Australian landed gentry model evolved differently to its spiritual parent. William died in 1850, only 13 years after his father.

William and Rebecca's second son, James, was much more in the adventurous mould of his father and has been described as a man of outstanding ability and a true pioneer.[32] Alfred considered he was strikingly like their father in face and figure and 'had his father's energy, the same clear head, and as strong a determination when he took a matter in hand to go through with it'. He moved to Van Diemen's Land in 1814, with his wife Mary Connell, where he created a career and an estate in ways of which his father would have fully approved. He told Alfred years later, in 1847, presumably when Alfred was working in Tasmania, that the move was because, when William was away in England (from 1806 to 1809) he had been 'his father's representative and sole manager'. He felt, on his father's return, that 'it would be well to think out a course for himself'. He certainly had been running the farm with Rebecca and been a leading signatory of the Hawkesbury residents' addresses to Bligh.

Soon after his arrival James acquired land at Port Dalrymple and in 1817 he had become a wholesale merchant, with a government contract to supply meat to the garrison, and was appointed a magistrate. In 1819, around the time of Commissioner Bigge's visit, James was granted a total of 6700 acres on the South Esk River at Morven (renamed Evandale in 1836) which he named Clarendon after his father's estate, but for fear of bushrangers and Aborigines moved into Launceston to live.

In April 1820 he wrote an account of the Port Dalrymple and Launceston area for Bigge, noting that he paid his convict labourers £25 a year in clothing, necessaries and food, which was comparable to the more generous masters in mainland New South Wales.[33] Bigge recorded in his Report on Agriculture and Trade: 'At Port Dalrymple there are four individuals who possess considerable quantities of stock, and of these Mr Cox Jnr is making some attempt to improve both his land and the quality of his wool'.[34] Bigge had made extensive enquiries about agricultural improvements on the mainland and would have seen greater attempts there, hence his disparaging tone. In his letter James also bemoaned the large number of unprincipled ex-convicts in the area. Bigge bemoaned that 'Three magistrates at Launceston, Mr Archer, Cox and Captain Beverly, were occupied largely in agriculture or trade with the exception of Mr

Archer [one of them] did not command the respect of the inhabitants'.[35]

That must have changed, if it was ever correct, since James came to prosper greatly as a pastoralist, bringing merino sheep from the Macarthur flock at Camden, and establishing a stud breeding from an Arab stallion, Hadji Baba. Between 1834 and 1838 he built one of the greatest mansions of Australia at Clarendon, also creating a deer park with imported fallow deer. The house is described as having 'simplicity, taste and imagination … grand without being overpowering'.[36]

Clarendon, James Cox's mansion on the banks of the South Esk River, Tasmania (Author's photo)

His first wife had died and he had then married the daughter of Lieutenant Governor Collins, Eliza. He acquired other farms, naming some after his father's Dorset origins, notably Fernhill (which came to him through his second wife) and Winburn and founded the village of Lymington. After Tasmania became a colony in its own right in 1824 he was a member of the Legislative Council, later from 1851 to 1854 being a member of the first elected House of Assembly there. He also helped to found the Cornwall Bank.

James died on 17 March 1865, leaving life occupancy of the great house to Eliza. His grandson, also James, inherited next, but sadly two generations later the estate was acquired compulsorily by the government in 1915 under the Closer Settlement Acts with £22,000 compensation, following the early death of the third inheritor, John Claud Cox. It was divided into nine lots. The widow of John Claud was able to keep the homestead block, but eventually found it untenable with only 687.5 acres. The house was endangered by its weight being too great for the foundations and in 1962 the then owner donated the homestead to the National Trust of Australia (Tasmania), which has gradually restored it to the original state, including reconstructing the magnificent – but overweight – portico. James and his descendants had lived there for a century and his descendants have been active ever since with agricultural pursuits. James had been, in every way, a chip off the old block.

Henry Cox, the fourth son, had been born at Devizes in 1796 and, like George, had travelled out with his parents on the *Minerva*. He assisted at the first depot during the mountain road building, where William recorded him helping to count what proved to be a satisfactory 75 pieces of pork in a cask, but did not mention him again. He married in 1823 and settled initially with his wife Frances at The Cottage – a house that was much in demand and at times was shared – until in 1825 he built Glenmore at

Glenmore, Henry Cox's house at Mulgoa (Author's photo)

Mulgoa, a sandstone bungalow with attic rooms beneath a hipped roof and with large wine cellars, today a golf clubhouse. Here, like George, he cultivated vines, orchards and wheatfields and eventually bought some of Captain Waterhouse's famed sheep and cattle. However this was not on the 400 acres, named as being at Bringelly, granted to him by Macquarie in 1821, because that land lacked water.[37] In the early 1850s he transferred most of the sheep to his estate of Broombee at Mudgee, but appears to have leased the run to his brother George (it was only eight miles from Burrundulla). He was not a magistrate and seems to have taken little interest in public affairs, although he did join his father and his brother George in the address by Landed Proprietors and Merchants in July 1825 supporting Governor Darling.

Henry was involved in an historically interesting potential conflict with the local Aborigines in 1848 on another run he owned near Wellington on the Barwon River, where the natives had extensive fish trap enclosures. The Commissioner of Crown lands advocated creating a reserve for them of one square mile. There was no suggestion that Henry had acted improperly towards the Aborigines, although others might have done so, but the idea of such a reserve was novel. The Attorney General declined to allow it.[38] Henry died on 1 April 1874, having made no great impact on the society around him, nor does he seem to have been active in the construction of St Thomas' church at Mulgoa, which Edward and George had strongly supported.

In many ways the life of Edward, William and Rebecca's youngest son, reveals more about the society they all lived in, while his son made a real impact on the colony. As already mentioned, Edward's first grant of land at Mulgoa had been obtained for him at the age of four by Rebecca. As a 16-year-old he was sent by William to learn sheep farming in Yorkshire. On his return his father obtained the farm which they called Rawdon on the Bathurst plains for him, as detailed in Chapter 10. Edward then obtained for himself a far rarer colonial commodity – a locally born heiress. This was Jane Maria Brooks, the daughter of an exploitative and rich ship owner and trader, Richard Brooks. Once she had acquired a gentleman husband her

Edward Cox, seen in middle age

memoirs show her as having become something of a snob, but not as talented a letter writer or hostess as her sister-in-law, Elizabeth.

Jane Maria's 'Reminiscences', which were only compiled by her between 1870 and 1880, when she was old, described both her upbringing and the early days of her marriage. Her father, captaining a ship with a letter of marque, meaning he was an authorized privateer, also made 'a great deal of money' when chartered to bring prisoners out in 1808. She remembered Elizabeth Macquarie and dinners given by John Piper at Piper Point, and enjoyed five or six very happy years before she married, which positions her in the era. She married Edward in the mid to late 1820s and, if as an heiress she looked for a handsome husband, as well as a gentleman, she obtained one. A portrait of Edward in middle age shows him as good looking, with wavy hair, elegantly dressed in a well-cut suit with a wing collar and extravagant bow tie, holding a gold (?) knobbed cane.

Jane Maria had been born in London in 1806, 'the year Mr Pitt died', and after she married Edward they 'went to live at Mulgoa Cottage, it was a very pretty place … and my two brothers in law [were] about two miles on either side [Henry and George], so that my dear parents were not concerned for my safety, besides we had a grand neighbour in Sir John Jamison'. This must have been after George vacated The Cottage and built Winbourne, not far down the road. After many years at The Cottage, Edward embarked on building what would become one of the colony's most distinguished houses, probably in 1839. He brought 20 stonemasons from Ireland to build this house, Fernhill, the name yet again echoing his father's Dorset beginnings.

The internationally known architect Philip Cox, another descendant, describes Fernhill as 'one of the grander houses built by the early settlers … on a gently rising hill from which panoramic views along the Nepean Valley are gained'. He refers to its magnificent circular verandah and single shaft stone columns, and remarks, in a sentence that reinforces the view of the second generation proposed above: 'There is a magic in these buildings which dispels all thought of an earlier Australia which had to be tamed. Instead, a languor prevails, and a sense of belonging, suggesting a gentle life by the early settlers, which is far from the truth.'[39] Indeed it was extremely tough, as George's letters from Mulgoa in the 1840s show.

Broadbent remarks that the house reflects 'the confidence, wealth and social status of the "pure merino" pastoralist who built it'. Even in its unfinished state 'it is one of the grandest and most impressive country houses built in colonial New South Wales'. During the years of depression building work somehow continued, although in 1840 Jane Maria feared they would never complete the house, and it may not have been until 1845 that the family moved in. It is thought to have been designed by the architect Mortimer William Lewis, who also designed W. C. Wentworth's Vaucluse.

Of their earlier days at Fernhill Jane Maria wrote 'I remember Sir Francis Forbes, William Charles Wentworth and many other military men'. She then said cattily of Forbes, 'He was persuaded to give a Grand Fancy Ball, but it was like a great many other foolish things, a failure'.[40] Her memories, like Elizabeth Cox's letters, conjure up a very different style of domestic living to that of the previous generation. Even so, the hardships of expanding estates beyond the mountains, as Edward continued to do, were still considerable, although in the 1820s quite a few settlers around Bathurst were simply living the life of country gentlemen, rather than pioneers, as John Piper did. This said, there were frequent ambushes on the road by bushrangers and George always sent cheques in two halves by different mail coaches.

Living grandly and farming sheep at Rawdon were by no means everything that Edward achieved. He became both a magistrate at Mulgoa and a member of the Legislative Council, while he gave five acres of land for the Mulgoa

Edward's Cox's mansion, Fernhill, at Mulgoa (Courtesy of Philip Cox)

church in 1836. Records show that he made wine, being given permission to import vine dressers from Europe in 1847, as were his brother George and James King, his father's long-serving aide, who also lived at in The Cottage at Mulgoa for a time but moved out when it became too crowded.[41] The Cottage, incidentally, later became know as Claremont Cottage and was lived in by the solicitor Francis Beddek, after he married Anna Cox's sister in 1828.

Although the 1840s brought disasters for many, they were happily not fatal for Edward. He, along with his late father, was a shareholder in the Bank of Australia, having 18 shares of £50 each and 12 of £100, making a total of a substantial £2100. In 1843 the bank went under. As Governor Gipps explained in a despatch to Lord Stanley, the bank having been formed on the joint stock principle, 'every Shareholder in it is liable for the debts of the Bank to the full amount of his property'.[42] So shareholders not only lost their capital, they had to pay the bank's debts. William Snr had owned 10 shares of £100 each and his executors paid up, even though this was so long after his death, as George Cox's letters show. Edward was one of a committee set up to sort out the shareholders' affairs. He was not bankrupted, although the intended upper storey of Fernhill was never built. But this was a great deal better than it was for families like that of

John Blaxland, who lost everything. Fernhill, Glenmore, Winbourne and the Burrundulla estate at Mudgee survived, when Blaxland's administrators were paying 5s in the pound on the debts of Luddenham in the Mulgoa valley and Newington. To repeat Bennett's remark: 'Castles in the air had suddenly faded'. Happily, the dream did not fade for Edward's children either.

His son, Edward King Cox, born in 1829, inherited the Rawdon merino stud and became an outstanding breeder of stud stock, winning many awards for his wool, particularly the grand prize at the Exposition Universelle in Paris in 1878. He also bred shorthorn cattle and racehorses, winning the Sydney and Melbourne Cups. Racing was a tradition in the family too, William having been a co-founder of the Racing Club in 1825. He was appointed to the Legislative Council in 1874.[43] So this grandson of William was, like his uncle George Cox, a true inheritor. He was fortunate in having a rich mother and became more distinguished than his father, earning a place in the *Australian Dictionary of Biography*, which his father has not. Another son, James Charles Cox, became a distinguished medical practitioner, presaging the move of later generations into the professions.

A candid personal account of those catastrophic 1840s was left by George Cox in a series of letters to his sons unearthed among old papers at Burrundulla, having lain unread for 100 years. They have been edited by a descendant, Edna Hickson. George was William Snr's fourth son. He married Eliza Bell, a daughter of Archibald Bell, a family friend who has featured frequently in this account, in 1822. They lived for a time at The Cottage at Mulgoa, before Edward and his new wife did, until building their own mansion, Winbourne, in 1824, the year their son Henry George Cox was born. A visitor described it in 1836 as 'a substantial mansion, having the features of an Englishman's park'.[44] George added a second storey in 1842 to meet the needs of his growing family, which eventually totalled four girls and six boys. He had been a JP at Mulgoa since 1827.[45] He donated 38 acres of land for the construction of a parsonage, after Edward had given land for the church, where many Coxes lie buried. What was more remarkable about him was his uncomplaining fortitude.

George Cox was an obviously thoughtful man and concerned with agricultural improvements, who emulated his father in his organization of the Winbourne estate, which was not only self supporting and raised stock, but had extensive vineyards. In 1846 George produced 1000 gallons of wine, largely from the burgundy grape, which he presumably marketed. He also produced 'Shiraz, Sherry and Oportos'. The following year he won third prize for one of his wines at the Richmond Show, one of the local agricultural shows which survived the demise of the Agricultural Society. He worked hard to improve the quality of the wool from his flocks, collaborating with his son George Henry, who ran the estate at Mudgee.

The 1840s depression hit George very badly. He does not seem to have been a shareholder in the ill-fated Bank of Australia, in fact was an executor dealing with its affairs, and he shared the burden of dealing with his father's liabilities. But he was hit by the fall in the value of sheep and cattle, with rapidly rising interest rates on bank loans. Eventually a cow would fetch only £2 10s from a butcher, if a buyer could be found at all. George was reduced to boiling down carcasses for tallow, a disgusting job which he did himself on the farm, in order to get £26 a ton for the resulting product.

Most of George's letters were sent across the mountains to George Henry at Burrundulla, where he built the present homestead in 1864 and which is now the Coxes' only surviving estate. His son became a national

Mulgoa church, endowed by the Coxes (Author's photo)

Edward Cox's tomb at Mulgoa (Author's photo)

figure, who at the same time maintained that the ownership of land carried social and political obligations. He became the first mayor of Cudgegong in 1860, after having been a member for Wellington on the first Legislative Assembly at the age of 32. In 1863 he was appointed to the Legislative Council, where he sat until his death. He continued family support for the church at Mulgoa as well as promoting the construction of one at Mudgee. His grandson describes him as having 'combined Parliamentary and Church obligations with supervising the conduct and improvement of thousands of acres and such menial tasks as classing his extensive merino flocks'.[46] He built the present Burrundulla mansion in 1864. But in a way it was George who had already saved Burrundulla in 1847 when he 'set up a system of tenant farmers, but continued to work most of it himself'. He also sold some of the farms to tenants.[47] These were 40 acre plots on the Cudgegong River, where the tenants were able to buy later on a similar system to Edward Gibbon Wakefield's ideas. This also served the expansion of food production needed locally after the gold rush of 1851 at Gulgong.

In 1822 Commissioner Bigge wrote to the Secretary of State: 'In the colony of New South Wales there exists a Spirit of jealousy and animosity amongst the higher Classes of the Inhabitants, that has destroyed the comfort of Private Society and impeded the advancement of Public Institutions'.[48] This has been described in some detail in the last chapter. Happily it seems as though this 'spirit' did not motivate the second generation of the Cox family in their relationships with others, even though some of that generation were more politicized than their forbears. The catalogue of their achievements is more constructive. If this chapter has emphasized the country houses which William's sons built it is because they represented a large part of the sons' ambitions in life. But they did not fall into the trap of overweening ambition that caused George Hobler's equally magnificent Aberglasslyn to be abandoned and which gave 'a lesson on the pride, pretensions, avarice and eventual downfall of the high flying pastoralists of the 1830s and 1840s'.[49]

One important part of his sons' inheritance from William was commonsense and, as was especially shown in George's reactions to adversity, a quiet determination to get on with the job in hand, which had also characterized James. As Dyster has remarked, if those who survived the disastrous 1840s – Australia's first depression – 'no longer played the *undisputed* role that they had twenty years before … In their home districts they were still the men given pride of place.'[50] In 1867 Bennett was still able to list the Coxes among 30 families who were 'the landed gentry of that part of the colony.'[51] Geographically this left out the one estate still in Cox hands today, Burrundulla.

In 1901 the authors of the *Memoirs* reckoned that William had a thousand descendants. Even allowing for the families of the early days having been much larger than in the twentieth century – William had ten children, his son Thomas fathered ten, George also ten – after a further century or so the number must have greatly multiplied. Most have pursued professional careers. Many have been military officers – a Cox fought and was killed at El Alamein. Among the men, and more recently women, there have been academics, architects, authors, at least one spy, lawyers (many), diplomats, property developers and even – perish the thought – a stage entertainer. The family at Burrundulla still breeds racehorses and sheep and now makes wine. William's genes run strong and many of his descendants, in all generations, have displayed his two great qualities: organizational ability and determination.

Burrundulla, the one remaining estate still in family hands (Courtesy of Christopher Cox)

Bibliography

1. Printed Primary Sources

Army List, 1795–1835, National Archives, Kew, London.

Bennett, Samuel, *History of Australian Discovery and Colonisation*, Hanson & Bennett, Pitt Street, Sydney, vol. 1, 1865.

Bigge, John Thomas, Report of the Commissioner of Inquiry into the State of the Colony of New South Wales, its Government and Police; Management of the Convicts, their character and habits; State of Society; Agriculture and Trade, *British Parliamentary Papers*, (448), vol. 10, 539, June 1822.

Bigge, John Thomas, Report of the Commissioner of Inquiry on the state of Agriculture and Trade in the Colony of New South Wales, *British Parliamentary Papers*, vol. 10, 136, 13 March 1823.

Burke, Sir John Bernard, *A Genealogical and Heraldic History of the Colonial Gentry*, Harrison, London, 1891, pp. 74–76, 2nd ed. 1895, pp. 781-84.

Burke, Sir John, *Heraldic History of the Commoners of Great Britain and Ireland*, H. Colburn, London, 1835, vol. 4, subsequently updated and republished.

Census of New South Wales, 1822, 1828.

Colonial Secretary Index 1788–1825 in Mitchell Library. References after 1826, not printed, State Records, Kingswood, NSW.

Cunningham, Peter, Surgeon R.N., *Two Years in New South Wales*, Henry Colburn, London, 1827.

Eden, Sir Frederick Morton, *The State of the Poor*, 3 vols, J. Davis, London, 1797.

Historical Records of Australia, Series 1, 3.

Historical Records of New South Wales, vols v, vi.

Holt, Joseph, *Memoirs of Joseph Holt*, ed. T. Crofton Croker, vol. 2, Henry Colburn, London, 1838.

Lang, Gideon Scott, *Land and Labour in Australia*, Melbourne, 1845.

London Gazette, 1795–1809, National Archives, Kew, London.

Macarthur, James, *New South Wales, its Present State and Future Prospects*, D. Walther, London, 1837.

Marsden, Samuel, *Statement chiefly relating to the Formation and Abandonment of a Mission to the Aboriginals of New South Wales*, R. Howe, Government Printer, Sydney, 1828.

Marshall, William, *On the Landed Property of England*: an elementary and practical treatise, concerning the purchase, the improvement and the management of Landed Estates, G. and W. Nicol, G. and J. Robinson, R. Faulder, Longman and Rees, Cadell and Davies, and J. Hatchard, London, 1804.

Pickering, William, *A Guide to Wimborne Minster*, Pickering, London, 1830

Royal Kalenders 1784, 1789, 1793, National Archives, Kew.

Wentworth, William Charles, *Statistical, Historical and Political Description of the Colony of New South Wales and in Van Diemen's Land*, printed for G. & W. B. Whittaker, London, 1819.

White's Directory of Christchurch, White's, Christchurch, 1859.

Newspapers and Newsletters

Sydney Gazette, 1803–28.

Hobart Gazette, 1818–21.

News from the State Records of New South Wales, 2010–11.

2. Primary Printed Sources Later Reprinted

Bannister, Saxe, late Attorney General in New South Wales, *Humane Policy or Justice to the Aborigines of New Settlements*, London 1838, republished by Dawsons of Pall Mall, London, 1968.

Cobbett, William, *Selections from William Cobbett's Illustrated Rural Rides, 1826–1832*, ed. Christopher Norris, Webb and Bower, London, 1984.

General Muster and Land and Stock Muster of New South Wales 1822, ed. Carol Baxter, Australian Biographical and Genealogical Record, North Sydney, 1988.

Cox, George, *George Cox of Mulgoa and Mudgee: Letters to his Sons 1846–49*, with notes by Edna Hickson, privately printed, 1980.

Cox, William, *Memoirs of William Cox J.P.*, William Brooks and Co., Sydney, 1901. Facsimile reprint, Library of Australian History, North Sydney, 1979.

Mudie, James, *The Felonry of New South Wales*, 1837, ed. Walter Stone, Angus & Robertson, London, 1995

Report from the Select Committee on Transportation, 1838, together with the Minutes of Evidence, Appendix and Index, House of Commons, *British Parliamentary Papers*, 14 July 1837, facsimile edition, Irish University Press, Shannon. Proceedings, Chronological Series, 1968.

The Universal British Directory of Trade, Commerce and Manufacture, sold by C. Stalker, London, 5 vols, 1791–98.
Threlkeld, L. E., *Australian Reminiscences and Papers of L. E. Threlkeld, Missionary to the Aborigines 1824–1859*, ed. Niel Gunson, Aboriginal Studies No. 4, Australian Institute of Aboriginal Studies, Canberra, 1974.

3. Unpublished Primary Sources
Banks, Sir Joseph, Banks Papers, Mitchell Library, Sydney, vol. 22.
Bigge, John Thomas, Appendices to the Parliamentary Commissioners Report, CO 201/120, CO 201/121, CO 201/1123, Bonwick Transcripts, Boxes 5, 14, 15, 16, 18, 20, 24, 25, 26, 28, Mitchell Library, Sydney.
Bonwick Transcripts of New South Wales official correspondence.
Campbell, John Thomas, 'Report of the Governor's Tour of Inspection', April 1815, Colonial Secretary Index, reel 6038, SZ 159.
Certificate of William Cox's Army Commission, ML Mss 6079, Mitchell Library, Sydney.
Courts Martial Records, 1806–09, National Archives, Kew, WO 71/145,212.
Cox, Alfred, 'Family Reminiscences, 1884', transcribed by Bryan Cox, New Zealand, 1997.
Cox, George, correspondence, 1846–67, ML Mss 1150.
Cox, George, 'A Journal kept by Mr George Cox on his late Tour to Northward and Eastward of "Bathurst"', 1821, transcribed 28.3.1974, National Library of Australia, Canberra, NLA ref M71224.
Cox, George Henry Frederick, 'A History of Mudgee', unpublished, written 1909 or 1910, typed copy in Mudgee Library, NSW.
Cox, William, 'Last Will and Testament of William Cox of Fairfield, Windsor', 21 December 1836, typed copy and photocopy made by Thelma and Matthew Birrell, undated, Priest's House Museum, Wimborne, Dorset.
Macquarie, Lachlan, 'Journal of a Tour in the newly Discovered Country, 25 April – 19 May 1815', ML reel CY 33, A 779.
Macquarie, Lachlan, 'Journal of a Tour of Inspection 1810–1811', Mitchell Library, CY reel 302, A 778.
New South Wales Corps, correspondence, WO 4/486, National Archives, Kew, London.
Piper Papers, vols 2 and 3, 1832, Mitchell Library ref A255, 256.
Price, John Washington, 'A Journal kept on board the Minerva Transport from Ireland to New South Wales', British Library, Mss 13380.
Registry of Baptisms, Marriages and Deaths, Dorset History Centre, Dorchester, England.
Various documents re William Cox stored in three envelopes, ML, Ac 42/1-3. These include bills of exchange and W. C. Wentworth's counsel's opinion of 9 August 1832.
Wiltshire Historical Records, County Records and Parish Records, Wiltshire & Swindon History Centre, Chippenham, Wiltshire, England.
Youll, Anne, letter of 11 December 1903 from Balham, London, to Winfred Cox at Cann River, Orbost, Victoria, ML Mss 6731.

4. Unpublished Secondary Manuscripts
Cox, David, 'Historian's Report 1986', William Cox Fellowship, privately distributed by David Cox, Blackheath, NSW.
'Cox, of Clarendon, N. S. Wales', 35 pages unpublished and unsigned typescript, giving family genealogy 1400 to approx 1900, copy held by Priest's House Museum, Wimborne, Dorset.

5. Printed Secondary Sources (Books, Chapters, Articles)
Books
Atkinson, Alan, *Camden*, Oxford University Press, Melbourne, 1988.
Atkinson, Alan, *The Europeans in Australia*, Oxford University Press, Melbourne, vol. 1, 1997, vol. 2, 2004.
Australian Council of National Trusts, *Historic Homesteads of Australia*, vol. 1, Cassell Australia, Stanmore, NSW, 1969.
Australian Historical Statistics, ed. Wray Vamplew, Fairfax, Syme &Wilson, Broadway, NSW, 1987.
Barkley-Jack, Jan, *Hawkesbury Settlement Revealed: A New Look at Australia's Third Mainland Settlement 1793– 1802*, Rosenberg, Kenthurst, NSW, 2009.
Bassett, Marnie, *The Governor's Lady*, 2nd ed., Oxford University Press, Oxford, 1956.
Bateson, Charles, *The Convict Ships 1787–1868*, Brown, Son and Ferguson, London, 1969.
Beamish, Derek, Dockerill, John, and Hillier, John, *The Pride of Poole 1688–1851*, Poole Historical Trust, Poole, Dorset, 1988.
Bettey, J. H., *Rural Life in Wessex 1500–1900*, Moonraker Press, Bradford on Avon, Wiltshire, 1977.
Blainey, Geoffrey, *A Land Half Won*, Macmillan, South Yarra, Victoria, 1980.
Bowd, D. G., *Macquarie Country: A History of the Hawkesbury*, Library of Australian History, Sydney, 1994.

Broadbent, James, *Elizabeth Farm*, Historic Houses Trust of NSW, Glebe, NSW, 1995.

Broadbent, James, *The Australian Colonial House*, Hordern Rare Books, Sydney, 1997.

Brooke, Alan, and Brandon, David, *Bound for Botany Bay: British Convict Voyages to Australia*, National Archives, Kew, 2000.

Cameron, Roderick, *Australian History and Horizons*, Weidenfeld & Nicolson, London, 1971.

Clark, C. M. H., *A History of Australia*, vol. 1, Melbourne University Press, Carlton, 1962; vol. 2, Melbourne University Press, Carlton, 1968; vol. 3, Melbourne University Press, Carlton, 1973.

Clayton, Anthony, *The British Officer*, Pearson Longman, London, 2006.

Clemons, G. M. W., *Historic Homesteads of Australia*, Cassell Australia, 1969.

Clendinnen, Inga, *Dancing with Strangers*, Text Publishing, Melbourne, 2003.

Clune, Frank, *Bound for Botany Bay: Narrative of a Voyage in 1798 Aboard the Death Ship Hillsborough*, Angus & Robertson, Sydney 1965.

Concise History of National Biography, Oxford University Press, Oxford, vol. 1, 1992.

Connor, John, *The Australian Frontier Wars, 1788–1838*, UNSW Press, Sydney, 2002.

Cox, Cornelia, and Rose, *Life at Clarendon* (nineteenth-century account), National Trust of Australia (Tasmania), 1988.

Cox, Philip, and Stacey, Wesley, *The Australian Homestead*, Lansdowne Press, Melbourne, 1972.

Cunningham, Chris, *The Blue Mountains Rediscovered: Beyond the Myths of Early Australian Exploration*, Kangaroo Press, East Roseville, NSW, 1996.

Daniels, Kay, *Convict Women*, Allen & Unwin, Sydney, 1998.

Darwin, John, *The Empire Project: The Rise and Fall of the British World System, 1830–1970*, Cambridge University Press, Cambridge, 2009.

de Serville, Paul, *Port Phillip Gentlemen*, Oxford University Press, Melbourne, 1980.

Draper, Jo, *The Georgians*, Dovecote Press, Wimborne, Dorset, 1998.

Ellis, M. H., *Lachlan Macquarie*, Angus & Robertson, Sydney, rev. ed., 1972.

Fletcher, Brian, *Colonial Australia Before 1850*, Nelson, London, 1976.

Fletcher, Brian, *Landed Enterprise and Penal Society: A History of Farming and Grazing in New South Wales Before 1821*, Sydney University Press, Sydney, 1976.

Fletcher, Brian, *Ralph Darling*, Oxford University Press, Melbourne, 1984.

Gascoigne, John, *The Enlightenment and the Origins of European Australia*, Cambridge University Press, Cambridge, 2002.

Grey, Jeffery, *A Military History of Australia 1788–1870*, Cambridge University Press, Cambridge, 1990.

Hampson, Norman, *The Enlightenment*, Penguin, London, 1990.

Hillier, John, *Ebb Tide at Poole 1815–1851*, Poole Historical Trust, Poole, Dorset, 1985.

Hirst, J. B., *Convict Society and its Enemies*, Allen & Unwin, North Sydney, 1983.

Hughes, Robert, *The Fatal Shore*, Knopf, New York, 1987.

Jeans, D. N., *An Historical Geography of New South Wales to 1901*, Reed Education, Sydney, 1972.

Jordanova, Ludmilla, *History in Practice*, 2nd ed., Hodder Education, London, 2006.

Karskens, Grace, *The Colony*, Allen & Unwin, Sydney, 2009

Kass, Terry, Liston, Carol, and McClymont, John, *Parramatta: A Past Revealed*, Parramatta City Council, Parramatta, 1996.

King, Hazel, *Richard Bourke*, Oxford University Press, Melbourne, 1971.

Kociumbas, Jan, *Oxford History of Australia*, vol. 2, Oxford University Press, Oxford, 1996.

Leeson, Eric, *William Cox – a Short Biography*, privately published, Wimborne, Dorset, 2008.

Light, Richard Upjohn, *A Study in Ancestry*, 2 vols, privately printed, Ann Arbor, Michigan, 1990.

McBurney, Yvonne, and Cox, David, *The Road to Bathurst*, Education Material Aid, Strathfield, NSW, 1988.

MacLaughlin, Eugene, and others, *Criminological Perspectives*, 2nd ed., Sage Publications, London, 2003.

Mant, Gilbert, *The Big Show*, Horowitz Publications, North Sydney, 1972.

Mowle, Percy Conrad, *A Genealogical History of the Pioneering Families of Australia*, 5th ed., Rigby, Adelaide, 1978.

Mulgoa Progress Association, *Mulgoa! Mulgoa! Where is That?*, privately printed, 1988.

Mumby, Lionel, *How Much is That Worth?*, Phillimore Books, Chichester, 1989.

Nicholas, Stephen, and Shergold, Peter R., eds, *Convict Workers: Re-Interpreting Australia's Past*, Cambridge University Press, Cambridge, 1988.

Oxford Dictionary of National Biography, Oxford University Press, Oxford, 2004.

Oxley, Deborah, *Convict Maids: The Forced Migration of Women to Australia*, Cambridge University Press, Melbourne, 1996.

Payne, Donald, *Dorset Harbours*, Christopher Johnson, London, 1953.

Popham, David, *The Book of Wimborne*, Barracuda Books, Buckingham, 1983.
Ritchie, John, *Lachlan Macquarie*, Melbourne University Press, Carlton, 1986.
Ritchie, John, *Profit and Punishment*, Heinemann, Melbourne, 1970.
Ritchie, John, *The Evidence to the Bigge Reports: New South Wales Under Governor Macquarie*, vol. 1, *The Oral Evidence*, Heinemann, Melbourne, 1971.
Roberts, Stephen, *The Squatting Age in Australia 1835–1847*, Melbourne University Press, Carlton, 1935.
Robson, L. L., *The Convict Settlers of Australia*, 2nd ed., Melbourne University Press, Carlton, 1994.
Roe, Michael, *The Quest for Authority in Eastern Australia 1835–1851*, Melbourne University Press, Carlton, 1965.
Rolls, Eric, *A Million Wild Acres*, Penguin Australia, Ringwood, Victoria, 1984.
Rudé, George, *Protest and Punishment: The Story of the Social and Political Protestors Transported to Australia 1788–1868*, Clarendon Press, Oxford, 1978.
Selzer, Anita, *Governors' Wives in Colonial Australia*, National Library of Australia, Canberra, 2002.
Shaw, A. G. L., *Convicts and the Colonies*, Melbourne University Press, Carlton, 1977.
Smith, Babette, *A Cargo of Women: Susannah Watson and the Convicts of the Princess Royal*, rev. ed., Rosenberg, Dural, NSW, 2005.
Spiers, Hugh, *Landscape Art and the Blue Mountains*, Alternative Publishing Co-operative Ltd, Chippendale, NSW, 1981.
Steven, Margaret, *John Macarthur*, Great Australians series, Oxford University Press, Melbourne, 1988.
Thompson, F. M. L., *English Landed Society in the Nineteenth Century*, Routledge & Kegan Paul, London, 1963.
Walker, William, *Old Hawkesbury Celebrities: William Cox of Clarendon and Family*, printed by C. M. Davies, Windsor, NSW, 1896.
Ware, Sydney, *Who Was Who on the Liverpool Plains*, 1841, Colonial Museum, Mudgee, December 1998.
Waterhouse, Richard, *Private Pleasures, Public Leisure: A History of Australian Popular Culture Since 1788*, Longmans Australia, South Melbourne, 1995.
Waterhouse, Richard, *The Vision Splendid: A Social and Cultural History of Rural Australia*, Curtin University Books, Fremantle, 2005.
Watkins, Susan, *Jane Austen's Town and Country Style*, Thames & Hudson, London, 1990.
Watson, Frederick, 'Introduction', *Historical Records of Australia*, Series I, vol. vii, pp. i–xiii.
White, Allen, *The Chain Makers: A History of the Watch Fusee Chain Makers*, published by the author, Wick Lane, Christchurch, Hants, 1967.
Wyndham. The Hon. H. A., *A Family History 1688-1837*, Oxford University Press, Oxford, 1950.
Yarker, Gwen, *Georgian Faces: Portrait of County*, Dorset Natural History and Archaeological Society, Dorchester, 2010.
Young, John, *Wiltshire Watch and Clockmakers*, Sedgehill Publishing, Trowbridge, Wiltshire, 2006

Journal Articles and Chapters in Edited Books
Atkinson, Alan, 'Master and Servant at Camden Park', *The Push From the Bush*, no. 6, May 1980, pp. 42–60.
Atkinson, Alan, 'The Parliament in the Jerusalem Warehouse', *The Push From the Bush*, no. 12, June 1982, pp. 76–98.
Blair, Sandra J., 'The Revolt at Castle Forbes: A Catalyst to Emancipist Emigrant Confrontation', *Journal of the Royal Australian Historical Society*, vol. 64, pt 2, September 1978, pp. 89–107.
Bolton, G. C., 'The Idea of a Colonial Gentry', *Historical Studies*, vol. 13, no. 5, October 1968, pp. 307–28.
Borch, Merete, 'Rethinking the Origins of *Terra Nullius*', *Australian Historical Studies*, vol. 32, no. 117, October 2001, pp. 222–39.
Broome, Richard, 'Aboriginal Workers on South Eastern Frontiers', *Australian Historical Studies*, vol. 26, no. 103, October 1994, pp. 202–15.
Carisbrooke, Donald, 'The Influence of the "Gentlemen Settlers" in Australia in 1838', *The Push From the Bush*, no. 11, November 1981, pp. 23–35.
Damousi, Joy, 'Chaos and Order: Gender, Space and Sexuality on Convict Ships', *Australian Historical Studies*, vol. 26, no. 104, April 1995, pp. 351–72.
Dickinson, H. T., 'Democracy', in *The Oxford Companion to the Romantic Age: British Culture 1776–1832*, ed. Iain McCalman, Oxford University Press, Oxford, 1999.
Dyster, Barrie, 'The Fate of Colonial Conservatism on the Eve of the Gold Rush', *Journal of the Royal Australian Historical Society*, December 1968, vol. 4, September 1980, pp. 329–55.
Dyster, Barrie, 'Public Employment and Assignment to Private Masters', in *Convict Workers*, ed. Stephen Nicholas, Cambridge University Press, Cambridge, 1988, Chapter 9.
Fink, David and Averill, 'Harlequin of the Hunter – "Major" James Mudie of Castle Forbes', *Journal of the Royal*

Australian Historical Society, vol. 54, pt 4, December 1968, pp. 368–86.

Fletcher, Brian H., 'The Hawkesbury Settlers and the Rum Rebellion', *Journal of the Royal Australian Historical Society*, vol. 54, pt 3, September 1968, pp. 217–37.

Gascoigne, John, 'Empire', in *The Oxford Companion to The Romantic Age: British Culture 1776–1832*, ed. Iain McCalman, Oxford University Press, Oxford, 1999, p. 56.

Garton, Stephen, 'The Convict Origins Debate: Historians and the Problem of the "Criminal Class"', ed. Stephen Garton, Reading 5, *Australia and New Zealand Journal of Criminology*, vol. 94, 1991, pp. 66–82.

Gilchrist, Catie, '"This Relic of the Cities of the Plain": Penal Flogging, Convict Morality and the Colonial Imagination', *Journal of Australian Colonial History*, vol. 9, 2007, pp. 1-28.

McGillivery, Angus, 'From Sods to Seed-Beds: Cultivating a Familiar Field at Port Jackson', *Journal of Australian Colonial History*, vol. 5, 2004, pp. 1–29.

McSween, Angus, 'Some Lawson Letters 1819–1824', *Journal of the Royal Australian Historical Society*, vol. 50, pt 3, August 1964, pp. 231–39.

Nichol, W., 'Ideology and the Convict System in New South Wales, 1788–1820', *Australian Historical Studies*, vol. 22, no. 86, April 1986, pp. 1–20.

Parsons, T. G., 'Does the Bigge Report Follow From the Evidence?', *Historical Studies*, vol. 15, no. 58, April 1972, pp. 268–75.

Roberts, David, 'The Bells Falls Massacre and Bathurst's History of Violence', *Australian Historical Studies*, vol. 26, no. 105, October 1995, pp. 616–27.

Rubinstein, Bill, 'The Top Wealthholders of New South Wales, 1830–44', *The Push From the Bush*, no. 8, December 1980, pp. 41–47.

Spigelman, J. J., *The Macquarie Bicentennial*, Annual History Lecture, History Council of New South Wales, Sydney, 2009.

Ward, John. M., 'James Macarthur, Colonial Conservative, 1798-1867', *Journal of the Royal Australian Historical Society*, vol. 66, pt 3, December 1980, pp. 149–62.

Woodruff, Douglas, 'Expansion and Emigration', *Early Victorian England 1830–1865*, vol. 2, Oxford University Press, London, no named editor, 1934, pp. 375–92.

Maps

British Ordnance Survey Old Series 1811, Cassini Publishing, 2007.

6. Electronic Resources

Australian Dictionary of Biography, online edition, various authors.

Notes

Abbreviations
ADB *Australian Dictionary of Biography*
AHS *Australian Historical Studies*
HRA *Historical Records of Australia*
HRNSW *Historical Records of New South Wales*
JACH *Journal of Australian Colonial History*
JRAHS *Journal of the Royal Australian Historical Society*
ML Mitchell Library

Foreword
1 Joseph Holt, *Memoirs of Joseph Holt*, ed. T. Crofton Croker, Henry Colburn, London, 1838, vol. 2, p. 134.
2 *London Gazette*, issue 16137, p. 535, British National Archives.
3 Governor Macquarie to Earl Bathurst, 24 June 1815, *HRA*, Series 1, vol. viii, p. 360.
4 Bonwick Transcripts, Box 22, pp. 4220–31.
5 Bonwick Transcripts, Box 10, p. 4078, evidence taken by Bigge at Mulgoa.
6 Cox to Bigge, Bonwick Transcripts, Box 25, pp. 5328–35.
7 Chris Cunningham, *The Blue Mountains Rediscovered*, Kangaroo Press, East Roseville, NSW, 1996, p. 145.
8 John Thomas, Report of the Commissioner of Inquiry on the State of Agriculture and Trade in the Colony of New South Wales, *British Parliamentary Papers*, vol. 10, 136, 13 March 1823, hereafter called Bigge Report, Agriculture.
9 Michael Roe, *The Quest for Authority in Eastern Australia, 1855–1851*, Melbourne University Press, Carlton, 1965, p. 6.

Chapter 1
1 *Memoirs of William Cox J.P.*, William Brooks and Co., Sydney, 1901, facsimile reprint by the Library of Australian History, North Sydney, 1979, p. iv.
2 Macarthur's father was a mercer and draper in Plymouth. D'Arcy Wentworth was connected to Lord Fitzwilliam, although his father was an innkeeper. Piper was of an army family and the son of a doctor. Marsden was the son of a Yorkshire blacksmith, persuaded to go by William Wilberforce, but later became a pastoralist as well.
3 Donald Payne, *Dorset Harbours*, Christopher Johnson, London, 1953, p. 20.
4 John Hillier, *Ebb Tide at Poole 1815–1851*, Poole Historical Trust, Poole, 1985, p 12.
5 Jo Draper, *The Georgians*, Dovecot Press, Wimborne, Dorset, 1998, p. 20.
6 The official presided over a consistory court, which sat in the Minster and had powers covering not only religious matters and personal morals, but also financial affairs of tithes and wills. David Popham, *The Book of Wimborne*, Barracuda Books, Buckingham, 1983, p. 81.
7 The house has been restored by the council, as being the oldest inhabited house in Wimborne.
8 *Memoirs of William Cox J.P.*, op. cit., p. 12. They consist of: Or, three bars azure, on a canton

argent a lion's head erased gules. Crest a griffin's head, erased pp pierced by arrow. Motto: 'Fortitudo in Adversis'.

9   'Cox of Clarendon, N.S. Wales', 35 page unpublished typescript genealogy, until c.1900, provided by James. C. Cox, Anglesea, Victoria, pp. 1, 2.

10 *A Genealogical and Heraldic History of the Colonial Gentry*, Bernard Burke, London, 1895, p. 75, reprinted edition p. 781.

11 Reproduced in Gwen Yarker, *Georgian Faces: Portrait of a County*, Dorset Natural History and Archaeological Society, 2010, p. 6.

12 Ordnance Survey Old Series, 1811, Sheets 11 and 15 map ref 975017, scale 1:50,000, and sheet 329 of 1909 reprinted by Cassini Publishing, Southampton, 2007.

13 Clarendon was built by James Cox in 1834–38. It has been restored by the National Trust of Australia. The portraits are on loan from Tim Cox, of Victoria. See Chapter 13.

14 These styles were illustrated in a 2011 exhibition at the Dorchester Museum, called 'Georgian Faces: Portrait of a County', which exhibited portraits of aristocrats and gentry of the eighteenth century.

15 Nigel Cox joined the Royal Navy as a cadet in 1912, at the age of 12, and returned to Australia in the mid-1960s. His son does not know how he acquired the portraits.

16 In February 1802, but he was removed from the magistracy in October by Governor King, for disobeying the Commander in Chief's orders that officers should not farm.

17 *A Guide to Wimborne Minster*, William Pickering, London 1830, p. 38.

18 William Rees-Mogg in *The Times*, 24 June 2001, p. 31.

19 Draper, *op. cit.*, p. 73.

20 Yarker, *op. cit.*, p. 58.

21 Thomas eventually stayed in England, becoming a country rector in Somerset, as described in Chapter 13.

22 David Popham, *The Book of Wimborne*, Barracuda Books, Buckingham, 1963, p. 64.

23 'Cox of Clarendon', *op. cit.*, p. 3. The school was rebuilt in the 1860s, but closed along with other grammar schools in 1980. The Priest's House museum has some Cox records.

24 *White's Directory of Christchurch*, Christchurch, Hampshire, 1859. Chain making ceased around 1814, but watchmaking continued. Allen White, *The Chain Makers*, Christchurch, 1967, p. 16.

25 *Memoirs of William Cox J.P.*, *op. cit.*, pp. 15, 16. They were married in February 1789. Robert Cox died in 1815.

26 Letter from Jim Cox to the author, 20 June 2011, from 29 Parker Street, Anglesea, Victoria, recounting research done by Barry Cox in 1991.

27 Paul de Serville, *Port Philip Gentlemen*, Oxford University Press, Melbourne, 1980, p. 82.

28 Susan Watkins, *Jane Austen's Town and Country Style*, Thames & Hudson, London, 1990, p. 57. Although Austen's first novel, *Sense and Sensibility*, was not published until 1811, she was already 25 when William left for the colony and acutely sensitive to the social situation of her time.

29 Yarker, *op. cit.*, p. 14.

30 J. H. Bettey, *Rural Life in Wessex 1500–1900*, Moonraker Press, Bradford on Avon, Wiltshire, 1977, p. 33.

31 It is has not been possible to trace any specific land belonging to William as a farmer in the County Records at the Wiltshire and Swindon History Centre.

32 In the National Gallery, London.

33 Popham, *op. cit.*, p. 107.

34 Draper, *op. cit.*, p. 9.

35 *The Concise Dictionary of National Biography*, Oxford University Press, Oxford, 1992, vol. 1, p. 883.

36 Sir Frederic Morton Eden, *The State of the Poor*, 3 vols, printed by J. Davis, London, 1797, vol. 2, p. 146.

37 William Marshall, *On the Landed Property of England*, G. and W. Nicol and others, London, 1804, pp. 29, 113, 119, 125, 128.

38 William Cobbett, *Selections From William Cobbett's Illustrated Rural Rides 1826–32*, ed. Christopher Norris, Webb & Bower, 1984, pp. 127, 130.

39 Eden, *op. cit.*, 2. p. xix.

40 Marshall, *op. cit.*, p. 335.

41 Bettey, *op. cit.*, p. 50.

42 *Royal Kalenders*, British National Archives and Kingston Lacy, The National Trust, 1994, pp. 9, 12, 23.

43 The Parish Register of St Peter and Holy Trinity, Shaftesbury, shows a number of Upjohns as being labourers. Several were transported for theft and founded an Australian Upjohn family. One descendant, Sir William George Dismore Upjohn (1888–1979), became Chancellor of the University of Melbourne.

44 Dorset History Centre records, conveyance of 20/21 March 1721. Unfortunately the church is deconsecrated and used for offices and the internal monuments cannot be seen.

45 *A Short Account of the Life and Travels of James Upjohn of Red Lion Street Clerkenwell., 1784*, privately printed, Ann Arbor, Michigan, 1990, vol. 2, pp. 7, 11.

46 *Ibid.*, p. 13.

47 The unreliable *Memoirs of William Cox J.P., op. cit.*, state wrongly that she was born in Bristol.

48 Parish records of Devizes St John, Wiltshire Historical Records, Chippenham, A1 345/141A and 142/A. The house is now No. 4.

49 John Young, *Wiltshire Watch and Clockmakers*, Sedgehill Press, Trowbridge, Wiltshire, 2006, p. 113.

50 *The Universal British Directory of Trade, Commerce and Manufacture*, sold by C. Stalker, London, 1791, pp. 777, 779.

51 *Memoirs of William Cox J.P., op. cit.*, p. 16.

52 Letter to the author from Major Peters, The Rifles (Berkshire and Wiltshire) Museum, Salisbury, 18 September 2007.

53 *Memoirs of William Cox J.P., op. cit.*, p. 17.

54 *Burke's Colonial Gentry*, reprinted from the 1891 edition by Heraldry Today, London, 1970, p. 781.

55 Wiltshire Records Archives, A1 336/1.

56 Wiltshire County Records, Militia Accounts, A1 712/1-29 and documents 109/795/807.

57 *Richard Upjohn Light, A Study in Ancestry*, privately printed, Ann Arbor, Michigan, 1990, vol. 1, pp. vi, 121, vol. 2, pp. 7, 13, 14, 62.

58 Anthony Clayton, *The British Officer*, Pearson Longman, London, 2006, p. 57.

59 War Office circular of 14 March 1795 relative to recruiting, Wiltshire and Swindon History Centre, Chippenham, documents 109/795/807.

60 Register of baptisms, parish of Devizes St John, Wiltshire Historical Records, Chippenham, Wiltshire.

61 The *Memoirs* explain this as being due to 'a woful [sic] time of peace and his opportunity for war was not', but admit that the terms offered for the New South Wales Corps were 'very good', pp. 17, 18.

62   Brian Fletcher, *Colonial Australia Before 1850*, Nelson, London, 1976, p. 44.
63   Geoffrey Gray, *A Military History of Australia*, Cambridge University Press, Cambridge, 1990, pp. 10, 11.
64   Letter from Anne Youll in Balham, London, of 11 December 1903, to Winifred Cox at Cann River, Orbost, Victoria, ML Mss 6731.
65   Joseph Holt, *Memoirs of Joseph Holt*, ed. T. Crofton Croker, vol. 2, Henry Colburn, London, 1838, pp. 45, 46.
66   John Washington Price, 'A Journal kept on board the Minerva transport from Ireland to New South Wales', British Library Mss 13380, hereafter referred to as Surgeon's Log. The baby is not included in the passenger list on p. 36.
67   Land Tax assessments for the Parish of Devizes St John, Wiltshire Records A1/345/143. Their house ceased to be on the tax registers after July 1798.
68   Holt, *Memoirs*, *op. cit.*, p. 36.
69   'Cox of Clarendon', *op. cit.*, p. 8.
70   *Burke's Heraldic History of the Commoners of Great Britain and Ireland*, H. Colburn, London, 1835 and revised, vol. 4, p 577.
71   Cox to Piper, letter of 29 July 1804, Piper Papers, ML, CYA 358.
72   Surgeon's Log, 17 March 1799, p. 6.
73   It had been John Macarthur's, as evidenced by Elizabeth Macarthur's letters.
74   Douglas Woodruff, 'Expansion and Emigration', *Early Victorian England*, Oxford University Press, Oxford, vol. 2, p. 375.
75   By November 1802 Macarthur held 3950 acres, Laycock held 1348 and Lieutenant Thomas Hobby 660. *HRA* Series 1, vol. 3, p. 614.

Chapter 2

1 Holt, *Memoirs*, *op. cit.*
2   Surgeon's Log, p. 10. Price was young, but men at both the London and Dublin colleges started their surgical training at 16.
3   *Ibid.*, p. 2.
4   These are discussed in Alan Brooke and David Brandon, *Bound for Botany Bay: British Convict Voyages to Australia*, British National Archives, London, 2005, pp. 189–215.
5   *Ibid.*, p. 7.
6   *Ibid.* The dates do not make sense.
7   Surgeon's Log pp. 6, 6 verso.
8   *Ibid.*, p. 31.
9   *Ibid.*, p. 2.
10   Robert Hughes, *The Fatal Shore*, Knopf, New York, 1987.
11   Colonial Office Correspondence, Secretary of State, CO 201/20, British National Archives.
12   Brooke and Brandon, *Bound for Botany Bay*, *op. cit.*, p. 37.
13   *Ibid.*, pp. 25–31, 51–5, 168.
14   Surgeon's Log, p. 37.
15   E.g., Frank Clune, *Bound for Botany Bay: Narrative of a Voyage in 1798 Aboard the Death Ship Hillsborough*, Angus & Robertson, Sydney, 1965.
16   Brooke and Brandon, *Bound for Botany Bay*, *op. cit.*
17   Surgeon's Log, p. 30.
18   *Ibid.*, p. 12.

19 *Ibid.,* p. 10.
20 Brooke and Brandon, *Bound for Botany Bay op. cit.,* p. 169.
21 *Memoirs of William Cox J.P., op. cit.,* p. 19.
22 Surgeon's Log, p. 1.
23 National Maritime Museum and also Eric Leeson, *William Cox – a Short Biography,* privately published, Wimborne, 2008.
24 The normal deck height in convict transports was 5 feet 10 inches.
25 Bigge Report, Agriculture, pp. 2, 6, 7.
26 Surgeon's Log, p. 35.
27 *Ibid.,* p. 43.
28 Holt, *Memoirs, op. cit.,* p. 36.
29 Surgeon's Log, p. 38.
30 *Ibid.,* p. 44 verso.
31 *Ibid.,* p. 39.
32 *Ibid.,* p. 39.
33 *Ibid.,* p. 37.
34 Quoted in Roderick Cameron, *Australian History and Horizons,* Weidenfeld & Nicolson, London, 1971, p. 57.
35 Bigge Report, Agriculture, p. 4.
36 Joy Damousi, 'Chaos and Order: Gender, Space and Sexuality on Convict Ships', *AHS,* vol. 26, no. 104, April 1995, p. 355.
37 *Ibid.,* p. 352.
38 Surgeon's Log, p. 42.
39 *Ibid.,* p. 43.
40 Holt, *Memoirs, op. cit.,* pp. 49–51.
41 Surgeon's Log, p. 44.
42 Holt, *Memoirs, op. cit.,* pp. 45–46.
43 *Ibid.,* pp. 45, 62, 86.
44 Holt, *Memoirs, op. cit.,* pp. 45,46.
45 Surgeon's Log, p. 52.
46 *Memoirs of William Cox J.P., op. cit.* p. 23.
47 Surgeon's Log, p. 69 verso.
48 Holt, *Memoirs, op. cit.,* p. 86.
49 Surgeon's Log, p. 83.

Chapter 3

1 Grace Karskens, *The Colony,* Allen & Unwin, Sydney, 2009, pp. 74, 75.
2 This and much other of the information that follows is derived from *Parramatta: A Past Revealed,* by Terry Kass, Carol Liston and John McClymont, Parramatta City Council, 1996.
3 Roe, *The Quest for Authority, op. cit.,* p. 35.
4 Margaret Steven, *John Macarthur,* Great Australians series, Oxford University Press, Melbourne, 1988, pp. 3–6.
5 Holt, *Memoirs, op. cit.,* p. 87.
6 *Ibid.,* p. 90.
7 *Ibid.,* p. 89.
8 Cox to King, 24 December 1804, Philip Gidley King, letters 1794–1807, ML.
9 Holt, *Memoirs, op. cit.,* p. 132.

10 *Ibid.*, p. 97.

11 *Ibid.*, p. 95.

12 King to Portland, 1 March 1802, *HRA* Series 1, vol. iii, p. 422.

13 This is Holt's description, see next reference. A part of Brush Farm at Ryde is today a public park and the house, much enlarged, is a Prison Service Training College.

14 Holt, *Memoirs, op. cit.*, p. 135.

15 This translation of Peron's *Voyage de découvertes aux Terres Australes* (published in English by B. Macmillan, Bond Street, Covent Garden, London in 1809) is taken from *Memoirs of William Cox JP, op. cit.*, pp. 37, 38.

16 Rowley to Capt Waterhouse, Bonwick Transcripts, vol. 4, p. 1094, ML A 2,000-4.

17 Holt, *Memoirs, op. cit.*, p. 90.

18 *Ibid.*, p. 169.

19 *Ibid.*, p. 141.

20 *Ibid.*, p. 95.

21 *Memoirs of William Cox J.P., op. cit.*, pp. 38, 39.

22 Clayton, *op. cit.*, pp. 30, 43.

23 Alan Atkinson, *The Europeans in Australia*, Oxford University Press, Melbourne, vol. 1, 1997, pp. 203–14.

24 John Ritchie, *Lachlan Macquarie*, Melbourne University Press, Carlton, 1986, pp. 32–34.

25 James Broadbent, *Elizabeth Farm*, Historic Houses Trust of NSW, Glebe, NSW, 1995, pp. 9–11.

26 Samuel Bennett, *History of Australian Discovery and Colonisation*, Sydney, 1867, p. 167.

27 Frederick Watson, *HRA* Series 1, vol. vii, Introduction p. vi.

28 Colonial Secretary Index, 13 January 1810, fiche 3003; 4/1821 No 73. Rebecca's reason was that the fertility of the land on the Hawkesbury was becoming exhausted.

29 Bennett, *History of Australian Discovery, op. cit.*, p. 173.

30 Camden to King, 31 October 1804, *HRA* Series 1, vol. v. p. 161, and subsequent letters in 1805.

31 Cunningham, *The Blue Mountains Rediscovered, op. cit.*, p. 85.

32 For example, Camden to King, 31 October 1804, *HRA* Series 1, vol. v, p. 161 and subsequent correspondence in 1805 King to Camden and King to Macarthur.

33 King to Castlereagh, 27 July 1806, *HRA* Series 1, vol. v, pp. 748, 749.

34 Bligh reported William's departure on the *Buffalo* to Windham (now spelt Wyndham) on 19 March 1807, *HRA* Series 1, vol. vi, p. 131.

35 Holt, *Memoirs, op. cit.*, pp. 134, 135, 170.

36 ML, reel CY 2727, Ap. 13-1 and 13-2, also Ac 42, doc 358, pp. 97–161, containing Cox's bills on the New South Wales Corps.

37 These details come from a local booklet entitled *Some Well Known Pioneers*, p. 23, among the Cox papers in the Mitchell Library. A guinea was £1 1s. It is not clear whether this was Sterling or Currency.

38 *Sydney Gazette*, 25 June 1803.

39 Holt, *Memoirs, op. cit.*, 20 May 1803, p. 187.

40 *Sydney Gazette*, 1 May 1804, p. 2.

41 King to Hobart, 17 September 1803, *HRA* Series 1, vol. iv, p. 392.

42 King to Hobart, 1 March 1804, enclosure no. 8, *HRA* Series 1, vol. v, pp. 546–7.

43 Court Martial Records, British National Archives, Kew, WO 71/145.

44 King to Camden, 1 November 1805, *HRA* Series 1, vol. v, pp. 604–5.

45   Jan Barkley-Jack, *The Hawkesbury Settlement Revealed: A New Look at Australia's Third Mainland Settlement, 1793–1802*, Rosenberg, Kenthurst, 2009, p. 283.

46   Letter of 28 July 1804 to Captain John Piper, Piper Papers, microfiche CYA 358, ML.

47   *Sydney Gazette*, 6 January 1805.

48   ML, Ac 42, *op. cit.*

49   An old spelling for Wimbourne, where William had been born.

50   Macarthur to Piper, 9 November 1803, Piper Papers, vol. 3, CYA 256, ML.

51   Gascoigne, *The Enlightenment and the Origins of European Australia*, Cambridge University Press, Cambridge, 2002, p. 25.

52   Bligh to Wyndham, 7 February 1807, *HRA* Series 1, vol. vi, p. 127.

53   *London Gazette*, 14 April 1808.

54   W. Merry to Cox, 28 January 1808, and Merry to H C Litchfield, 8 December 1808, WO 4/846, NSW Corps 1803–1810, p. 94, British National Archives.

55   Colonial Secretary Index, reel 6040, 9/2673, pp. 13, 14, 19, 61 and reel 604, 4/1723, p. 91.

Chapter 4

1   Bligh to Windham, 7 February 1807, *HRA* Series 1, vol. vi, p. 127.

2   *Sydney Gazette*, 7 January 1810, p. 1. There were gubernatorial orders in almost every issue.

3   *Sydney Gazette*, 24 February 1810, p. 1.

4   Holt, *Memoirs, op. cit.*, p. 130.

5   F. M. Thompson, *English Landed Gentry in the Nineteenth Century*, Routledge & Kegan Paul, London, 1963, p. 109.

6   Colonial Secretary Index, reel 6021, 4/1819, pp. 531, 533.

7   Colonial Secretary Index, reel 6042, 4/1725, p. 66.

8   *Sydney Gazette*, 7 January 1810, p. 3.

9   Colonial Secretary Index, reel 6038, SZ758, pp. 122, 128.

10   *ADB*, vol. 2, pp. 187–95.

11   *HRNSW*, vol. vii, p. 464. It is misquoted in the *Memoirs*.

12   Colonial Secretary Index, 29 October 1810, reel 6002, 3490/D, p. 33.

13   *HRA* Series 1, vol. vii, p. 399.

14   *Sydney Gazette*, 30 January 1813, p. 2.

15   Karskens, *op. cit.*, p. 128.

16   James Broadbent, *The Australian Colonial House*, Hordern House, Sydney, 1997, p. 151.

17   Macquarie to Castlereagh, 30 April 1810, *HRA* Series 1, vol. vii, p. 276.

18   NSW Corps papers, WO 4/846, British National Archives.

19   John Ritchie, *Profit and Punishment*, Heinemann, Melbourne, 1970, p. 24.

20   Colonial Secretary Index, reel 6002, 4/3490D, pp. 50, 51.

21   Cox to Campbell, 7 March 1811, Colonial Secretary Index, reel 6043, 4/1726, pp. 101–2.

22   Portland to Hunter, 18 September 1798, *HRA* Series 1, vol. ii, p. 226.

23   Eugene MacLaughlin, John Muncie, Gordon Hughes, *Criminological Perspectives*, 2nd ed., Sage Publications, London, 2003, p. 1.

24   'Journal of a Tour of Inspection 1810–1811', pp. 7, 17, 28, 44, 45.

25   Supplement to the Journal of the 'First Tour of Inspection'.

26   D. G. Bowd, *Macquarie Country*, Library of Australian History, Sydney, 1994, p. 6.

27   *Ibid.*, p. 7.

28   Barkley-Jack, *Hawkesbury Settlement Revealed, op. cit.*, many references.

29   Blaxland to Banks, 22 October 1807, Banks Papers, vol. 22, p. 191, ML.

30 Bigge Report, Agriculture, p. 11.
31 Macquarie to Bathurst, 28 April 1814, *HRA* Series 1, vol. viii, p. 150.
32 Macquarie to Bathurst, 7 October 1814, *HRA* Series 1, vol. viii, p. 314.

Chapter 5

1 Gutenberg.net.au/ebooks04/0400191.txt. Page numbers for the diary are not given, only dates.
2 Colonial Secretary Index, 10 June 1815, reel 6038, SZ759, p. 100.
3 Realignment was being discussed again near Mount Victoria early in 2010, when the author
    was last there.
4 Macquarie to Bathurst, 7 October 1814, *HRA* Series 1, vol. viii, p. 314.
5 J. B. Hirst, *Convict Society and its Enemies*, Allen & Unwin, North Sydney, 1988, p. 39.
6 Colonial Secretary Index, 10 June 1815, reel 6038, SZ759, p. 114.
7 Macquarie to Bathurst, 24 June 1815, *HRA* Series 1, vol. viii. p. 576.
8 Bigge Report, Agriculture, pp. 123, 124.
9 Macquarie to Bathurst, 24 June 1815, *HRA* Series 1, vol. viii, p. 570.
10 Macquarie to Bathurst, 24 June 1815, *HRA* Series 1, vol. viii, pp. 571–76; also Lachlan
    Macquarie, 'Journal of a Tour to the New Discovered Country, 25 April–19 May 1815', ML,
    reel CY 33, A779. References to the pages are not given in this chapter.
11 Campbell, 'Report of the Governor's Tour of Inspection April 1815', Colonial Secretary
    Index, 10 June 1815, reel 6038, SZ759, pp. 102, 105–6, 112–113.
12 Macquarie to Bathurst, 28 April 1814, *HRA* Series 1, vol. viii, p. 150, and enclosure.

Chapter 6

1 Lachlan Macquarie's journal, 'Tour to the New Discovered Country', April 1815, ML.
2 Macquarie to Bathurst, 24 June 1815, *HRA* Series 1, vol. viii, pp. 571–76.
3 John Thomas Campbell's report of the Governor's tour of inspection, *op. cit.*, numerous
    references.
4 Colonial Secretary Register, 15 January 1815, reel 6004, 4/1730, pp. 362–63.
5 Campbell, 'Report of the Governor's Tour of Inspection April 1815', *op. cit.*
6 John Thomas Campbell, letter of 10 June 1815 from Government House, Sydney, Colonial
    Secretary Index, reel 6038, SZ759, pp. 102, 105–6, 112–113.
7 Macquarie to Bathurst, 24 June 1815, *HRA* Series 1, vol. viii, pp. 558–560.

Chapter 7

1 Bathurst to Macquarie, 30 January 1817, *HRA* Series 1, vol. ix, p. 201.
2 Bathurst to Macquarie, 24 July 1818, *HRA* Series 1, vol. ix, p. 824.
3 Macquarie to Bathurst, 16 May 1818, *HRA* Series 1, vol. ix, p. 797.
4 *HRA* Series 1, vol. x, p. 1.
5 Ritchie, *Profit and Punishment*, *op. cit.*, pp. 92–93.
6 Macquarie to Bathurst, 28 November 1821, *HRA* Series 1, vol. x, p. 568.
7 Cunningham, *op. cit.*, p. 152.
8 Macquarie to Bathurst, 30 November 1821, *HRA* Series 1, vol. x, p. 574.
9 Bigge Report, Agriculture, p. 14.
10 Bonwick Transcripts, Box 10, p. 4078, ML.
11 'Last Will and Testament of William Cox of Fairfield, Windsor', 21 December 1836. Typed
    copy made by Thelma and Matthew Birrell, undated, Priest's House Museum, Wimborne,
    Dorset.

12   Brian. H. Fletcher, *Landed Enterprise and Penal Society*, Sydney University Press, Sydney, 1976, p. 73. There are numerous references to William Cox in this work.

13   It can be argued that the enclosures in England were altering the character of estates and farms there, but not to a fundamentally new model.

14   Holt, *Memoirs, op. cit.* p. 36.

15   Bigge Report, Convicts, Evidence, pp. 9, 12, 16.

16   Bathurst to Bigge, 6 January 1819, *HRA* Series 1, vol. x, p. 10.

17   Bigge Report, Agriculture, pp. 13, 16.

18   Colonial Secretary Index, 1823, fiche 3062, 4/1834B, p. 461. The map is at the State Records at Kingswood.

19   Bigge Report, Agriculture, p. 71 (old numbering p. 38).

20   Alfred Cox, 'Reminiscences', privately transcribed by Bryan Cox, 2007. Alfred was William's third son by his second marriage.

21   Kenyan farming families on Laikipia continue to quarry stone on their ranches and extend their houses, as needed, many decades after the 1963 independence.

22   Woodruff, 'Expansion and Emigration', *op. cit.*, p. 375.

23   Broadbent, *Colonial House, op. cit.*, p. 151.

24   Sydney Ware, *Who was Who on the Liverpool Plains, 1841*, Mudgee Colonial Museum, p. 11.

25   *Memoirs of William Cox, J.P., op. cit.*, pp. 141, 142.

26   *George Cox of Mulgoa and Mudgee: Letters to his sons 1846–49*, ed. Edna Hickson, privately published 1980, printed by Ambassador Press, Granville, Sydney, pp. 37, 38.

27   This Clarendon has been restored by the National Trust of Australia, Tasmania.

28   Newspaper cuttings on the Cox family in the Mitchell Library.

29   Holt, *Memoirs, op. cit.*, p. 130.

30   Colonial Secretary Index, reel 6043, 4/1727, p. 388.

31   The author has visited St Mathew's church on several occasions, most recently on 10 April 2010.

32   Bigge Report, Agriculture, Evidence, p. 41.

33   Alan Atkinson, 'Master and Servant at Camden Park', *The Push From the Bush*, no. 6, May 1980, p. 44.

34   Colonial Secretary Index, 2 July 1818, reel 6065, 4/1798, p. 85. The abstract was the accounting for the personnel and property.

35   Hassall to Gorman, 5 October 1816, Bonwick Transcripts, Box 15, p. 1486.

36   Colonial Secretary Index, 16 August 1815, reel 6004, 4/3494, p. 142.

37   *Ibid.*, 23 August 1819, reel 6048, 4/1742, p. 395.

38   Bonwick Transcripts, Box 18, p. 2458. In this flood only young maize was affected, no wheat or stock being lost.

39   Cox to Bigge, 7 May 1820, Bonwick Transcripts, Box 22, p. 4222.

40   Richard Waterhouse, *The Vision Splendid*, Curtin University Press, Fremantle, 2005, p. 100.

41   Macarthur to Bigge, February 1821, Macarthur Papers, no. 12, CY 927, Box 12, ML.

42   Alan Atkinson, *Camden*, Oxford University Press, Melbourne, 1988, pp. 21, 23.

43   Christopher Cox, email of 11 October 2010.

44   Colonial Secretary Index, reel 6004, 4/3493, p. 346.

45   Barrie Dyster, 'Employment and Assignment', in *Convict Workers: Reinterpreting Australia's Past*, ed. Nicholas and Peter R. Shergold, Cambridge University Press, Cambridge, p. 145.

46   John Ritchie, *The Evidence to the Bigge Reports: The Oral Evidence*, 'Roguery: The Conduct of William Cox', p. 184.

47 Bigge Report, Agriculture, Evidence. p. 71.

48 William Cox to George Cox, Clarendon, 17 May 1823, Bonwick Transcripts, fiche 3062, 4/1834B, No. 73, p. 463. Goulburn was acquiring a reputation as an interfering bureaucrat.

49 Colonial Secretary Index, reel 6059, 4/1773, pp. 159a–159b.

50 Analysis made by this author of convict indents at the State Records. The number of mechanics was assessed on the basis of a 50 percent sample.

51 Colonial Secretary Index, 1821, reel 6052, 4/1751, p. 258–89.

52 The Muster simply specifies who they worked for, not where.

53 Colonial Secretary Index, 24 August 1811, reel 6002, 4/3491, p. 54.

54 Deposition, Cox to Bigge from Clarendon, 7 May 1820, Bonwick Transcripts, Box 22, pp. 4222, 4223.

55 Hertfordshire County Records, Calendar to the Sessions Book of 1658, Lionel Mumby, *How Much is That Worth?*, Phillimore Books, Chichester, 1989, p. 29.

56 Thompson, *English Landed Gentry in the Nineteenth Century*, op. cit., p. 194.

57 Kay Daniels, *Convict Women*, Allen & Unwin, Sydney, 1988, p. 80.

58 Bonwick Transcripts, fiche 3062, 4/1834D, no 73, p. 443.

59 Colonial Secretary Index, 27 January 1820, reel 6007, 4/3501, p. 213, ML.

60 Atkinson, *Europeans in Australia*, op. cit, vol. 1, p. 199.

61 Gascoigne, *The Enlightenment and the Origins of European Australia*, op. cit., p. 13.

62 Atkinson, *Europeans in Australia*, op. cit., p. 270.

63 *Mudgee Guardian*, 2 March 1917, Cox family papers, ML, quoted in *Richard Upjohn Light: A Study in Ancestry*, op. cit., p. 126.

64 Holt, *Memoirs*, op. cit., 10 May 1803, p. 187.

65 *HRA* Series 1, vol. vi, pp. 577–79, 28 January 1807 and 25 February 1807.

66 Atkinson, *Europeans in Australia*, op. cit., p. 263.

67 *Ibid.*, p. 277.

68 Marnie Bassett, *The Governor's Lady*, Oxford University Press, Oxford, 1956, p. 59.

69 Brian Fletcher, 'The Hawkesbury Settlers and the Rum Rebellion', *JRAHS*, vol. 54, pt 3, September 1968, pp. 218, 219.

70 Roderick Cameron, *History and Horizons*, Weidenfeld and Nicolson, London, 1971, p. 150.

71 Taken from Kate Hunter's review of *The Vision Splendid* by Richard Waterhouse, *Australian Journal of Politics and History*, vol. 52, no. 1, March 2006, p. 496. Her remarks are equally true of a slightly earlier period than Waterhouse describes.

72 Enquiries made to various members of the family have all met with the same response; no one has any of Rebecca's correspondence.

73 Rebecca Cox to Macquarie, 13 January 1810, Colonial Secretary Register, fiche 3003, 4/1821, no. 73.

74 Letter Edward Cox to Colonial Secretary, 31 May 1825 from Mulgoa, Colonial Secretary Index, fiche 3125, 4/1841, no. 170, pp. 105–07. This stated that he had wealth of £1000 stg and further begged to 'refer you to my Father … as to what he purposes to invest me with'.

75 Mulgoa Progress Association, *Mulgoa! Mulgoa! Where is That?*, Mulgoa, 1988, pp. 19, 25–27.

76 Macquarie, 'Journal of a Tour of Inspection 1810–1811', ML, CY reel 302, A778, pp. 45, 62.

77 Macquarie, 'Journal of a Tour of Inspection to Bathurst 15 December 1821–26 December 1821', CY reel 303, A 783, p. 2.

78 Atkinson, *Europeans in Australia*, op. cit., p. 270.

79 'Cox of Clarendon, N.S. Wales', privately distributed typescript, undated, p. 8.

80 Cox to Piper, 28 July 1804, Piper Papers, ML doc. CY 358.

81 Atkinson, *The Europeans in Australia, op. cit.*, p. 8.
82 Fulton, Henry (1761–1840) was educated at Trinity College, Dublin, implicated in the 1798 rebellion and transported for life. Governor Hunter was perplexed over how to employ him, but when the Reverend Richard Johnson departed in 1800, it enabled Fulton to resume his profession. He served as Bligh's private chaplain and went to England to testify at the trial of Lieutenant Colonel Johnston. He died at Castlereagh on 17 November 1840. *ADB*, vol. 1, 1966, pp. 421–22.
83 Wentworth, *Statistical, Historical and Political Description of the Colony, op. cit.*, pp. 11, 12.
84 Cox to Macquarie, Colonial Secretary Index, 7 April 1820, reel 6049, 4/1247, p. 228.
85 Alfred went to New Zealand with his mother after she remarried. Thomas (the author's great grandfather) went to Cambridge, then to Oxford, and became a country rector at Monksilver in Somerset, although earlier on he did spend time on the estates west of the mountains.
86 State Records, SRNSW 907, reel 1114, letters 2929, 5852.
87 *ADB*, vol. 1, pp. 515–16.
88 Alfred Cox, 'Reminiscences', *op. cit.*, p. 5.
89 *Ibid.*, pp. 5, 5.
90 Jeans, *An Historical Geography of New South Wales, op. cit.*, p. 88.
91 Bigge Report, Agriculture, Evidence, p. 57.
92 Wentworth, *Statistical, Historical and Political Description of the Colony, op. cit.*, p. 98.
93 John Gascoigne, 'Empire', in *The Romantic Age, British Culture 1776–1832*, ed. Iain McCalman, Oxford University Press, Oxford, 1999, p. 55.
94 *Sydney Gazette*, 12 July 1822.
95 *Mulgoa! Mulgoa! Where is That?, op. cit.*, p. 2.
96 *Sydney Gazette*, 31 August 1816.

Chapter 8

1 Bigge Report, pp. 102, 96.
2 M. H. Ellis, *Lachlan Macquarie*, Angus & Robertson, London, 2nd ed., 1952, p. 275.
3 Cox to Bigge, Bonwick Transcripts, Box 25, pp. 5328–35, ML.
4 *Ibid.*, p. 123.
5 Bigge Report, Agriculture, Evidence, p. 91.
6 Appendix to Bigge Report, 1822, Police. Evidence, B, no 1-7, document 6, CO201/131, p. 368.
7 Colonial Secretary Index, reel 6053, 4/1756, p. 104.
8 *Ibid.*, reel 6062, 4/1783, p. 86.
9 Bigge Report, Police, Evidence, document B. 27, p. 376.
10 *Ibid.*, p. 375.
11 Colonial Secretary Index, reel 6053, 4/1756, p. 103.
12 Bigge Report, Agriculture, Evidence, p. 91.
13 W. Nichol, 'Ideology and the Convict System in New South Wales 1788–1820, *AHS*, no. 86, p. 14.
14 Darling to Bathurst, 9 September 1826, enclosure no. 1, *HRA* Series 1, vol. xii, pp. 556–58.
15 Atkinson, *Camden, op. cit.*, p. 22.
16 Colonial Secretary Index, 14 February 1811, reel 6002, 4/3490D, p. 107.
17 Macquarie to Bathurst, 22 February 1820, *HRA* Series 1, vol. x, pp. 239–44.
18 Bigge Report, Agriculture, Evidence, p. 91.
19 *Ibid.*, p. 91.
20 Memorandum of 7 May 1820, Bonwick Transcripts, Box 22, p. 4220.

21 T. Atkins, *Reminiscences of Twelve Years Residence in Tasmania and New South Wales, Norfolk Island and Morton Bay*, 1869, p. 48, quoted by Catie Gilchrist, '"This Relic of the Cities of the Plain": Penal Flogging, Convict Morality and the Colonial Imagination', *JACH*, vol. 9, 2007, p.13.

22 Bigge Report, Police, Evidence, document B 27, p. 375. Although Cox should not have been sentencing his own employee, the record is clear.

23 Bigge Report, Police, Evidence, p. 373.

24 Colonial Secretary Index, reel 6060, 4/1777, p. 191.

25 Bigge Report, Agriculture, p. 20.

26 Colonial Secretary Index, reel 6002, 4/3491, pp 481–83. Two thirds were to sent to Windsor.

27 *Ibid.*, 28 September 1819, reel 6006, 4/3500, p. 280.

28 *Ibid.*, 5 February 1816, reel 6004, 4/3494, p. 338; 21 March 1817 reel 6005, 4/3496, p. 78; convicts employed 1819 reel 6058, 4/1769, pp. 86a–86b; convicts employed 1821 reel 6052, 4/1751, pp. 258–59.

29 Bigge Report, pp. 123, 124.

30 Cox to McLeay, 30 July 1827, SRNSW 907, reel 1114, letters 2563, 7213, State Records Kingswood.

31 Bigge Report, p. 124.

32 Bigge Report, Agriculture, Evidence, p. 96.

33 Ritchie, *The Evidence to the Bigge Reports, op. cit.*, vol. 1, p. 117.

34 A. G. L. Shaw, *Convicts and the Colonies*, Faber & Faber, London, 1966, p. 92.

35 Campbell to Allan, Colonial Secretary Index, 14 June 1817, reel 6005, 4/3496.

36 *Ibid.*, 29 October 1817, reel 6005, 4/3497. p. 112.

37 *Ibid.*, 10 June 1815, reel 6038, SZ759, p. 114.

38 Bigge to Cox, Bonwick Transcripts, Box 25, frames 1–453.

39 Charles Frazer (1788?–1831), visited the 'interior' with Bigge and was highly respected for his scientific work. *ADB*, vol. 1, pp. 416–17.

40 Ritchie, *Evidence to the Bigge Reports, op. cit.*, p. 167.

41 Cox to Macquarie, 13 July 1818, Colonial Secretary Index, reel 8065, 4/1798, pp. 79–81.

42 Ritchie, *Evidence to the Bigge Reports, op. cit.*, pp. 175–85.

43 Colonial Secretary Index, reel 6065, 4/1798, p. 97. William had recommended three men for conditional pardons and later, p. 107, 16 prisoners for mitigation of sentence.

44 Campbell to Hassall, 3 February 1816, Colonial Secretary Index, reel 6065, 4/1798, p. 11.

45 Colonial Secretary Index, 25 October 1817 and return for 14–21 February 1818, reel 6031, 4/7028A, pp. 49, 83.

46 Ritchie, *Evidence to the Bigge Reports, op. cit.* Emblett, pp. 181, 182; Kippas, p. 184; Hangaddy, p. 185; Cheetham, p. 187; Smith, pp. 180, 181; Price, pp. 184, 185.

47 *Ibid.*, pp. 175, 176.

48 Evidence to the Bigge Report, Bonwick Transcripts, Box 26, p. 6047.

49 Colonial Secretary Index, 17 December 1816, reel 6046, 4/1736, pp. 200–01 and 30 April 1817, reel 6038, SZ759. p. 346.

50 Bonwick Transcripts, Box 25, pp. 5328–35.

51 Evidence to the Bigge Report, 30 January 1821, Bonwick Transcripts, Box 26, p. 6042.

52 Cox to Hassall, 17 December 1816, Colonial Secretary Index, reel 6046, 4/1736, p. 210.

53 The use of the bullocks had been repeatedly authorized: for example, Campbell to Hassall, 3 February 1816, Colonial Secretary Index, reel 6065, 4/1798, p. 11.

54 Colonial Secretary Index, reel 6065, 4/1798, p. 11.

55 Hassall to Gorman, 5 October 1816, Bonwick Transcripts, reel 15, p. 1486.
56 Ritchie, *Evidence to the Bigge Reports, op. cit.*, pp. 215, 216.
57 Colonial Secretary Index, 3 February 1816, reel 6065, 4/1798, p. 11.
58 Bigge Evidence, Bonwick Transcripts, Box 25, p. 5770, also Bonwick Transcripts, Box 26, p. 5766.
59 Bigge Report, pp. 124, 125.
60 Bathurst to Bigge, 6 January 1819, *HRA* Series 1, vol. 10, pp. 4, 6, 7.
61 Bigge Report, p. 125.
62 Macquarie to Goulburn, 24 November 1821, *HRA* Series 1, vol. x, p. 561.

Chapter 9

1 Bathurst to Bigge, 6 January 1819, *HRA* Series 1, vol. x, pp. 7–8.
2 Atkinson, *Europeans in Australia., op. cit.*, p. 30.
3 *ADB*, vol. 1, pp. 99–100.
4 Bigge Report.
5 Bigge Report, Agriculture.
6 Commission of 30 January 1819, *HRA* Series 1, vol. x, p. 3.
7 Bathurst to Bigge, 6 January 1819, *HRA* Series 1, vol. x, pp. 4, 6, 7.
8 *Ibid.*, pp. 8–11.
9 *Ibid.*, p. 18.
10 George Rudé, *Protest and Punishment*, Oxford University Press, Oxford, 1978, p. 166.
11 Portland to Hunter, 31 August 1797, *HRA* Series 1, vol. ii, pp. 107–08.
12 Camden to King, 31 October 1804, *HRA* Series 1, vol. v, p. 161 (Davidson and Macarthur). Castlereagh to King and King to Castlereagh, 27 July 1806, *HRA* Series 1, vol. v, p. 748, 749 (Gregory Blaxland).
13 Barrie Dyster, 'Public Employment and Assignment to Private Masters, 1788–1821', in *Convict Workers*, ed. Stephen Nicholas, Cambridge University Press, Cambridge, 1988, p. 127.
14 A. G. L. Shaw, *Convicts and the Colonies*, Melbourne University Press, Carlton, 1977, p. 92.
15 Report from the Select Committee on Transportation, together with the Minutes of Evidence, Appendix and Index, *British Parliamentary Papers*, 3 August 1838, p. xxxvi, British Library.
16 John Thomas Bigge, *ADB*, vol. 1, pp. 99, 102.
17 Portland to Hunter, 18 September 1798, *HRA* Series 1, vol. ii, p. 226.
18 Eugene MacLaughlin, John Muncie, Gordon Hughes, *Criminological Perspectives*, 2nd ed., Sage Publications, London, 2003, p. 1.
19 Select Committee on Transportation, *Minutes of Evidence*, 14 July 1837, *British Parliamentary Papers* online, 2006, pp. 9, para. 118.
20 Macquarie to Bathurst, 24 June 1815, *HRA* Series 1, vol. viii, p. 558.
21 *Bigge Report*, pp. 123, 124.
22 Bigge Report, Agriculture, Evidence, and Convicts, Evidence.
23 Even the interview with John Oxley, the Deputy Surveyor, was brief.
24 Ritchie, *Lachlan Macquarie, op. cit.*, p. 173.
25 Bigge Report, Evidence Agriculture, CO1/123, 25 November 1819, p. 49.
26 Quoted in Jeans, *An Historical Geography of New South Wales, op. cit.*, 1972, p. 88.
27 Angus R. McGillivery, 'From Sods to Seed-Bed: Cultivating a Familiar Field at Port Jackson', *JACH*, vol. 5, 2004, p. 24.
28 Bigge Report, Agriculture, Evidence, p. 41.
29 *Ibid.*, pp. 57, 59.

30 Bigge Report, Convicts, Evidence, p. 11.

31 *Ibid.*, p. 11.

32 Jane Austen, *Persuasion*, Alan Wingate, London, 1948, p. 17 *et seq*.

33 Commentary, *HRA* Series 1, vol. x, p. 808. Enclosure with letter from Bathurst to Lord Sidmouth, of 23 April 1817.

34 Macquarie to Bathurst, 16 May 1818, *HRA* Series 1, vol. ix, p. 794.

35 T. G. Parsons, 'Does the Bigge Report Follow From the Evidence?', *Historical Studies*, vol. 15, no. 58, 1972, p. 270.

36 Bigge Report, Agriculture, Evidence, pp. 53, 71. The records show that in 1818 William himself employed 73 convicts, 'free of expense to the Crown', Colonial Secretary Index, fiche 3062, 4/1834B, no. 73, p. 443.

37 Colonial Secretary Index, fiche 3062, 4/1834B, no. 73, p. 463.

38 Bigge Report, Agriculture, Evidence, p. 71.

39 Hirst, *Convict Society and its Enemies*, *op. cit.*, p. 34 *et seq*.

40 Nicholas, *Convict Workers*, *op. cit.*, p. 132.

41 Bigge Report, Agriculture, Evidence, p. 24.

42 *Ibid.*, p. 71.

43 Cox to Bigge, 7 May 1820, Bonwick Transcripts, Box 22, p. 4220.

44 Cobbett, *Illustrated Rural Rides*, *op. cit.*, p. 130.

45 Holt, *Memoirs*, *op. cit.*, vol. 2, p. 36.

46 Bigge Report, Evidence, Convicts, pp. 9, 12, 16.

47 Ritchie, *Lachlan Macquarie*, *op. cit.*, p. 130.

48 L. L. Robson, *Convict Settlers of Australia*, Melbourne University Press, Carlton, 1994, p. 146, quotes Bateson's figures from *Convict Ships*.

49 Deborah Oxley, *Convict Maids*, Cambridge University Press, Cambridge, 1996, pp. 119, 120.

50 Hirst, *Convict Society and its Enemies*, *op. cit.*, pp. 53, 55.

51 Elizabeth Macarthur to her mother, 22 August 1794, Macarthur Papers, AS 2908.

52 Joy Damousi, 'Beyond the Origins Debate: Theorising Sexuality and Gender Disorder in Convict Women's History', *AHS*, vol. 27, no. 106, April 1996, p. 60.

53 Babette Smith, *A Cargo of Women*, Rosenberg Publishing, Dural, NSW, 2005, pp. 36, 50.

54 Bigge Report, Agriculture, Evidence, p. 87 (original numbering 13).

55 Ritchie, *The Evidence to the Bigge Reports*, *op cit.*, pp. 185, 186.

56 *Ibid.*, p. 158; Cartwright, *ADB*, vol. 1, pp. 211–12.

57 Macquarie to Bathurst, 7 October 1814, *HRA* Series 1, vol. vii, p. 315.

58 Bigge Report, Agriculture, Evidence, p. 91.

59 Colonial Secretary Index, 10 November 1819, reel 6007, 4/3501, p. 28.

60 Campbell to Commandant, Newcastle, 4 May 1820, Colonial Secretary Index, reel 6007, 4/3502, p. 17.

61 Ritchie, *The Evidence to the Bigge Reports*, *op. cit.*, p. 213.

62 Bigge Report, Agriculture, p. 125.

63 Bigge Report, Agriculture, Evidence, p. 91, and Bigge Report, p. 644.

64 Letter Macquarie to Bigge, 6 November 1819, *HRA* Series 1, vol. x, p. 222.

65 Bigge Report, Agriculture, Evidence, p. 86: Archibald Bell (1773–1837). In 1820 he was appointed chief police magistrate: *ADB*, vol. 1, pp. 78–80.

66 Ritchie, *Profit and Punishment*, *op. cit.*, p. 24.

67 Bigge Report, Convicts, Evidence, p. 9.

68 Ritchie, *Lachlan Macquarie*, *op. cit.*, pp. 176, 177.

69   Colonial Secretary Index, 7 March 1811, reel 6043, 4/1726, p. 101–02.

70   Bigge Report, Convicts, Evidence, p. 9.

71   Bigge Report, Agriculture, Evidence, p. 59.

72   *Ibid.*, p. 65.

73   Bigge, Report, p. 173.

74   Letter of 7 May 1820 addressed to Bigge. Bonwick Transcripts, Box 22, p. 4220, ML.

75   Stephen Nicholas and Shergold, *Convict Workers*, *op. cit.*, p. 82.

76   Robson, *The Convict Settlers of Australia*, *op. cit.*, pp. 156, 159, 166 (table 5d), 169 (table 6a), p. 174 (table 6f).

77   *Sydney Gazette*, Saturday 20 March 1819, p. 3; Macquarie to Bathurst 24 March 1819, *HRA* Series 1, vol. x, pp. 52–65.

78   Ellis, *Lachlan Macquarie*, *op. cit.*, p. 466.

79   Bigge Report, Agriculture, Evidence, p. 39.

80   *Ibid.*, p. 22.

81   Ritchie, *Profit and Punishment*, *op. cit.*, p. 228.

82   Bigge Report, Agriculture, Evidence, p. 39.

83   Cunningham, *op. cit.*, vol. 2, p. 49.

84   Atkinson, *The Europeans in Australia*, *op. cit.*, vol. 1, p. 68.

85   J. J. Spigelman, *The Macquarie Bicentennial*, Annual History Lecture, History Council of New South Wales, Sydney, 2009, p. 29.

86   Ellis, *Lachlan Macquarie*, *op. cit.*, pp. 212, 213.

87   Spigelman, *op. cit.*, pp. 28, 29, 34.

Chapter 10

1   *Memoirs of William Cox J.P.*, *op. cit.*, p. 137.

2   Colonial Secretary Index, 23 August 1819, reel 6048, 4/1742, pp. 395–395c.

3   'Journal' of June 1815, p. 18, ML.

4   Cunningham, *The Blue Mountains Rediscovered*, *op. cit.*, p. 152.

5   Lawson to Hoper, 29 March 1819, Angus McSween, 'Some Lawson Letters 1819–1824', *JRAHS*, vol. 50, pt 3, August 1964, p. 230.

6   Bigge Report, Agriculture, 183, p. 14.

7   *Memoirs of William Cox, J.P.*, *op. cit.*, p. 121.

8   Geoffrey Blainey, *A Land Half Won*, Macmillan Australia, South Yarra, Victoria, 1980, p. 51.

9   Bigge Report, Agriculture.

10   Ritchie, *Profit and Punishment*, *op. cit.*, pp. 92–3.

11   Bonwick Transcripts, Box 10, p. 4078.

12   John Darwin, *The Empire Project: The Rise and Fall of the British World System 1830–1970*, Cambridge University Press, Cambridge, 2009, p. 50.

13   H. T. Dickinson, 'Democracy', in *The Oxford Companion to the Romantic Age*, ed. Iain McCalman, Oxford University Press, Oxford, 1999.

14   Manning Clark, *A History of Australia*, vol. 1, Melbourne University Press, Carlton, 1962, p. 27.

15   *Sydney Gazette*, 12 February 1814, p. 1.

16   Wentworth, *Statistical, Historical and Political Description of the Colony*, *op. cit.*, pp. 60–62.

17   Darling to Goderich, 1 September 1831, *HRA* Series 1, vol. xvi, p. 342.

18   Jeans, *An Historical Geography of New South Wales*, *op. cit.*, p. 90.

19   Fletcher, *Colonial Australia*, *op. cit.*, p. 120.

20 Bigge Report, Agriculture, p. 18.

21 *Ibid.*, pp. 398, 399.

22 Jeans, *op. cit.*, p. 35

23 Bigge Report, pp. 16, 18.

24 'A Journal kept by Mr George Cox on his late Tour to Northward And Eastward of "Bathurst"', National Library of Australia, Canberra, ref. M712224, transcribed 1974.

25 Eric Rolls, *A Million Wild Acres*, Penguin Australia, Ringwood, Victoria, 1984, p. 50.

26 Ware, *Who Was Who on the Liverpool Plains, op. cit.*

27 Fletcher, *Landed Enterprise, op. cit.*, pp. 179–80.

28 Bigge Report, Agriculture, p. 13.

29 Bathurst to Brisbane, I January 1825, *HRA* Series 1, vol. xi, pp. 439, 440.

30 Frederick Goulburn (1788–1837) was officious and alienated many leading settlers. *ADB*, 1966, pp. 463–64.

31 Goulburn to Cox, 5 January 1822, Colonial Secretary Index, reel 6008, 4/3504A, p. 239.

32 Colonial Secretary Index, 21 March 1822, reel 6009, 4/3505, p. 51.

33 *ADB*, vol. 2, pp. 96, 97.

34 *The 1822 Muster*, ed. Carol Baxter, Australian Biographical and Genealogical Record, North Sydney, 1988, p. 112.

35 Spigelman, *The Macquarie Bicentennial, op. cit.*, p. 25.

36 Oxley retired from the Navy to become surveyor general in 1812. In 1824 he drafted regulations for land sales for Governor Brisbane. *ADB*, vol. 2, pp. 305–07.

37 Brian Fletcher, *Ralph Darling*, Oxford University Press, Melbourne, 1984, p. 140.

38 Oxley to Ovens, 23 May 1825, *HRA* Series 1, vol. xi, pp. 692– 97.

39 Ritchie, *Profit and Punishment, op. cit.*, p. 249.

40 Spigelman, *op. cit.*, p. 32.

41 Darling to Bathurst, *HRA* Series 1, vol. xii, p. 377.

42 *Ibid.*, pp. 536–39.

43 *Ibid.*, p. 376.

44 The counties were each of 40 square miles, divided into parishes of 100 square miles and further divided into hundreds of 25 square miles, on the English pattern.

45 Colonial Secretary Index, April/May 1825, fiche 3125, 4/1841 A, p. 117, ML.

46 *Ibid.*, 5 June 1825, reel 3125, 4/1841, p. 107.

47 Alexander McLeay (1767–1848), a Fellow of the Royal Society, went out with Governor Darling, arriving in January 1826, continuing under Bourke. *ADB*, vol. 2, pp. 177–80.

48 Oxley to Colonial Secretary, 18 December 1826, SRNSW 907, reel 1114, letter 8506, State Records, Kingswood.

49 Fletcher, *Darling, op. cit.*, p. 147. Bathurst had resigned in 1827.

50 Ritchie, *Profit and Punishment, op. cit.*, p. 251.

51 William Cox to Colonial Secretary, 3 April 1830, SRNSW 907, reel 1114, letter 30/2818, State Records, Kingswood.

52 Goderich to Darling, 9 January 1831, *HRA* Series 1, vol. xvi, pp. 19–22.

53 *ADB*, vol. 2, pp. 559–62. *A Letter from Sydney, the Principal Town of Australasia*, was published in December 1829.

54 Hazel King, *Richard Bourke*, Oxford University Press, Melbourne, 1971, p. 190.

55 Forbes to Darling, 2 April 1831, *HRA* Series 1, vol. xvi, pp. 341–44.

56 Darling to Goderich, 1 September 1831, *HRA* Series 1, vol. xvi, p. 345.

57 Clark, *History of Australia, op. cit.*, vol. 1, pp. 105, 182.

58 Sir Frances Forbes (1784–1841), *ADB*, vol. 1, pp. 392–99.
59 Letter from William McPherson, collector of Internal Revenue to Colonial Secretary, 20 September 1831, SRNSW 907, reel 1114, letter no. 31/7685, State Records, Kingswood.
60 McPherson to Colonial Secretary, SRNSW 907, reel 1114, letter 33/2832, State Records, Kingswood.
61 Atkinson, *Camden, op. cit.*, p. 38.
62 King, *Richard Bourke, op. cit.*, p. 180.
63 *News from the State Records of NSW*, number 44, June 2010. The 1836 Act was published in the *Government Gazette*, 5 October 1836, pp. 745–46.
64 Stephen Roberts, *The Squatting Age in Australia 1835–1847*, Melbourne University Press, Carlton, 1935, p. 13.
65 *ADB*, vol. 2, pp. 334–35.
66 Piper Papers, vol. 2, CY A 255, p. 53, ML.
67 *Ibid.*, pp. 171, 457, 477.
68 George Henry Frederick Cox, 'A History of Mudgee', written c.1919/10, typed copy in the Mudgee Library, p. 3.
69 *ADB*, vol. 2, p. 157.
70 'Last Will and Testament of William Cox of Fairfield, Windsor', 21 December 1836. Typed copy made by Thelma and Matthew Birrell, undated, Priest's House Museum, Wimborne, Dorset. There were also codicils dated 21 and 25 February 1837.
71 Certified copy from the honorary archivist, Jenny Pearce, 24 August 2008.
72 Ian Hawkins Nicholson, *Shipping Arrivals and Departures, Tasmania, 1803–1833*, Roebuck, Canberra, 1983, p. 63.
73 *Hobart Gazette*, 23 September 1820.
74 Bryan Cox to author, email of 28 August 2007.
75 Piper Papers, *op. cit.*, vol. 2, p. 484.
76 Darling to Secretary of State from Parramatta, 22 December 1828, *HRA* Series 1, vol. xiv, p. 535.

Chapter 11

1 *ADB*, vol. 2, 1967.
2 Evidence given by Bell at Windsor 27 November 1819, Bonwick Transcripts, Box 5, p. 2032.
3 Inga Clendinnen, *Dancing with Strangers*, Text Publishing, Melbourne, 2003, p. 285.
4 Merete Borch, 'Rethinking the Origins of Terra Nullius', *AHS*, vol. 32, no. 117, October 2001.
5 *ADB*, vol. 2, pp. 55–61.
6 Macquarie to Bathurst, 8 October 1814, *HRA* Series 1, vol. viii, pp 368–69.
7 Atkinson, *The Europeans in Australia, op. cit.*, vol. 1, p. 135.
8 Richard Broome, 'Aboriginal Workers on South Eastern Frontiers', *AHS*, vol. 26, no. 103, October 1994, p. 213.
9 This paragraph derives from Barkley-Jack, *Hawkesbury Settlement Revealed, op. cit.*, chapter 9.
10 Karskens, *The Colony, op. cit.*, p. 123.
11 Colonial Secretary Index, reel 6065, 4/1799.
12 ML, reel CY 2743, DL Add. 81 and original letters.
13 Colonial Secretary Index, 9 May, reel 6004, 4/3494, 483; 26 July, reel 6005, 4/3494, p. 55; 19 October, reel 6046, 4/1736, pp. 140–2; 2 November, reel 6005, 4/3495, p. 245.
14 Nor can it have been the long established Society for the Propagation of the Christian Gospel.
15 Colonial Secretary Index, 24 August 1819, reel 6048, 4/1743.

16 Saxe Bannister, *Humane Policy on Justice to the Aborigines of New Settlements*, London, 1830, republished by Dawsons of Pall Mall, London, 1968, appendix No. 5, p. ccxl.

17 Colonial Secretary Index, reel 6065, 4/1798, p. 121.

18 William Cox to Brisbane, 7 February 1822, Colonial Secretary Index, 6065, reel 4/1798, p. 121.

19 Bigge Report, Agriculture, Evidence, p. 46.

20 Cox to Goulburn, Colonial Secretary Index, 7 December 1823, reel 6017, 4/5783, pp. 481–82.

21 Colonial Secretary Index, reel 6065, 4/1799, p. 10.

22 *Ibid.*, pp. 73–76.

23 His name was also spelt Chamberlane.

24 Hirst, *Convict Society and its Enemies, op. cit.*, pp. 55, 56.

25 *ADB*, vol. 2, pp. 260, 261.

26 David Roberts, 'The Bells Falls Massacre and Bathurst's History of Violence', *Australian Historical Studies*, October 1995, vol. 26, no. 105, p. 620.

27 *Ibid.*, p. 622.

28 Morisset to Goulburn, 26 July 1824, Colonial Secretary Index, reel 6065, 4/1800, p. 125.

29 Based on *Sydney Gazette*, 16 and 24 September 1824, both p. 2.

30 John Connor, *The Australian Frontier Wars 1788–1838*, UNSW Press, Sydney, 2002, pp. 59, 61.

31 Iris Clayton, 'Wiradjuri Identity', *Australian Aboriginal Studies*, 1988, no. 1, p. 54.

32 *Sydney Gazette*, 14 October 1824, p. 2.

33 McSween, 'Some Lawson Letters', *op. cit.*, p. 239.

34 L. E. Threlkeld, *Australian Reminiscences and Papers of L. E. Threlkeld, Missionary to the Aborigines 1824–1859*, ed. Niel Gunson, Aboriginal Studies No. 4, Australian Institute of Aboriginal Studies, Canberra, 1974, p. 14.

35 Threlkeld first reported this in a letter to George Burder and W. A. Hankey at the London Missionary Society, received by them on 20 June 1825. L.M.S Australia letters, p. 178.

36 *ADB*, vol. 1, pp. 55, 56. A succession of defeats in court lessened confidence in him as attorney general and in 1826 he returned to England.

37 Bannister, *Humane Policy or Justice to the Aborigines, op. cit.*

38 Samuel Marsden, *Statement chiefly relating to the Formation and Abandonment of a Mission to the Aboriginals of New South Wales*, R. Howe, Government Printer, Sydney, 1828.

39 Jan Kociumbas, *Oxford History of Australia*, vol. 2, Oxford University Press, Oxford, 1996, p. 144.

40 *Sydney Gazette*, 30 September 1824, p. 3, col. 2. The whole skirmish was reported.

41 Kociumbas, *op. cit.*, endnote 34.

42 *Ibid.*, p. 239.

43 George Cox of Mulgoa and Mudgee, *op. cit.*, p. 1, obituary p. 49.

44 Rolls, *A Million Wild Acres, op. cit.*, p. 56.

45 Goulburn to Bathurst, 3 November 1824, *HRA* Series 1, vol. xi, p. 410.

46 Cox to Macquarie, 13 July 1818, Colonial Secretary Index, reel 6065, 4/1798, pp. 79–81.

47 Brisbane to Bathurst, 1 November 1824, *HRA* Series 1, vol. xi, p. 406.

48 Threlkeld, *Reminiscences, op. cit.*, p. 322.

49 Bigge Report, Agriculture, Evidence, 27 November 1820, doc. 4, p. 75.

50 Roe, *The Quest for Authority, op. cit.*, p. 66.

51 *Sydney Gazette*, 21 May 1827, pp. 2, 3.

52 Peter Cunningham, *Two Years in New South Wales*, Henry Colburn, London, 1827, vol. 2, p. 6.

53 Karskens, *The Colony, op. cit.*, p. 537.

54 Bigge Report, Agriculture, Evidence, 27 November 1819, Bonwick Transcripts, Box 5, p. 2032.

55 Broome, *op. cit.*, p. 214.

Chapter 12

1 Roe, *The Quest for Authority, op. cit.*, pp. 6, 88.

2 *Ibid.*, p. 51.

3 This was James Mudie's scornful phrase in his book, *The Felonry of New South Wales*, 1837, republished by Angus & Robertson, London, 1995.

4 Manning Clark, *A History of Australia.*, vol. 2, Melbourne University Press, Carlton, 1968, p. 155.

5 *Australian Historical Statistics*, ed. Wray Vamplew, Fairfax, Syme & Wilson, Broadway, NSW, 1987, pp. 4–5.

6 *HRA* Series 1, vol. xvii, pp. 171–75.

7 *HRA* Series 1, vol. xxv, p. 294, 30 December 1846.

8 Cobbett, *Illustrated Rural Rides, op. cit.*, pp. 127, 130.

9 Roe, *The Quest for Authority, op. cit.*, p. 71.

10 Atkinson, *Camden, op. cit.*, pp. 36, 37.

11 King, *Richard Bourke, op. cit.*, p. 182.

12 Gideon Scott Lang, *Land and Labour in Australia*, Melbourne, 1845, p. 14.

13 Donald Carisbrooke, 'The Influence of the "Gentlemen Settlers" in Australia in 1838', *The Push From the Bush*, no. 11, November 1981, pp. 28, 29.

14 Hon. H. A. Wyndham, *A Family History 1688–1837*, Oxford University Press, Oxford, 1950.

15 *HRA* Series 1, vol. XX, p. 54, 5 March 1839.

16 Carisbrooke, 'The Influence of the "Gentleman Settlers"', *op cit.*, pp. 28, 29.

17 Sandra J. Blair, 'The Revolt at Castle Forbes: A Catalyst to Emancipist Emigrant Confrontation', *JRAHS*, vol. 64, pt 2, September 1978, p. 96.

18 Clark, *History of Australia, op. cit.*, vol. 2, p. 214.

19 John Ward, 'James Macarthur, Colonial Conservative', *JRAHS*, vol. 66, pt 6, p. 155.

20 Roe, *The Quest for Authority, op. cit.*, pp. 40, 47.

21 Bigge Report, Agriculture, Evidence, p. 84.

22 *Ibid.*, p. 2044.

23 Sir John Jamison (1776–1844) was a physician, who had been knighted for curbing scurvy in the Swedish navy and inherited his father's property in the colony. *ADB*, vol. 2, pp. 10–12.

24 Colonial Secretary Index, reel 6038, SZ759, pp. 359–61.

25 Correspondence, ML, CY 762, A 264, pp. 7, 43.

26 Rolls, *A Million Wild Acres, op. cit.*, p. 77.

27 Colonial Secretary Index, reel 6057, 4/1768, p. 23, ML.

28 Cox to Brisbane, 2 February 1823, Colonial Secretary Index, reel 6058, 4/1769, p. 72.

29 *Sydney Gazette*, 20 March 1819, p. 3. Also, Macquarie to Bathurst, 24 March 1819, *HRA* Series 1, vol. x, pp. 52–65.

30 Macquarie to Bathurst, 22 March, 1819, *HRA* Series 1, vol. x, pp. 55–65. Also Clark, *History of Australia, op. cit.*, vol. 1, pp. 322, 323.

31 Ward, 'James Macarthur', *op. cit.*, p. 151.

32 Quoted by Fletcher, *Colonial Australia, op. cit.*, p. 79. Bell's evidence to Bigge revealed him as

opposed to emancipists holding public office.

33 Introduction, *HRA* Series 1, vol. xvi, p. viii.

34 Bigge Report, Agriculture, Evidence, p. 84.

35 Barron Field (1786–1846) had replaced Jeffrey Hart Bent in February 1817. *ADB*, vol. 1, pp. 373–76.

36 *Sydney Gazette*, 12 July 1822, p. 2.

37 Roe, *The Quest for Authority, op. cit.*, pp. 38, 39.

38 Colonial Secretary Index, 20 August 1822, reel 6052, 4/1753, p. 174/174a, ML.

39 Gilbert Mant, *The Big Show*, Horwitz Publications, North Sydney, 1972, p. 21.

40 Rachel Pintado at the RASNSW, email of 7 October 2010.

41 *Sydney Gazette*, 16 February 1827, p. 3.

42 Brisbane to Bathurst, 9 February 1825, *HRA* Series 1, vol. xi, pp. 520, 937. Commentary and note 136 on p. 937. Marsden's speech was printed by Robert Howe in 1824.

43 Brisbane to Bathurst, 9 February 1825, *HRA* Series 1, vol. xi, p. 520.

44 Geoffrey Moorhouse, *Sydney: Portrait of a City*, Phoenix, Sydney, 2000, p. 93.

45 Brisbane to Bathurst, 9 February 1825, *HRA* Series 1, xi, p. 519, with enclosures.

46 Brisbane to Bathurst, 23 May 1825, *HRA* Series 1, vol. xi, pp. 606, 609, 612.

47 *Oxford Dictionary of National Biography*, Oxford University Press, Oxford, 2004, vol. 7, p. 679.

48 Brisbane to Bathurst, 18 November 1825, *HRA* Series 1, vol. xi, p. 903.

49 Brisbane to Bathurst, 21 May 1825, *HRA* Series 1, xi, p. 596 and note 172, p. 944.

50 Royal Agricultural Society of New South Wales website, February 2011.

51 Cox, *George Cox of Mulgoa and Mudgee, op. cit.*, p. 27.

52 Darling to Bathurst, 31 June 1827, *HRA* Series 1, vol. xiii, pp. 50, 51.

53 Darling to Goderich, 14 December 1827, *HRA* Series 1, vol. xiii, p. 638.

54 *HRA* Series 1, vol. xvi, p. 317.

55 Forbes to Hay, 12 November 1827, *HRA* Series 1, vol. 1, legal papers 1786–1827, pp. 749, 750.

56 Darling to Hay, 17 December 1827, *HRA* Series 1, vol. xiii, p. 657.

57 Alan Atkinson, 'The Parliament in the Jerusalem Warehouse', *The Push From the Bush*, no. 12, June 1982, p. 76.

58 Darling to Twiss, 7 July 1829, enclosure, *HRA* Series 1, vol. xv, pp. 71–73.

59 'Australia: a Poem written for the Chancellor's medal at the Cambridge Commencement, July 1823'. It came second.

60 *ADB*, vol. 2, pp. 570–72.

61 Brisbane to Bathurst, 12 January 1825, *HRA* Series 1, vol. xi, p. 470, 471.

62 *ADB*, vol. 2, p. 583.

63 *ADB*, vol. 2, p. 584.

64 *Sydney Gazette*, 15 September 1828, p. 2.

65 Colonial Secretary Index, 30 June 1820, fiche 3024, 4/1824B, No. 445, p. 641, and fiche 3031, 4/1825B, No. 670, p. 575, ML.

66 *Sydney Gazette*, 27 July 1827, p. 3.

67 *Sydney Gazette*, christening, 5 April 1822, p. 3; races 19 April 1822, p. 3; ball 4 September 1823, p. 3. The dining room is recorded by Broadbent, *Colonial House, op. cit.*, p. 151.

68 Atkinson, 'Jerusalem Warehouse', *op. cit.*, pp. 76–79.

69 Blair, 'The Revolt at Castle Forbes', *op. cit.*, p. 89.

70 Mudie, *The Felonry of New South Wales, op. cit.*, p. 7.

71 *HRA* Series 1, vol. xix, p. 115, 10 Oct 1837.

72 Roe, *The Quest for Authority, op. cit.*, pp. 6, 76.
73 *Ibid.*, p. 54.
74 Spigelman, *The Macquarie Bicentennial, op. cit.*, p. 16.
75 Ward, 'James Macarthur', *op. cit.*, p. 150.
76 Colonial Secretary Index, Sec. letters, SRNSW, reel 1114, 35/2608, 7 April 1835, Stare Records, Kingswood.
77 *Ibid.*, reel 1114, 36/345, 28 December 1835, and 41/0799, 12 June 1837, State Records, Kingswood.
78 Barrie Dyster, 'The Fate of Colonial Conservatism on the Eve of the Gold Rush', *JRAHS*, December 1968, vol. 54, part 4, p. 334.
79 Bennett, *History of Australian Discovery, op. cit.*, vol. 1, 1865, vol. 2, pp. 527, 627, 628.
80 *Ibid.*, p. 578.
81 Wentworth, *Historical and Political Description of the Colony, op. cit.*, p. 101.
82 *ADB*, vol. 1, p. 118.
83 Broadbent, *Colonial House, op. cit.*, p. 376.
84 Bennett, *History of Australian Discovery, op. cit.*, pp. 527, 628.
85 *Ibid.*, p. 629.

Chapter 13

1   *George Cox of Mulgoa and Mudgee, op. cit.*, p. 10.
2   State Records Kingswood, Land, reel 1114, 36/345.
3   SRNSW, 907, reel 1114 and 1114 no. 420, State Records Kingswood.
4   Broadbent, *Colonial House, op. cit.*, p. 150.
5   Alfred Cox, 'Reminiscences', *op. cit.*, p. 2.
6   Last will and testament of William Cox of Fairfield, Windsor, copy at the Priest's House Museum, Wimborne, Dorset.
7   Legal notice, *Sydney Morning Herald*, 17 June 1918.
8   Letter from George Cox to George Henry Cox of 2 January 1848, in *George Cox of Mulgoa and Mudgee*.
9   *George Cox of Mulgoa and Mudgee, op. cit*, p. 56.
10 This is derived from a website account by Birrell headed 'Rebecca and Anna', which has to be treated with reserve since it contains errors, such as referring to James Cox as Edgar's uncle when they were half- brothers.
11 Colonial Secretary Index, 26 April 1824, reel 6060, 4/1777, p. 194.
12 Various family accounts call it the Edward VI school. County records show that there was no such grammar school in Wiltshire. It must have been the City Grammar School.
13 Colonial Secretary Index, 16 July 1804, fiche 3268; 9/2731, p. 140.
14 Alfred Cox, 'Reminiscences', *op. cit.*, p. 7.
15 Contrary to Edna Hickson's accounts.
16 Attachment to a letter from Mrs Anne Youll to Winifred Cox, *op. cit.*
17 Colonial Secretary Index, 29 April 1818, reel 6006, 4/3498, p. 195.
18 State Records Kingswood, Land, reel 1114, 35/2608, 7 April 1835.
19 Broadbent, *Colonial House, op. cit.* pp. 152–54.
20 'Reminiscences of J. M. Cox', ed. Andrew Houison, *The Cox Family* c. 1912, ML, vol. 2, p. 175.
21 *George Cox of Mulgoa and Mudgee, op. cit.*, p. 19.
22 Piper Papers, vol. 2, p. 178, ML.
23 Quoted in Rachel Roxburgh, *Early Colonial Houses of Australia*, but she has named the wrong

bride. The letter is in the Mitchell Library.

24 Smith, *A Cargo of Women, op. cit.*, pp. 36, 50.

25 Archives Office of New South Wales, 4/2127.5, reel 72.

26 Smith, *Cargo of Women, op. cit.*, pp. 131 *et seq.*

27 Author's visit, 2009.

28 Alfred Cox, 'Reminiscences', *op. cit.*, p. 7.

29 *HRA* Series 1, vol. xviii, p. 252, 26 December 1835.

30 *HRA* Series 1, vol. xx, p. 54, 5 March 1830.

31 *HRA* Series 1, vol. xxii, p. 16, 16 April 1842.

32 G. M. W. Clemons, *Historic Homesteads of Australia*, vol. 1, Cassell Australia, 1969, p. 95.

33 *HRA* Series 1, Series III, vol. iii, pp. 843–845, 20 April 1820.

34 Bigge, Report Agriculture, 13 March 1823.

35 Bigge Report, p. 117.

36 Clemons, *Historic Homesteads, op. cit.*, p. 95.

37 *HRA* Series 1, vol. x, p. 561, 24 November 1821.

38 *HRA* Series 1, vol. xxvi, p. 635, report of the Commissioner of 1 June 1848.

39 Philip Cox and Wesley Stacey, *The Australian Homestead*, Lansdowne Press, Melbourne, 1972, p. 130 *et seq.*

40 'Reminiscences of J. M. Cox', *op. cit.*

41 *HRA* Series 1, vol. xxvi, p. 10, Fitz Roy to Grey, 14 October 1847.

42 *HRA* Series 1, vol. xxv, pp. 164–167, 1 January 1845.

43 *ADB*, vol. 3, 1969.

44 *Mulgoa! Mulgoa! Where is that? op. cit.*, p. 9.

45 *HRA* Series 1, vol. xiii, p. 59, Darling to Bathurst, list of magistrates 31 January 1827.

46 Christopher Cox, email of 11 October 2010.

47 Christopher Cox, email of 11 October 2010.

48 Bigge to Bathurst, 6 May 1822, *HRA* Series 3, vol. 4, p. 679.

49 Broadbent, *Colonial House, op. cit.*, p. 378.

50 Barrie Dyster, 'The Fate of Colonial Conservatism on the Eve of the Gold Rush', *Journal of the Royal Australian Historical Society*, December 1978. vol. 54, part 4, p. 334.

50 Bennett, *History of Australian Discovery, op. cit.*, pp. 628, 629.

Index